Vile Bodies

Vile Bodies

The Body in Christian Teaching,
Faith and Practice

Adrian Thatcher

scm press

Published in 2023 by SCM Press
Editorial office
3rd Floor, Invicta House,
108–114 Golden Lane,
London EC1Y 0TG, UK

www.scmpress.co.uk

SCM Press is an imprint of Hymns Ancient & Modern Ltd
(a registered charity)

H
Y Ancient
M
N &Modern
S

Hymns Ancient & Modern® is a registered trademark of
Hymns Ancient & Modern Ltd
13A Hellesdon Park Road, Norwich,
Norfolk NR6 5DR, UK

British Library Cataloguing in Publication data

A catalogue record for this book is available
from the British Library

ISBN 978-0-334-06360-5

Typeset by Regent Typesetting
Printed and bound by
CPI Group (UK) Ltd

Contents

Acknowledgements

I thank my friends and former colleagues in Religion and Theology at the University of Exeter for my continued association with them. Now part of the Department of Classics, Ancient History, Religion and Theology in the Faculty of Humanities, Arts and Social Sciences, these talented colleagues are first for world-leading research in theology and religious studies in the UK. By allowing me to continue among them as Honorary Professor I have been able to carry on researching and writing, long after my retirement from their department in 2011. I am most grateful to them and their head of department for proposing, and to the Vice Chancellor of the university for approving, my present appointment as Honorary Professor, thereby enabling me to make further contributions to constructive and liberal theology. Without access to the university's library with its ever-growing number of academic databases, it would have been impossible to continue to research and write.

I have benefited from the advice of several academics during the writing of this book. Michael Lawler, Amelia and Emil Graff Professor Emeritus of Catholic Theology at Creighton University, Omaha, Nebraska, commented helpfully on several chapters. Dr Rachel Starr, Director of Studies at the Queen's Foundation, Birmingham, UK, and Johanna Stiebert, co-lead for the Shiloh Project and Professor of Hebrew Bible at the University of Leeds, gave valuable advice on particular areas of the book where their fields of expertise much exceed my own. Helen King, Professor Emerita of Classical Studies at the Open University, read the whole manuscript. Her advice, especially on classical, medieval and indeed modern understandings of bodies, was most encouraging and fruitful. Francesca Stavrakopoulou, Professor of Hebrew Bible and Ancient Religion at the University of Exeter, pored extensively over the full manuscript and made scores of helpful suggestions, not merely on the Hebrew Bible chapters but on the whole script. I thank them all. The remaining errors and omissions are mine.

I'm grateful to Modern Church, the main advocate for liberal theology in the British churches, for its persistence. Membership of Modern Church has kept me in touch with thoughtful Christians determined that modern evangelicalisms should not have the last word, especially in the Church of England.

Last but never least, Caroline Major, my life partner for over 20 years, has been unflagging in her interest in this, my current project, like many others before. I'm most grateful to her for her support, encouragement and understanding of my motivation for continuing to immerse myself in theology, when I could have let it go long ago.

Introduction:
Why 'Vile Bodies'?

This book is about human bodies as they are perceived and understood in Christian faith and thought. Why then a title that confronts readers with a sense of disgust?

Because far too many human bodies have been imbued with a sense of disgust in Christian teaching, and this teaching continues to revile ('re-vile') them. The book asks why so many bodies were and still are regarded as vile, and what a more positive theology of the body looks like.

The apostle Paul referred to his own 'vile body' (Phil. 3.21 KJV) as he approached the end of his life, anticipating its transformation into the 'glorious body' that it would become after his anticipated death. 'Vile body' was a term interred in the Order for the Burial of the Dead, in the Book of Common Prayer (1662), and is still in use. The novelist Evelyn Waugh used the title *Vile Bodies* for his 1930 novel, well aware of its biblical derivation and its association with death. The all-powerful idea in the Christian tradition that the human body, and especially the female body, is vile – that is, disgusting and shameful – has had an incalculably negative influence on millions of people past and present. This book explores why this happened, continues to happen, and what can be done about it.

Paul may not have had quite the sense of disgust that the term conveys in English. The NRSVA renders it 'the body of our humiliation', which might refer to the adverse circumstances of Paul, languishing in prison, perhaps in Rome, around 58 CE. However, the human body, and especially the female body, soon came to have the visceral character that the middle-English word 'vile' conveys. Something or someone vile is 'physically repulsive, especially through filth or corruption'; 'horrid, disgusting'; 'held in no esteem or regard'; 'despicable on moral grounds'; 'deserving to be regarded with abhorrence or disgust; characterized by baseness or depravity'; 'of a low, base, or despicable character; morally depraved or degraded; capable of the basest conduct' (*Oxford English Dictionary*, hereinafter *OED*). The judgement that something or someone is vile incorporates an emotional or 'visceral' component too. The *viscera* were the internal organs or bowels that were thought to be the seat of our deepest feelings or emotions, beyond language and reason. Our deepest loves and longings, we might say, are visceral, but so are our deepest negative emotions like disgust or fear. There can be little doubt that many human bodies quickly came to be viewed in all these ways among Christians.

Whose Bodies?

But *whose* bodies? All bodies are specific bodies, yet every body (yes, everybody) already finds itself constructed within specific social and cultural frameworks, and within these frameworks there are specific bodies that have been regarded as particularly vile: those of a particular sex, race, religion, tribe, sexual orientation, disability or age. Thankfully there is now an array of dissenting theologies – feminist, queer, black, liberationist, womanist, political, post-colonial – which, despite their differences, have a common method. They begin with people who are in some way forgotten, persecuted, oppressed, excluded, and ask about how they got to where they are and what can be done about it. They speak from experience out of the pain that oppression, often multiple, causes them. Such theologies are not merely optional add-ons, nor are they academically suspect. They all ask about the redemptive possibilities that faith may be able to provide in specific social situations. But they also examine, where necessary, how their various predicaments are already a consequence of the bad faith of others. Powerful Christians have regarded as abhorrent not merely the bodies of women but the bodies of many other perceived 'others', for example Jews, Muslims, homosexuals, people of colour, heretics.

So a theology book about bodies must always ask *whose* bodies are being talked about, and – no less important – who is doing the talking. That requires theologians to swim in deep and unfamiliar waters as we listen to historians, sociologists, psychologists and others, and dare to read our own traditions through critical eyes. An intersectional approach to these prolonged historical maladies requires a studied concentration on the beliefs that authorized and encouraged indefensible conduct towards them, and still does.

Hundreds of books have been written about the struggles of the churches with sex and gender. I have contributed to the pile myself. As long as justice is denied to women and to sex and gender minorities throughout the world, the pile will only grow bigger. But as I reflect on what I have learned and written over 40 years since my first effort (Thatcher, 1993), I have come to see how, while working, writing and praying for sexual and gender justice, religious beliefs in all traditions are intrinsically connected with violence of many kinds and towards many people (Thatcher, 2021). It has been a most uncomfortable discovery, which, in the main, Christians do not want to make for themselves, and congregations do not want to hear. Our leaders dare not confront much that lies in our common past, while programmes of theological study for ministry generally provide little clue. The appalling and never-ending violence against women in contemporary life is partly a continuation of the misogyny that was authorized by certain biblical texts and what pious male theologians did with them.

But the violence is not confined to women. It extends to all people without power. White-majority societies still do not dare to confront the depths of suffering, evil and death caused by modern slavery (Chapter 12). The Holocaust was preceded by centuries of Christian anti-Semitism, and cannot be disentangled from it (see Cohn-Sherbok, 2015; Sweeney, 2008) (Chapter 15). The assumption of the superiority of the white race, endorsed by Christian teachings and believed by most white people to be a self-evident truth, gave it authority to treat 'others' with disdain (Chapters 12, 15 and 16). Colonized countries and peoples continue to be harmed by the havoc inflicted on them by colonizing Europeans (Chapter 16). How can a Christian read Luther's *On the Jews and their Lies* (Chapter 15), one of the most distressing and offensive anti-Semitic works ever written, without feeling nauseous at the theologically fuelled contempt and hatred for a whole people? Indeed, in the flourishing discipline of Holocaust studies, a debate continues among scholars about whether the Nazi treatment of Jews represents a continuation and intensification *of the behaviour of the Christian colonizing powers* towards the colonized (the 'continuity thesis'), and not the single event that, conveniently remembered as such, evades interrogation of earlier European and Christian history on Holocaust Memorial Day (Tollerton, 2021, pp. 87–95). Here the waters are so deep and dangerous, it is no surprise that theologians generally keep their toes dry.

There have been many church reports about sexuality in the last 45 years, and I have found them all evasive. There is almost never a serious discussion of history in these writings. The latest sexuality report from the Church of England, *Living in Love and Faith* (House of Bishops, 2020), deserves notoriety in this respect. Nor is there any willingness to acknowledge, still less to own, the continuing influences of body-negativity, suspicion of difference, and outright disgust, well encapsulated by the phrase 'vile bodies'. Peter Damian's *Book of Gomorrah* (Chapter

13), written in 1051, may still be influencing Christians a millennium later since it burned on to the historical imagination of Christians the association between men having sex with men and the worst punishments hell can eternally provide. Yes, we may remember the misogyny of, say, Jerome or Augustine (Chapters 9—12), and then seek to excuse their extreme views as a product of their times. But during their times their views were *not* extreme (both of them were canonized), and their baleful misogynistic legacy lingers on, still largely unacknowledged and unrecognized. Who remembers the misogyny that drove thousands of women to imprisonment, torture and death as witches? Why was the *Hammer of Witches* (Chapter 14) one of the most misogynistic works ever written, never withdrawn or apologized for? The book will weave together unwelcome threads of historical continuity between past and present. These will help to illumine the inadequacy of basic beliefs and doctrines that lend their support for sexism, racism and colonialism (Chapter 16), and to suggest (Chapter 22) how they may (fairly easily) be reconceived.

Key terms will be explained as the pages turn. But several contested terms have already found their way in. 'Patriarchy' is a key term in feminist theology, and in this book. It derives from Latin and Greek words meaning 'father' and 'rule'. Abraham, Isaac and Jacob (all characters in Genesis), the ancestors of the Jewish faith, are known as 'the patriarchs'. In the Orthodox Churches a patriarch is a senior bishop. Patriarchy was used for the rule of the pope and archbishops, but by the seventeenth century it came to mean 'a form of social organization in which the father or oldest male is the head of the family, and descent and relationship are reckoned through the male line; government or rule by a man or men' (*OED*). It tends to be used most often (in biblical studies) to refer to the tendency for authority and power to be centred with older males – often to the detriment of younger persons and women. It became widespread in the 1970s, especially in feminist theology, where it stood for 'the predominance of men in positions of power and influence in society, with cultural values and norms favouring men. Frequently with pejorative connotation' (*OED*). That is how it is used here. Churches remain primary exemplifiers of patriarchy in countries influenced by Christianity. Take a look at a papal entourage, or press coverage of episcopal conferences, convocations, synods and so on in Catholic, Orthodox and many Anglican Churches, and try to find a woman.

Everyone knows that 'misogyny' (from two Greek words meaning 'woman' and 'hatred') is the 'hatred or dislike of, or prejudice against women' (*OED*). It expresses itself in male suspicion, contempt, disgust, disparagement, silencing and so on. But misogyny is not merely an unfortunate disposition that particular males happen to harbour. It is a *social* phenomenon,

> a property of social systems or environments as a whole, in which women will tend to face hostility of various kinds *because they are women in a man's world* (i.e., a patriarchy), who are held to be failing to live up to patriarchal standards (i.e., tenets of patriarchal ideology that have some purchase in this environment). (Manne, 2018, p. 33, author's emphasis)

Patriarchy *enables* misogyny and is prior to it. In *Down Girl: The Logic of Misogyny*, Kate Manne suggests a helpful distinction between misogyny and *sexism*: the former being 'the "law enforcement" branch of a patriarchal order' and the latter its '"justificatory" branch'. This branch is the ideology of patriarchy that has 'the overall function of *rationalizing* and *justifying* patriarchal social relations' (Manne, 2018, pp. 78–9, author's emphases). Translated into theology, the church is the patriarchal order: misogyny is the power that keeps women in their place, while sexist theology justifies patriarchy by rationalizing and justifying it in the name of God. 'Ideology' is a 'systematic scheme of ideas, usually relating to politics, economics, or society and forming the basis of action or policy; a set of beliefs governing conduct. Also: the forming or holding of such a scheme of ideas' (*OED*). It is obvious that theology is the bearer of an ideology. The internal theological task is to abolish the sexism it carries, in the name of a just God and a more just ecclesial order, free of its patriarchal spoilers.

Vilified Bodies: some examples

Here are several *contemporary* examples of the bodily vilification of human beings in today's churches. I will argue in the book that only by laying bare their historical and theological roots can action be taken to understand and remedy them. The examples are influenced by my situatedness in the Church of England, but my sights are broader and similar examples are surely present and recognizable throughout the world. There's nothing parochial about what follows. They are the justification for the inquiry that follows in subsequent chapters. They are deep-seated moral wrongs that must be challenged and removed.

Abuse survivors

The unbearable scandals of child abuse, deepening over 40 years of cover-ups, the evasion of justice and the denial of responsibility, is stupefying in its turpitude and has led to the characterization of the church itself as a 'vile body' (Chapters 20—21). The abuse crisis of the churches is a moral one, but it is the tip of a *theological* iceberg. Beneath the tip there is an icy mass of historical thinking that has contributed to the abuse, and projected contempt on to the bodies of whole groups of 'others', beginning with women and children, but also on to many 'otherized' groups – 'sodomites', indigenous and colonized bodies, disabled bodies, heretical bodies – or, as we now see in the churches today, on to people whose bodies and whose desires do not coincide with strict notions of heterosexuality or binary gender. Abusers may already be partly formed by a theology that distorts attitudes to their own bodies and those of their victims. Inadequate teaching about bodies, sexuality and gender may be one of the reasons why Christian influence is fast disappearing at least in Europe, weakening in the USA (despite the noise of emergent Christian nationalism there), and why it is fuelling controversy, fear, victimization and death where it is still influential.

As I started to write this book during the second lockdown of the Covid-19 crisis in the autumn of 2020, Anglicans in England and Wales endured the prolonged embarrassment of two reports on child sexual abuse in the Church of England. Indeed, the embarrassment was in danger of drawing attention away from the victims and recommendations of the reports. An Independent Inquiry into Child Sexual Abuse (IICSA) was set up by the government of the United Kingdom because many historical cases of abuse had come to light throughout the country, and the government had 'some very grave concerns that some organizations were failing and were continuing to fail to protect children from sexual abuse' (IICSA, n.d.). Among these organizations were the Church of England (and the Church of Wales) and the Roman Catholic Church in England and Wales. In October 2020 the second report was published,[1] and it concluded:

> The culture of the Church of England facilitated it becoming a place where abusers could hide. Deference to the authority of the Church and to individual priests, taboos surrounding discussion of sexuality and an environment where alleged perpetrators were treated more supportively than victims presented barriers to disclosure that many victims could not overcome. Another aspect of the Church's culture was clericalism, which meant that the moral authority of clergy was widely perceived as beyond reproach. As we have said in other reports, faith organisations

such as the Anglican Church are marked out by their explicit moral purpose, in teaching right from wrong. In the context of child sexual abuse, the Church's neglect of the physical, emotional and spiritual well-being of children and young people in favour of protecting its reputation was in conflict with its mission of love and care for the innocent and the vulnerable. (IICSA, 2020b, p. vi)

This was a damning judgement. In October 2022 a further report by the Church of England admitted 400 previously undisclosed cases involving actions by clergy, officials and volunteers against children and vulnerable adults, uncovered in the most extensive review of personnel records ever undertaken (National Safeguarding Steering Group, 2022). The Archbishops of Canterbury and York expressed 'the great sadness and profound shame that we, again and again, come face-to-face with the brokenness and failings of our church'. The following month, IICSA published its report into safeguarding in the Roman Catholic Church in England and reached near-identical conclusions. It observed that:

faith organisations are marked out from most other institutions by their explicit moral purpose. The Roman Catholic Church is no different. In the context of the sexual abuse of children, that moral purpose was betrayed over decades by those in the Church who perpetrated this abuse and those who turned a blind eye to it. The Church's neglect of the physical, emotional and spiritual well-being of children and young people in favour of protecting its reputation was in conflict with its mission of love and care for the innocent and vulnerable. (IICSA, 2020a, p. v)

Between 1970 and 2015, the Roman Catholic Church in England and Wales received more than 900 complaints involving over 3,000 instances of child sexual abuse against more than 900 individuals connected to the church, including priests, monks and volunteers. Since 2016 there have still been more than 100 further allegations reported each year. The inquiry 'heard appalling accounts of sexual abuse of children perpetrated by clergy and others'. It described the psychological effects endured by victims. The inquiry found 'a sorry history of child sexual abuse', which was 'swept under the carpet. Resistance to external intervention was widespread.' It reported that:

Across the Inquiry's hearings on the Roman Catholic Church, weaknesses in leadership were significant in the failures to address child sexual abuse. The responses of Church leaders over time were marked by delay in implementing change as well as reluctance to acknowledge responsibility, to hold individuals to account or to make sincere apologies. They conveyed on occasions a grudging and unsympathetic attitude to victims. Failure in some of these areas contributed to more children experiencing actual abuse and many others being exposed to the risk of sexual abuse. (IICSA, 2020a, p. 8)

It found the very limited cooperation it received from the Vatican 'passes understanding'.

I wrote to IICSA to inquire whether any incidences, alleged or confirmed, had been committed by women. They replied: 'Having liaised with our research and legal departments to investigate your query, the Inquiry can confirm that we are not aware of any female perpetrators or alleged perpetrators in the Roman Catholic or Anglican Church investigations.'[2] It is a patriarchal problem, but we should not overlook that there *are* cases of female perpetrators and, even more, women who collude with or ignore abuse. *But abuse is a highly gendered crime combining male sexual gratification with male power.* Throughout the world the extent of sexual abuse in the Catholic Church is scarcely believable (see Chapter 20 for its extent), and compensation paid to victims has to be calculated in billions of dollars – money provided by believers for the work of God in the world.

LGBTIQ people[3]

Sexual minorities are regularly vilified. Indeed, the association of any sexual activity with shame remains widespread in the churches. Gay men are particularly singled out as objects of disgust and abhorrence, partly because of what they are thought to do with their bodies (Chapter 13). The Anglican Communion of churches at their Lambeth Conference in 1998,

> while rejecting homosexual practice as incompatible with Scripture, calls on all our people to minister pastorally and sensitively to all irrespective of sexual orientation and to condemn irrational fear of homosexuals, violence within marriage and any trivialisation and commercialisation of sex. (Anglican Communion, Resolution 1.10(d))

While some member churches within the Anglican Communion are taking steps to bless and/or solemnize same-sex unions, others, mainly from the Global South (and excluding the province of South Africa where Desmond Tutu was Archbishop), continue to support governments that persecute, exclude and imprison homosexual people. No connection was made between the 'irrational fear' of homosexuals and the abusive theology that continued to allow 'scripture' to be read in a fear-arousing way. There seems to be little pastoral and sensitive ministry here. But these churches represent about half of the 80 million active Anglicans worldwide, and they have responded to these theological disputes by declaring a state of impaired communion with their Western and Northern counterparts. Once more the task of combatting homophobia cannot be left to people whose lives are affected by it. Straight people need to get active, confront implicit and explicit forms of homophobia, within the churches and beyond them.

Many distinguished Roman Catholics have taken, and continue to take, issue with the dubious foundations of Catholic opposition to same-sex relations (most recently the *Wijngaards Report*, Wijngaards Institute for Catholic Research, 2018). But the Vatican's recent pronouncement denies that even a blessing of a same-sex couple is admissible, because the church is unable to 'approve and encourage a choice and a way of life that cannot be recognized as objectively ordered to the revealed plans of God'. God 'does not and cannot bless sin' (Congregation for the Doctrine of the Faith, 2021). A theology that begins with the experience of being despised, persecuted and misunderstood starts from a different place, where the wisdom of the Creator in creating sexual diversity is not questioned; where the required internalization of the disgust of others falls away; and where the shared love between partners is recognized as sharing in the love that God is.

Victims of racism

Racism 'is a set of unproven assumptions for indicating the notion of fixed categories of biological (and hierarchical) differences between differing groups of people, and is an invention, or fiction, of the era of modernism' (Reddie, 2009, p. xvi) (Chapters 15 and 16). But racism cannot be understood without making some attempt to grasp the growing anti-Semitism within the church during the medieval period (Chapter 15) that led to a further justification for enslavement in the early modern period. The scourge of racism in many churches is proving difficult even to acknowledge, still less to remove. In my own church, it remains a constant source of consternation. In the USA, Christian nationalism and white evangelicalism continue their hijack of the faith in their overt support for racism and homophobia. 'Racism is a sin', the Archbishops of Canterbury and York recently announced (Archbishops of Canterbury and York, 2021). They set up an Anti-Racist Taskforce to advise the church on how to deal with it. *From Lament to Action* (Church of England, 2021) was the result. But the authors of this commendable document reported that they first had to consider more than 20 reports from the mid-1980s onwards with a total of more than 160 recommendations. Since then, they wearily complained, 'the Church of England has considered motion after motion, debate after debate, yet we still find ourselves in the position where – throughout our life as a church – the flourishing of UKME/GMH [United Kingdom Minority Ethnic/Global Majority Heritage] Anglicans is hard to discern' (Church of England, 2021, p. 17). (Three months later, General Synod was told that a key recommendation – the appointment of Racial Justice Officers in every diocese – would not be funded.)

Robert Beckford, a leading black theologian in the UK, thinks the time has come for the white-majority church in the UK to 'face its demons'. The church, he rues,

> is oppressed by a negative, demonic force – in its thinking, in its theologising, and its performance and ministry. There needs to be a form of exorcism. This can't be done cognitively or rationally: it's so deeply embedded. It needs a spiritual awakening. (quoted in McDonald, 2022)

But the 'demons' that require exorcism are not confined to the removal of racism. The demons of patriarchy, of sexism, of hierarchy need exorcizing too. The same demons run rife in the secular world as well. They shape-shift. Closing down the spaces they occupy requires understanding how the 'thinking' and 'theologizing' that accommodates them came about. Its 'deep embeddedness' requires examining how particular bodies came to be regarded as inferior, malformed, vile, 'other', and how those traits came to be embedded in Christian 'performance and ministry'. That requires considerable cognitive and rational effort, beginning with the Bible and the uses to which its books have been put. Such effort does not run counter to the 'spiritual awakening' Beckford wants. It will help to bring it about, and this book is a small contribution to it. Combatting racism cannot be left to those people whose lives are directly affected by it because the problem lies more squarely with those perpetuating it (mainly white people). It will require some theological nerve to keep going to the end.

Victims of Spiritual Abuse

Recently the term 'spiritual abuse' has come into prominence accompanying investigations into the abusing behaviour of thousands of priests and ministers. A definition that finds favour with survivors calls it 'a form of emotional and psychological abuse' that 'is characterized by a systematic pattern of coercive and controlling behaviour in a religious context'. It 'can have a deeply damaging impact on those who experience it' (Oakley and Humphreys, 2019). Spiritual abuse is common among the religions of the world. It is a fitting label for the conduct of Christians and churches who attempt to enforce heteronormativity through 'conversion' therapy on LGBTIQ people; of pastors who form inappropriately close contact with members of their flock; and in one case, documented in the astonishing book *Bleeding for Jesus* (Graystone, 2021), of a powerful Christian leader and high-flying barrister who used his role in the church to beat severely over a hundred male victims he assaulted and betrayed, while senior Christian leaders who knew about it did – nothing. In England (in 2023), legislation to ban conversion therapy (Chapter 19) – a practice that has caused untold suffering and suicide – is being opposed and delayed by a group of churches that are members of the Evangelical Alliance.

Victims of marital and domestic violence

There are several types of violence or abuse apart from the obvious physical violence. There is psychological and emotional abuse, which takes many forms – controlling, undermining, blaming, yelling, insulting, stalking and so on. Less is heard about '*epistemic* violence'. From the Greek word for knowledge, 'epistemic violence' (a term not coined until 1998 (Spivak, 1987)), is the name given to the effect that overarching structures of knowledge have upon particular minorities of people who may be unable to challenge them (see Thatcher, 2020, pp. 17–19).

Everyone knows violence occurs in marriages, families and households, and here too the churches need to examine the contribution Christian beliefs make to its initiation and intensification. Marriage is celebrated as a sacrament, a holy ordinance, a covenant. Good theological sense can be made of these fine designations (Chapter 17), but surely not without also considering the shadow side of marriages, and the covert control and coercion lurking within many of them. Spousal bodies are not 'vile bodies', but many of them are *violated* nonetheless, nearly all of them female. Coercive control, manipulation, undermining and so on are all forms of violence, whether or not they are accompanied by physical expression. In so far as the violence is mandated, or believed to be mandated, by scripture, then it becomes epistemic as well.

Traditional marriage is also the locus of some appalling violence (Chapter 17), including by Christian husbands against their wives, worldwide, as Elizabeth Koepping reports in a shocking study (Koepping, 2021). Where does that sense of entitlement, assumed by domineering husbands, to inflict harm on their wives, come from? Partly from the Bible (Chapter 6). Exploring domestic violence in Argentina and England, Rachel Starr identifies among the risk factors to women '*dominant Christian teachings and practices around marriage*' (Starr, 2018, p. 2, emphasis added). Christian traditions are mostly silent about domestic violence, she thinks, because ambiguous attitudes to the body and sex have led to a 'spiritualization of marriage, the physical realities being pushed to one side', and because of the widespread influence of the doctrine of headship (Starr, 2018, p. 41). She explains how the depiction in the Hebrew Bible of God's relation to God's people as a marriage (Chapter 3) authorizes the inequality of partners in the marriage and the freedom of the more powerful partner to do what he likes. The assumption that procreation is a necessary purpose of marriage has led to the denial of contraception and abortion to women (Chapter 8), while the depiction of marriage as an 'indissoluble bond' still makes it difficult or impossible to exit failed or violent marriages. Even 'the denial of violence is a form of violence in itself'. There is a long list of deleterious consequences for women as a result of biblical teaching about, for example, Eve's disobedience, the silencing of women in churches, the prevention of their leadership, their definition as 'self-for-others and therefore suited to caring for others' (p. 143) (Chapters 5 and 6).

Starr made her criticism of Christian marriage because she can still see the possibility of developing a more helpful understanding of it. These observations about marriage gone wrong illustrate how the scheme just defined – patriarchy, misogyny, sexism – works: patriarchy the structure; misogyny the use of authority, biblical or ecclesial, to enforce the patriarchy; and sexist theology the justificatory practice. The Church of England report *Responding Well to Domestic Abuse* (Church of England, 2017) illustrates the veracity of Starr's analysis. The report is important within its limited readership, but I use it here to illustrate a failure of theology probably worldwide. A short appendix to the report provides a table of 'helpful' and 'unhelpful' 'applications' of problematic biblical texts (pp. 43–4), yet fails completely to acknowledge or critique the theology that utilizes and endorses the gender inequality, male headship and the enforcement of obedience that is based on them (Chapter 6).

The recent, and perhaps ongoing, Covid-19 pandemic has eclipsed a different pandemic, that of escalating worldwide violence against women (see Storkey, 2015; Thatcher, 2020). Indeed, the Covid-19 pandemic has made the incidence of domestic violence still worse. Prior to the lockdowns imposed as a consequence of the recent pandemic, gender violence had already 'reached endemic levels in many countries and communities around the world, where sexual violence, family violence, homophobia, biphobia, and transphobia have become a lived reality for many people' (Blyth, Colgan and Edwards, 2018). 'Rape culture' is the name associated with the global backgrounds that endorse gender violence. Some writers are now making disturbing connexions between the reading of sacred texts and the ability of 'rape cultures' to maintain themselves unremarked and unnoticed. 'Rape cultures create an environment in which gender violence can flourish; and the Bible – with its myriad traditions about gender violence and its endorsement of the patriarchal discourses that sanction such violence – plays an undeniable role in this process' (Blyth, Colgan and Edwards, 2018, p. 2).

Women priests – victims of epistemic violence

The exclusive and seemingly impermeable male priesthood in Catholic, Orthodox and many Anglican and Protestant Churches is a symptom of a deep moral and spiritual malaise. The so-called 'reservation' of priesthood to men alone (Pope John Paul II, 1994, para. 1) is an obvious form of epistemic violence (Medina, 2021). Powerful males inform powerless females that they are unworthy of male office, and adduce lots of proof -texts and works of dead male theologians whom they invest with divine authority. Because epistemic violence operates in systems or bodies of knowledge, it is also called 'systemic violence'. That women still cannot be ordained *throughout most of the worldwide church* is scandalous, a stark fact the implications of which extend far beyond the self-imposed restriction of the preaching of the gospel, disintegration of congregations through pastoral scarcity, and 'eucharistic famine' – the lack of a penis-possessing priest to consecrate and administer bread and wine.

This exclusion of women from ministry is strong evidence for the continuation of the classical, hierarchical view that men are superior to women in every respect (and women are especially unsuited to represent Christ because they are not part of the superior sex to which he temporarily belonged). This inferiority, and its apparent endorsement by the New Testament (see Chapter 6) and many other passages of the Bible (Chapters 2—6), has been consistently called out and exposed, yet with little hope of early success against the entrenched patriarchy of Catholic, Orthodox and Evangelical male gerontocracies (systems of government by old men: *gerōn* means 'old man' in Greek). No wonder humanists ask *Does God Hate Women?* (Benson and Stangroom, 2009). But a theology that begins with the exclusion from ministry of half the population of the world, impoverishes the church and fails to take seriously the harm and pain that follows the internalization of this exclusion is certain to read the Bible differently.

Abused bodies and abusive theology

Connexions are not being made between abusive behaviour in the churches and the abusive teachings and practices that tend to legitimize it. In November 2020 the Church of England published a series of materials, including a large book, entitled *Living in Love and Faith* (LLF). The project described itself as a 'church-wide learning together, listening to one another, and listening to God', as 'part of discerning a way forward for the Church of England in relation to matters of identity, sexuality, relationships and marriage' (Church of England, 2020). Three earlier reports had failed to discern a way forward. Neither had a protracted 'listening process', centrally organized. Meanwhile, the abuse did not stop. In 2018 alone, '449 concerns were reported to the Church about recent child sexual abuse, of which more than half related to church officers' (IICSA, 2020b, p. vi). But listening to the anguish of victims of sexual abuse, and hearing their distressing stories, *was never part of the purpose of LLF*, never part of the discernment sought. The connection between the immoral behaviour of hundreds of church officers over many years and the nexus of beliefs and attitudes that appeared to validate their actions and the cover-up by others *was never made*. Despite huge amounts of money now being spent on safeguarding and training,[4] the handwringing, apologizing (usually late, minimal and reluctant), and promising to do better (and of course to learn lessons), the legacy of this visceral tradition is scarcely recognized and still less owned.

That is why more is being heard of something called 'abusive theology' (Stiebert, 2023). As Stiebert explains:

> As with other kinds of abuse, power relations play a key role in abusive theology. Consequently, groups disenfranchised in terms of representation and agency – women, children, LGBT+ persons, persons with disabilities – are disproportionately targeted in spiritual abuse. Such abuse is predominantly perpetrated by hegemonic men in positions of authority: be that in faith communities, the family or the public sphere. (Stiebert, 2023, p. 9)

The Shiloh Project (Shiloh Project, 2023), which investigates the contribution of biblical texts to rape culture, lists over 200 major works that have been published since 1980, demonstrating the connexion. Indeed, 'trauma theology', another branch of contemporary theology, has grown out of the experience of multiple abuses, beginning with the experience of victims and examining theology and church from survivors' perspectives (O'Donnell and Cross, 2020). It is not possible to read any of these books without experiencing distress for victims, but also for the continuation of abusive theology within the churches and many of their training institutions.

Some established theologians are feeling their way 'toward a post-abusive theology', the subtitle of Un*knowing God* (Harvey and Woodhead, 2022). The authors share their unease about many facets of Christian doctrine – concepts of a punitive God, the Virgin Mary, the ambivalence of the cross, a sin-centred theology and so on. All these, they say, which we Christians thought we had known and inwardly digested, are implicated in abusive theology and have to be 'un-known' in moving towards a post-abusive theology and church.

It will become clear in the book that what I am calling the 'vilifying' or 'visceral' character of Christian teaching about bodies, past and present, is deeply implicated in the abuse crises, and the crises will never be understood, still less overcome, without owning and expunging them. A decade ago, when the crisis in Catholicism was already a generation old, one of the leading Catholic women theologians in England spoke of 'the poisonous legacy of a long tradition of contempt for human sexuality in an institution which has privileged secrecy and unaccountable power over transparency and participation'. This 'poisonous legacy' is the visceral tradition of Christian thought about sexed bodies and their desires (Chapter 18). The Catholic tradition, she continues, is one:

> in which sexual desire has been portrayed as the enemy of those who seek spiritual union with God. In a religion in which the main focus has been the development of men's spirituality through the suppression of their sexuality, this has meant that male priests and monks have regarded the sexual female body as the greatest threat to their spiritual well-being, and the control of female sexuality has been and continues to be a major preoccupation. (Beattie, 2010)

But the attempt to control the bodies of others is not limited to female sexuality. Since all sexual arousal and all desire (except of course desire for God) is perceived as potentially sinful, desiring bodies are considered sinful, requiring discipline or 'mortification', while desired bodies are perceived as objects of temptation, and the desire for them a soul-racking state of guilt (Chapter 18). The visceral tradition always has new bodies to vilify. The bodies of trans people are its latest victims.

The book will explore two millennia of Christian thinking about sexed and gendered bodies, attending particularly to its visceral, vilifying and potentially abusive character. It is *not* hostile to Christian faith *as such*, only to those elements of it that continue to damage and kill people. It *is* hostile towards versions of faith that attempt to require of individuals unnecessary suffering and then vest it with spiritual significance; or that lay on individuals burdens they do not need to carry; or that retain violence and injustice in their very accounts of who and what God is, all derived from the Bible. Jesus asked, 'Is there anyone among you who, if your child asks for a fish, will give a snake instead of a fish? Or if the child asks for an egg, will give a scorpion?' (Luke 11.11–12). Yes, there are versions of faith that are venomous, poisonous to body and soul.

Thankfully there are also millions of Christians who emphasize all that remains positive and attractive in their faith, including tireless work towards diversity and inclusion. But these elements go deep. It is not possible to say whether the required changes will ever happen. The book *is* hostile towards the preservation of many of the visceral, historical elements of Christian teaching about the body and sexuality, barely recycled as they reappear in the vilification of particular bodies, especially those of women, LGBTIQ people and people of colour. As the story unfolds it will throw light on modern sexism, homophobia, transphobia and racism; on the rapid loss of faith in 'the West'; on the polemics that continue to rage within the churches over the sexed body and its erotic desires; on the disgraceful and global outbreaks of sexual abuse in virtually every Christian denomination; and on the pathetic and culpable attempts to cover up the abuse to protect the churches' 'good name'. The bodies of *slaves*,[5] too (Chapter 12), will not be forgotten, as the vocabulary of hierarchy took hold, and domination became Christians' preferred notion of power. It will show that all the residual disparagement of bodies deemed strange and deviant is inconsistent with the teaching of the One in whose name it is proclaimed, and based on a patriarchal mindset that has no place either in a faithful church or an increasingly faithless world.

Notes

1 The third and final report was published in October 2022.
2 Email correspondence, 17 November 2020.
3 Is there a stable designation for sexual and gender minorities that is acceptable to all of them, that acknowledges real differences yet retains respect? LGBTQ+

remains in common use, but 'I' (for intersex people) is either missing or subsumed in the '+'. The Bishops of the Church of England (2023) now use LGBTQI+. LGBTQIA+ appears to be the latest, ever-lengthening assemblage of digits. It includes intersex people but adds 'A' (for 'asexual'). While asexual people are often wrongly overlooked, 'asexual' is a negative term. It is hard to see how or why people with no sexual desire or interest in sex should be included in a term specifying particular sexualities. Q (for people identifying as queer) runs the risk of being an anti-identity identity, refusing not only 'heterosexual' but also L, G, B, T and I as well. Equally some people mean by 'queer' an umbrella term *encompassing* all non-heterosexual identities. There is more about 'queer' in Chapter 19.

Whatever compound is adopted, the page-scanning eye of the straight cis-gender reader is likely to see a blur of identities, incomprehensibly expressed, inviting the very loss of difference the single designation purports to express. I want to avoid generating such responses. Above all, respect for all minorities must be maintained. My least unfavourite collective term is LGBTIQ, avoiding 'A' and the suffix '+' (because of its indefiniteness and catch-all character). I use the term sparingly and I hope respectfully, preferring to speak of sex and gender minorities, or specifying more precisely which minorities have become subjects in the text.

4 In 2013 the Archbishops' Council spent £37,000 on safeguarding. In 2020 its budget for safeguarding was £3,189,000. IICSA, 2020, p. 15.

5 Slaves were not regarded as persons. Should I therefore speak not of 'slaves' but of 'enslaved persons', 'enslaved people' instead? Perhaps, but it sometimes becomes cumbersome and awkward to do so (because of the 80 or so references to them in the book). Because it is assumed throughout the book that slaves *are* persons, I have retained the term. I think no harm is done if it also reminds readers that slaves were *once* treated as non-persons. For a contrary view, see Browning-Mullis, 2020.

2

Some Ancient Hebrew Bodies:
The Vilification Begins

All the early Christians, like Jesus, were Jews. The Jewish people at the time of Jesus had their own scriptures. Christians had no scriptures at all apart from the Jewish scriptures that they inherited. Out of respect for the Jewish people, and recognition that the Tanakh is for them a living religious text and so not 'Old' or superseded, most scholars no longer refer to it as the 'Old' Testament, though that name is still very common in the churches. It took the Christians at least a century to build a literature of their own, and another two centuries before they could more or less agree which writings were 'in' and which were 'out' (the ones that were in were called the 'canon'). From now on I will refer to the Tanakh as the Hebrew Bible, abbreviated to HB, and to the New Testament as NT. The roots of Christianity, then, are Jewish through and through and we need to look to the HB first to discover what early Christians did with it in developing their understanding of human bodies and of themselves.

Shamed and Shameful Bodies

The well-known creation myth, common to Jews and Christians alike, in the book of Genesis, associates the *naked* body with shame. Prior to eating the forbidden fruit in the garden in Eden, 'the man and his wife were both naked, *and were not ashamed*' (2.25). After their disobedience (which came to be known among Christians as 'the Fall'), 'the eyes of both were opened, and they knew that they were naked; and they sewed fig leaves together and made loincloths for themselves' (3.7). Nakedness, for Jews and Christians, has been a matter of shame ever since, both in public and in private.

It is no longer possible to understand the myth of the Fall as a historical event, with a paradise 'before' and a cosmic ruination 'after'. Christians still do this, and the habit dies hard, even though creatures that existed 'prior' to the Fall show many symptoms of 'fallen' humanity (disease, violence, death), and humanity as a species we now know has multiple origins, not just one. In the myth, the first human pair, having eaten the forbidden fruit, suddenly perceive themselves to be unclothed. Nakedness brings the burden of shame causing them to hide away from God (Gen. 3.9). Human genitalia must from now on be covered. Body parts made by the Creator become unfit objects for the divine gaze, and the human gaze also. Body shame becomes a 'primordial fact' in the human story, reaching as far back as theological history and the human imagination can go. It is not difficult to imagine the impact of these details on later generations of Jews and Christians.

Cursed and Racialized Bodies

Another myth in the early chapters of Genesis associates nakedness with a racial curse. Noah, better known as an ark builder and flood survivor, was also a vine grower. We are told he had three sons, Shem, Ham and Japheth, and one day one of them found him drunk, naked and incapable in his tent – the Bible's first drunkard. What happens next is among the strangest narratives in all ancient literature:

> And Ham, the father of Canaan, saw the nakedness of his father, and told his two brothers outside. Then Shem and Japheth took a garment, laid it on both their shoulders, and walked backwards and covered the nakedness of their father; their faces were turned away, and they did not see their father's nakedness. When Noah awoke from his wine and knew what his youngest son had done to him, he said,
> 'Cursed be Canaan;
>   lowest of slaves shall he be to his brothers.'
> He also said,
> 'Blessed by the LORD my God be Shem;
>   and let Canaan be his slave.
> May God make space for Japheth,
>   and let him live in the tents of Shem;
>   and let Canaan be his slave.' (9.22–27)

The problem seems to be that Ham (or Canaan – the text is confused) sees his father's penis, a sight so troublesome that all his descendants get cursed and are required to live in servitude. Was the old man's penis so revered that, almost like God, no one could look on it and live (Exod. 33.20)? Unlike Noah, we don't know 'what his youngest son had done to him'. Probably just catching an unwelcome glimpse of the old man's revered organ accidentally, rather than playing with it, or mocking its flaccid state, was his crime. The symbol of patriarchal order, however, is too holy to be glimpsed, limp, even accidentally. If seeing his father's nakedness is a euphemism for actual physical contact with him, that would explain the rabbinic and scholarly confusion about what Ham actually does to Noah. But this ancient broken text about the consequences of viewing the nakedness of a revered but drunken father had the most distressing and fatal repercussions for millions of people in the Christian era. Ham came to be associated with the Jewish people directly (Chapter 15), justifying the punitive regimes that persecuted and banished them. The same text was twisted to endorse both the believed inferiority of all black people, identified by white Christians as Canaanites, and their God-given status as slaves. In 1862 a man born in the United States to freed slaves claimed that the divine curse upon black people was the 'general, almost universal, opinion in the Christian world'. He found it

> in books written by learned men; and it is repeated in lectures, speeches, sermons, and common conversation. So strong and tenacious is the hold which it has taken upon the mind of Christendom, that it seems almost impossible to uproot it. Indeed, it is an almost foregone conclusion, that the Negro race is an accursed race, weighed down, even to the present, beneath the burden of an ancestral malediction. (Crummell, 1862, in Goldenberg, 2003, p. 176)

The origins of racism are found in one group of people regarding another group as inferior to them. Once inferiority becomes a 'category' the stage is set for multiple oppressions, particularly racism (Kaplan, 2019). That the story of Noah's nakedness became a root of the appalling ideologies of anti-Semitism and white racism indicates how dangerous the Bible is when hunters of proof texts get hold of it. The very possibility of understanding the story of Noah's nakedness this way indicates the visceral depth of disgust associated with the genitals, and the bizarre belief that God curses people for even looking at them.

Ejaculating and Menstruating Bodies

According to the law of Moses, found in the first five books (the Pentateuch) of the Bible, the shameful body is in constant danger of polluting other bodies and of being polluted. The term for pollution (in Hebrew the verbal root *tm'*) occurs 286 times in the HB (Kazen, 2002, p. 206). Like being 'vile', it 'describes a negative, contagious quality that is a product of disgust' (Feinstein, 2014, p. 8). Pollution is visceral: a subjective, emotional response from deep within the human being, recognized also as a universal human response and therefore framed and acknowledged in religious law.

The book of Leviticus asserts that a man always 'pollutes' himself when he ejaculates, whether by himself or with a partner:

> If a man has an emission of semen, he shall bathe his whole body in water, and be unclean until the evening. Everything made of cloth or of skin on which the semen falls shall be washed with water, and be unclean until the evening. If a man lies with a woman and has an emission of semen, both of them shall bathe in water, and be unclean until the evening. (15.16–18)

It is still widely thought that the Bible somewhere forbids (male) masturbation. It doesn't. But the moralizing name for it is 'self-pollution', and the origin of that term is here. The degree of pollution is mild. It takes a *ritual* form, not a moral one. It lasts a day. In Leviticus bodily pollutants are a *normal* fact of human life. It was Ezekiel who made menstrual blood an image of *moral* pollution. His visceral image of a boiling pot, contaminated with menstrual blood (24.2–14), stands for the moral condition of Jerusalem. He compares that city with 'an unclean woman immersed in her bloody filth' (Niditch, 2021, p. 33). Later generations of Christians, eager to find biblical justification for labelling masturbation a sin, had to be content with seizing upon the case of Onan who 'spilled his semen on the ground whenever he went in to his brother's wife, so that he would not give offspring to his brother' (Gen. 38.9). But Onan was no masturbator (at least not in this passage). Under the law of Levirate marriage he was expected to have sex with his dead brother's wife to produce children (see Ruttenberg, 2012, p. 391) who would perpetuate the dead man's lineage and name. By pulling his penis away from her prior to orgasm (his), he sought to avoid the end result that justified the practice – a child who would eventually care for their mother. The practice didn't end well for Onan. 'What he did was displeasing in the sight of the LORD, and he put him to death' (38.10). Christian masturbators would come to fear death as the divinely mandated punishment for the simple act of releasing the sexual tension to which their beliefs had probably contributed and failed to cure.

Men have probably always viewed the menstruation of women with disgust and fear of contamination. The ovarian cycle in women was not properly understood until the twentieth century (around 1930), so superstitious or pre-scientific beliefs about it before then were inevitable. But ignorance is different from disgust. This sense of disgust is confirmed in the passage from Leviticus, just cited. It continues:

> When a woman has a discharge of blood that is her regular discharge from her body, she shall be in her impurity for seven days, and whoever touches her shall be unclean until the evening. Everything upon which she lies during her impurity shall be unclean; everything also upon which she sits shall be unclean. Whoever touches her bed shall wash his clothes, and bathe in water, and be unclean until the evening. Whoever touches anything upon which she sits shall wash his clothes, and bathe in water, and be unclean until the evening; whether it is the bed or anything upon which she sits, when he touches it he shall be unclean until the evening. If any man lies with her, and her impurity falls on him, he shall be unclean seven days; and every bed on which he lies shall be unclean. (15.19–24)

Women throughout the world have to cope with the taboo surrounding their periods, and texts like these in the world's sacred writings are no help to them. This one is written by men, for men (and probably originally intended only for priests). 'Impurity', like pollution, is a heavily negative term. A menstruating woman is not only impure. She is a contaminant, contaminating everything and everyone she touches. She must be 'socially distant' from male family and friends. But social distancing is just one response. The other more practical response is the purification ritual set out to manage contact with menstruating women. Biblical writers, ever eager to express God's disgust at the behaviour of God's own people – political, social, ritual – had a ready illustration to hand. One of the prophets exclaimed, 'But we are all as an unclean thing, and all our righteousnesses are as filthy rags' (Isa. 64.6 KJV; see also Lam. 1.17; Ezek. 36.17). Much later the text would be commonly used by Protestant preachers to proclaim the worthlessness of good actions in helping to procure salvation. Doubtless hearers of the word would feel wretched when their efforts to be virtuous were compared to 'filthy rags', but they would not have been told about the earlier visceral resonance of the term. 'Filthy' translates the Hebrew term *iddah*, which more properly refers to 'the bodily fluids from a woman's menstrual cycle'. The object that illustrates God's repugnance is the precursor of a sanitary towel.

Regulations for men in contact with menstruating women were originally the product of ritual specialists, but as Torah became more authoritative they were increasingly applied to everyone. Laws and assumptions about purity have hideous consequences for the impure. The purity laws marginalized almost everyone: the uneducated and poor people who did not understand or have the resources to obey them; 'the sick, the lame, the blind, the deformed, lepers, and persons with various kinds of skin ailments and bodily fluxes ... vast numbers of people who made their living by means regarded as polluting and sinful, among them tax collectors, prostitutes, servants' (Ruether, 1998, p. 17). The division between pure and impure spread to the division between Jew and Gentile, 'while the inner and most intimate division between the holy and the unholy *divided male from female*' (Ruether, 1998, p. 17, emphasis added). James Cone thinks the sense of 'the purity of the white race' was so important to white Americans that it was instrumental in the lynching of thousands of black people (Cone, 2013, p. 99) in order to protect white people from contamination. The purity laws created religious elites, and elites are almost inevitably self-congratulatory, priding themselves on the differences between them and everyone else. That is how disdain and contempt arise, and once arisen, can quickly escalate. Purity and misogyny go hand in hand.

There is a lot more to disgust than the private sensation associated with it and named by it. Disgust is 'Strong repugnance, aversion, or repulsion excited by that which is loathsome or offensive, as a foul smell, disagreeable person or action, disappointed ambition, etc.; profound instinctive dislike or dissatisfaction' (*OED*). But disgust is like misogyny. It manifests itself *socially*. That is why it is 'particularly well-suited, *and hence recruited*, to play the role of regulating people's adherence to social norms, conventions, hierarchies, and so on' (Manne, 2018, p. 257, emphasis added). Disgust can be manipulated, exaggerated and encouraged in order to enforce required behaviour produced by it. It spreads 'by association', just as men's disgust towards women's periods can spread towards women themselves. Disgust keeps people in their closets. Why? Because 'the risk of becoming disgusting to others by engaging in socially taboo behavior acts as a further motivator, given a more or less universal aversion to shunning, shaming, and being ousted from one's community' (Manne, 2018, p. 257). Ask a closet gay (if you can find one, especially if they are a bishop). Disgust as a *social* phenomenon surrounds us. No wonder some LGBTIQ people internalize it, and then have to overcome it and the likely response to it when they come out. There can be little doubt that these biblical texts, understood as God-given law, have greatly influenced Christian attitudes to bodies.

Virginal Bodies

Unlike Catholic priests today, a priest in the HB is at least permitted (and indeed expected) to marry, but 'He shall marry only a woman who is a virgin. A widow, or a divorced woman, or a woman who has been defiled, a prostitute, these he shall not marry' (Lev. 21.13–14). Some scholars argue persuasively that the term *betulim* ('virginity') properly refers to an unmarried woman who has reached puberty but has not yet had her first child. Virginity, then, is less about sex and more about *potential fertility*. The context here is about a woman who has not belonged to another man (apart from her father, of course). The text is about men, here priestly men, and how they avoid self-defilement. A man defiles himself by taking another man's woman (be it his wife, his whore and so on). It is a property infringement.

There is a list of relatives in Leviticus 18 whom the reader, the male head of the clan or extended family, must not see naked. These are the prohibitions against incest:

> None of you shall approach anyone near of kin to uncover nakedness: I am the LORD. You shall not uncover the nakedness of your father, which is the nakedness of your mother; she is your mother, you shall not uncover her nakedness. You shall not uncover the nakedness of your father's wife; it is the nakedness of your father. (Lev. 18.6–8; and see Lev. 20.7–21)

The list goes on to include the man's mother, sister, granddaughter, aunt, daughter-in-law and sister-in-law. There is a clear reason given for these prohibitions: 'they are your flesh; it is depravity' (18.17). Uncovering nakedness is often a euphemism for having sex. A man may not have sex with any of these persons. The emphasis is on homosociality, on the boundaries a man must not step over in relation to the property of another man. So having sex with your mother is wrong because she belongs to your father (and thus belongs to his genitals). The sexuality of all female dependants is owned/controlled by the paterfamilias. There are two exceptions: no regulations against a man having sex with his daughter (because she is already his until she marries); and no regulation against a man having sex with his dead brother's wife (because her new partner is effectively acting as a legitimate substitute for his dead brother, perpetuating his line). So fully are women the permanent property of men, they cannot transfer their sexual assets to anyone else.

There is a risk to having sex. The risk is contamination, not in a literal or virological sense, but in the ritual sense. Purity – one of the roots of the valorization of virginity in the Christian tradition – may have grown more deeply in the soil of male disgust at the possibility of women's autonomous sexual behaviour than in the more fertile soil of divine revelation. Another surprise may lurk in the common idea, based on Genesis 2.24, that a married couple become 'one flesh'. There is no particular language in Hebrew for 'marriage' or 'wife' or 'husband'. What gets translated (in various contexts) as 'marry' is properly 'take' or 'seize' (the latter is also used of rape). A wife is simply 'woman'; a husband is usually 'man' (the closest word for husband is 'lord'). It has often been remarked that the one flesh is the husband's, which now includes the flesh of his wife (a perverse notion of inclusion!). But 'one flesh' is more than a usurpation of the wife's body. In Leviticus 18 there is a fear of contamination from any sexual contact not expressly authorized by divine law, and it cannot be expunged.

Foetal Bodies – sexed and gendered from the womb

Giving birth is not merely *intended* by God to be painful as a punishment for sin (Gen. 3.16). It is a polluting and polluted process in the ritual sense. A woman is not only polluted by her period. She is even polluted by giving birth. Not only that, the period of waiting prior to a ceremony of 'purification' after a birth differs according to the sex of the child. The period of waiting in the case of the birth of a baby girl is twice the length of the same period in the case of the birth of a boy, and pursuit of the likely reason for this provides an important insight into early ideas of gender.

According to Leviticus:

> If a woman conceives and bears a *male* child, she shall be ceremonially unclean *seven days*; as at the time of her menstruation, she shall be unclean. On the eighth day the flesh of his foreskin shall be circumcised. Her time of blood purification shall be *thirty-three days*; she shall not touch any holy thing, or come into the sanctuary, until the days of her purification are completed. If she bears a *female* child, she shall be unclean *two weeks*, as in her menstruation; her time of blood purification shall be *sixty-six days*. (12.2–5)

This piece of legislation has puzzled Jews and Christians ever since its compilation. It lies behind the rite of the churching of Women, which was practised by several churches until the 1960s. I remember a Baptist minister in the 1960s, a young woman, asking me at the front door of the manse if she could be 'churched'. I didn't even know then what she was asking for, but guessed she wanted to give thanks to God for the safe delivery of her son, and to seek a blessing from God for him. She was happy with this suggestion (and relieved, I recall, that she didn't need to feel unclean until the minister had said the appropriate prayers).

But we are now better placed to understand this utterly strange passage. Recently there has been much research into ancient embryology, and the probable reasons for the differing purification periods in Jewish law are becoming clearer. These reasons take us into yet more strange assumptions about the composition and reproduction of bodies in biblical times, but some of them will be mentioned now. First, there was a belief that achieved 'virtual ubiquity' (Thiessen, 2018, p. 309) in the ancient world: that male foetuses develop more quickly than female ones! A boy 'moves' first in the womb. That belief remained, at least in Europe, until 1723. The lack of evidence for it made no difference to its acceptance. Its counterpart is that men are more *perfect* than women. There was no evidence for that either, but it is a belief – more a deep-seated prejudice – that also enjoyed ubiquity. Aristotle affirms the belief explicitly. So does the Greek-speaking Jew, Philo of Alexandria, who may be making a direct connection between the Levitical text and Greek thought when he observes:

> Inasmuch as the moulding of the male is more perfect than, and double, that of the female, it requires only half the time, namely forty days; whereas the imperfect woman, who is, so to speak, a half-section of man, requires twice as many days, namely eighty. (Thiessen, 2018, p. 304)

The explanation is daft, not least because it relies on the assumption that 'something twice as good should take half as long to develop' (Thiessen, 2018, p. 305). But once conjecture and prejudice take hold, they are almost impossible to dislodge.

Another virtually ubiquitous belief about embryos in the ancient world was that menstrual blood provided the growing foetus with all the nutrition it required while *in utero*. Girl babies, being less perfect, are also colder and weaker. In the womb, so it was thought, they consume less of their mother's blood than boys. After birth the mother has excess blood to discharge because her body makes a constant amount, and a female baby doesn't need it all. The mother, then, takes longer to discharge any excess blood, so the period of purification must take into account a longer time to discharge the excess.

There is a further consideration unique to the Levitical text. In reality a woman will probably bleed for longer than seven days regardless of the sex of the baby. The baby boy's circumcision *seems to hasten the purification of his mother*. The blood shed in (male) circumcision acts as a 'ritual detergent' but female blood is a 'ritual pollutant' (of course). If there's no blood of circumcision, there's no hastening of the mother's purification.[1] These biblical materials, so out of sync with modern embryological, medical and social thought, and however they are read, helped to create the great lie of masculine superiority. They must all be understood, owned and superseded if abusive theology is to be overcome. We will encounter many more such materials in ensuing chapters.

Notes

1 I'm much indebted to Francesca Stavrakopoulou for her many suggestions, which have helped me make better sense of passages in the Hebrew Bible. I incorporate many of them in this and the next chapter. The remaining errors are mine alone.

3

Some More Hebrew Bodies:
Divine Violence and Human Misogyny

Abused and Dismembered Bodies – Gomer, Oholah, Oholibah

Linked with disgust about discharges from bodies is the association of
the bodies of women with disgusting sexual behaviour. Several of the
Hebrew prophets, in their attempts to depict their nation as unfaithful
to the covenant established between them and their God, compare the
covenant – where God is faithful and Israel, the people, is faithless – with
human marriage, where the long-suffering husband is faithful and the
wanton promiscuous wife is faithless. The prophet Hosea depicts himself
as instructed by the Lord to '"Go, take for yourself a wife of whoredom
and have children of whoredom, for the land commits great whoredom
by forsaking the LORD"' (Hos. 1.2). He marries Gomer, 'a worthless
woman' (1.3 NEB). They have three children, all of them given names
that are puns drawing attention to the nation's parlous plight in rejecting its God. In the next chapter God threatens his 'whoring' bride with
disturbing sexual violence. In chapter 3, the shortest chapter in the Bible,
Hosea gets a different call: '"Go, love a woman who has a lover and is
an adulteress, just as the LORD loves the people of Israel, though they
turn to other gods and love raisin cakes"' (3.1). Hosea obliges. He buys
a woman. 'So I bought her for fifteen shekels of silver and a homer of
barley and a measure of wine' (3.2). A market where women could be
bought and sold is no obvious moral deterrent to his action. The purpose
of the purchase is not to have sex with her. That's exactly it. Nothing
else. 'I said to her, "You must remain as mine for many days; you shall
not play the whore, you shall not have intercourse with a man, nor I with
you"' (3.3). The 'many days' of abstinence from sex (and presumably
from raisin cakes) is said to parallel and illustrate the 'many days' that
Israel must suffer God's abstinence from blessing them.

Scholars call such stories 'sign-acts' (Moughtin-Mumby, 2008, p. 210),
and some of them still debate whether Hosea had to marry both women
for the meaning of the sign-acts in the stories to convey meaning. But the
Christian tradition had no sophisticated reservations about the stories

then and now. Neither story commends marriage! Neither story shows regard for the wives or for the children. One doesn't need a theology degree to work out that these sign-acts are detrimental to women. The idea of a broken covenant is deeply asymmetrical. God retains all the attributes proper to God, like omnipotence, omniscience, perfection and so on (though none of these are attributed directly to God in the HB). And God is the husband. 'He' is *male*. He does no wrong. He is long-suffering, loving and, eventually, forgiving (he has all the positive human qualities as well). But his wife is a despicable character, arraigned by him in terms that would be condemned in a modern court of law as hate speech. But the prophet Ezekiel is easily the worst offender.

Anyone reading chapters 16 and 23 of Ezekiel must prepare themselves for extreme, offensive, violent language, and images that several commentators rightly describe as pornographic. Jerusalem is cast as a helpless foundling girl: 'on the day you were born your navel cord was not cut, nor were you washed with water to cleanse you, nor rubbed with salt, nor wrapped in cloths ... flailing about in your blood' (16.4, 6). The Lord comes across this infant and commands her to live. 'You grew up and became tall and arrived at full womanhood; your breasts were formed, and your hair had grown; yet you were naked and bare.' Then, when the child, still naked, was 'at the age for love', the Lord intervenes once more. 'I spread the edge of my cloak over you, and covered your nakedness' (16.8). With the Lord in attendance the child becomes a queen, but she uses her wealth and beauty to have sex with strangers. 'You ... lavished your whorings on any passer-by' (16.15). In the business of being paid for sex, she is so desperate for it that she pays her customers to have sex with her: 'So you were different from other women in your whorings: no one solicited you to play the whore; and you gave payment, while no payment was given to you; you were different' (16.34). The violence described next, intended by the Lord, is deeply distressing. He will gather Jerusalem's lovers and strip her naked in front of them. And then:

> I will deliver you into their hands, and ... they shall strip you of your clothes and take your beautiful objects and leave you naked and bare. They shall bring up a mob against you, and they shall stone you and cut you to pieces with their swords. They shall burn your houses and execute judgements on you in the sight of many women; I will stop you from playing the whore, and you shall also make no more payments. So I will satisfy my fury on you, and my jealousy shall turn away from you; I will be calm, and will be angry no longer. (16.39–42)

There are scores of critical feminist commentaries on these verses. Sexual violence is not merely condoned. The Lord is the very agent of it. His being angry is enough to justify it. He appears to delight in the violent sexual humiliation of a woman before she is stoned and hacked to death. Her violent end is allowed to become an object lesson and a threat to many other women. There are many references to female blood in the chapter (16.6, 9, 22, 36, 38), all of them disdainful. His 'fascination with female blood is one of its more disturbing features' (Moughtin-Mumby, 2008, p. 187). But in chapter 23 the pornographic imagery is yet more repulsive. The two nations of Israel are personified as daughters who 'played the whore in their youth; their breasts were caressed there, and their virgin bosoms were fondled' (23.3). The prophet appears to delight in the (for him) erotic detail. The Lord marries them both and the narrative graphically describes how one and then the other seduce the warriors, commanders and officials of the Assyrian army. The Lord declares:

> When she carried on her whorings so openly and flaunted her nakedness, I turned in disgust from her, as I had turned from her sister. Yet she increased her whorings, remembering the days of her youth, when she played the whore in the land of Egypt and lusted after her paramours there, whose members were like those of donkeys, and whose emission was like that of stallions. Thus you longed for the lewdness of your youth, when the Egyptians fondled your bosom and caressed your young breasts. (23.18–21)

Their punishment is to have their noses and ears cut off (23.25). Their former lovers will hate them, 'and they ... will make you feel their hatred ... [T]hat body with which you have played the whore will be ravished' (23.28–29 NEB).

Notwithstanding the disgusting images, the passage also affirms that the women were *abused as children*, and are culpably unable to recover from the traumas inflicted on them. They were not even given a voice. The images and the theology of Ezekiel, like his language, 'is problematic on every conceivable level, with the other prophetic texts paling in comparison to these violent narratives, which strive so brutally to force their negative assumptions about women onto the reader' (Moughtin-Mumby, 2008, p. 204).

It is easier to avoid examining these distressing narratives, as Christians invariably do. I have never heard them read in church. But here 'Bible believers' are in a bind because Ezekiel's misogynistic invective belongs to sacred scripture and is intended to be understood as the Lord's very words. 'Therefore, O whore, hear the word of the LORD' (Ezek. 16.35).

But the temptation to be spared embarrassment by ignoring them may be too closely associated with the attempt to be spared embarrassment by ignoring the many thousands of cases of abuse in the churches in the last 50 years. It is easier for Jews and Christians to avoid the problems for theology and belief of the depiction of the Lord as misogynistic, abusive and murderous than to admit the problem and begin to grapple with it. It is easier to let awkward silence win out. IICSA reported that church officers to whom complaints of abuse were made could not believe that the perpetrators, being holy, could conceivably have committed such crimes. But in abusive theology, even the holy God engages in criminal, abusive behaviour. Neither must 'He' be exempt from investigation, as the clergy now in jail for their violent crimes were not. Such passages cannot be overlooked. Beyond any direct influence they have exercised over men's minds, they contribute to the fear, disdain and disparagement of women that poisons much theology and belief today. They caricature real women as promiscuous and are an inevitable part of the shaping and endorsement of Christian misogyny.

Violated and Poisoned Bodies – the ordeal of bitter water

Feminist and womanist theologians have repeatedly shown how the Bible encourages gender and symbolic violence by, for example, 'trivializing the violence of rape and depicting females as property and female virginity as a commodity' (Stiebert, 2018, p. 32). There are around 500 terms for 'violence' in the HB, over 10,000 incidences of violence, of which 1865 are ascribed to God, averaging 'more than six instances of violence on every page of the Hebrew Bible' (Clines, 2020, no pagination). In Numbers 31, God commands Moses to exterminate the entire people of Midian. So the Israelites killed every Midianite man, and 'took the women of Midian and their little ones captive; and they took all their cattle, their flocks, and all their goods as booty' (Num. 31.9). Moses became angry that the women and children were classified as booty instead of being killed. Even limited 'gendered mercy' sparing their lives could not be tolerated. Next 'every male among the little ones' is to be killed, along with 'every woman who has known a man by sleeping with him' (31.17). Virgins, however, are exempt, and 'all the young girls who have not known a man by sleeping with him, keep alive for yourselves' (31.18).

There is a particularly strange and repellent narrative in Numbers 5 (the *Sotah* – a wife suspected of adultery). It is also known as the 'ordeal of the bitter water'. It contains assumptions that sustain and justify male jealousy and coercion, and, as we shall see in a moment, at least one conservative male theologian uses it now, to contribute directly to the misery of thousands of Christian women. A husband only has to be 'jealous of his wife' (5.14, 29) or to suspect her of adultery for the *Sotah* law to operate. The priest, in a Tabernacle ceremony, dishevels the woman's hair and mixes holy water with dust from the floor ('the water of bitterness that brings the curse' – 5.18). The wife is made to take an oath (5.19, 22). The oath is written down on parchment; the ink washed off into the water; the wife is required to drink the water, 'and the water that brings the curse shall enter into her and cause bitter pain' (5.24).

The shocking violence of the narrative has been extensively analysed. It is not just physical, but 'psychological and emotional' and gender based. As Johanna Stiebert comments:

> The potential for Numbers 5 to legitimate and justify jealousy, the policing of women, and what we nowadays call coercive control, is glaring. What is missing is outrage at how toxic the text is – especially in the midst of skyrocketing rates of domestic and intimate partner violence. (Stiebert, 2019, p. 95; Stiebert, 2023)

It is still used in the contemporary church to endorse the grovelling expectations that many earnest Christian men demand of their wives. A recent work revels in the 'Grand Asymmetries' (i.e. inequalities) displayed by the narrative, and understanding these is said to 'open up for us true womanliness and real manhood' (Andreades, 2015, p. 71). The violence of the narrative is said to have a positive, limiting function. It 'protect[s] a wife from abuse while upholding a husband's limited authority over her' (Andreades, 2015, p. 98). Women who have babies are 'unclean' through original sin, the book continues. They are unclean for twice the time if the baby is a girl (Lev. 12). This is OK, even just, because 'the principle of masculine representation explains the meaning of this law' (Andreades, 2015, p. 105). Liturgical and judicial violence against women is mandated by God (and Andreades) to protect women from even greater violence that unrestrained patriarchy might want to impose, whether or not she is guilty.

Alluring Bodies – the snare of mankind

The book of Proverbs contains erotic description, less lurid than Ezekiel's but along with appropriate condemnation of and contempt for women (see Jones, 2003). A 'wise' man spies (Prov. 7.6) on a tryst between a young man and a young woman. It is she who brings ruin on him. She is 'decked out like a prostitute, wily of heart' (7.10). She 'lies in wait' for him at every corner (7.12), and her mode of invitation is direct:

> so now I have come out to meet you,
>   to seek you eagerly, and I have found you!
> I have decked my couch with coverings,
>   coloured spreads of Egyptian linen;
> I have perfumed my bed with myrrh,
>   aloes, and cinnamon.
> Come, let us take our fill of love until morning;
>   let us delight ourselves with love!
> My husband is not at home … (7.15–18)

It turns out she is cheating on her absent husband, and the ogling narrator, peeping through his lattice, observes:

> With much seductive speech she persuades him;
>   with her smooth talk she compels him. (7.21)

She is entirely responsible for the doom awaiting her lover:

> Right away he follows her,
>   and goes like an ox to the slaughter,
> or bounds like a stag toward the trap
>   until an arrow pierces its entrails.
> He is like a bird rushing into a snare,
>   not knowing that it will cost him his life. (7.22–23)

The woman, now personified as womankind, is paraded as a death-inducing threat to men everywhere:

> And now, my children, listen to me,
>   and be attentive to the words of my mouth.
> Do not let your hearts turn aside to her ways;
>   do not stray into her paths.
> For many are those she has laid low,
>   and numerous are her victims.
> Her house is the way to Sheol,
>   going down to the chambers of death. (7.24–27)

At other times the unconscious androcentrism of the Wisdom literature,[1] its baleful eyeing of women as a separate species, its absorbed male selfishness, its resort to violence, its lack of self-criticism and its open contempt for women, strikes the modern reader, even those not yet open to feminist criticisms of androcentrism in the Bible and secular literature. The 'happy husband' is made so by 'a good wife' who 'doubles the length of his life' (Ecclus. 26.1 NEB). But 'there is nothing so bad as a bad wife; may the fate of the wicked overtake her!' (25.19 NEB) A series of sayings illustrates that a bad wife is an intolerable burden, with no awareness that marital discord takes two, or that 'nagging' (25.20 NEB) is often justified. It is clear that a good wife is a rare possession. That is because the female species is responsible for sin being in the world:

> Woman is the origin of sin,
> and it is through her that we all die.
> Do not leave a leaky cistern to drip
> or allow a bad wife to do what she likes.
> If she does not accept your control,
> divorce her and send her away. (25.23–26 NEB)

Some Queer Bodies – 'homosexuality' explained

A man is forbidden to have sex with a menstruating woman, a married woman among his kin, his near relatives and animals (Lev. 18.19–20). The list from Leviticus 18 continues with further prohibitions:

> You shall not give any of your offspring to sacrifice them to Molech, and so profane the name of your God: I am the LORD. You shall not lie with a male as with a woman; it is an abomination. You shall not have sexual relations with any animal and defile yourself with it, nor shall any woman give herself to an animal to have sexual relations with it: it is perversion. (18.21–23)

The prohibition of men having sex with men is repeated in a second list of prohibited relationships in Leviticus: 'If a man lies with a male as with a woman, both of them have committed an abomination; they shall be put to death; their blood is upon them' (Lev. 20.13). The command not to kill ('sacrifice') a child in order to appease a god draws attention to such a practice, which in turn draws attention to the stark and violent religious milieu of the period.

These two verses condemning men having penetrative sex with men (Lev. 18.22; 20.13) still feature in the culture wars of the last and present centuries. It is not immediately obvious why these two verses are thought to be so important when Christians have quietly disregarded other commandments as inapplicable in the Common Era. Leviticus permits the purchase of slaves, both male and female, provided they are obtained from neighbouring nations (25.44). Having sex with them is OK as well, provided they do not belong to anyone else. Sex with slaves means more slaves. People working on the Sabbath should be killed (Exod. 35.2). Women may be taken as 'booty' in war: 'You may enjoy the spoil of your enemies' (Deut. 20.15; and see 21.10–14), even when they are children (Num. 31). Leather goods must not be touched (Lev. 11.8), and shellfish, along with other creatures, must not be eaten (Lev. 10.10–11). These, and many other prohibitions, have been quietly sidelined. But the two passages about male–male sex acts have not. Why is that? Could homophobia be responsible? Again, attention to context helps to understand why these, and other, prohibitions may be found in the HB. Two lines of thought are especially helpful here: feminization, and the mixing of kinds.

When a man has anal sex with another man, one of them lets himself be penetrated. He lets himself become 'as a woman', and that was regarded as a perilous thing to allow. There seems to be broad agreement in the ancient world about this. It was probably as widely held as the belief that male foetuses develop more quickly than female ones. The sentence 'If a man has sexual relations with a man *as with a woman*' makes it fairly clear that penetration is at issue. But we now think we know why men having anal sex with men is a capital offence in the Levitical code. It is not because 'homosexual practice' (the euphemism found in Anglican documents) is something that God doesn't like. In the ancient world, if you are penetrated you are feminized. You have been treated as a woman. You abandon your masculinity whether by coercion or from choice. In a patriarchal society it is so much better and more perfect to be a man than to be a woman. Sex acts are governed by the gender hierarchy. If you are a man, you are favoured: your status is superior. If you are an Israelite man you belong to God's covenant people in a way women do not, and you have a shorn penis as a permanent sign of your elevated status. To behave as a woman when you are a man is to undermine and even relinquish your masculinity completely. For doing this you deserve to die.

One recent writer shows how, in Jewish thought, the prohibition of male–male anal sex in 'biblical culture' is based on the much broader series of prohibitions about the mixing of kinds. In Genesis 1, God is repeatedly said to make plants and animals 'according to their kinds' (1.11, 12, 21, 24, 25). The law of God forbids *hybrids* (cross-breedings, or mixings of, say, plants and animals of different types): 'one may not hybridize or even plant two species together, mate a horse to a donkey, weave linen and wool into linsey-woolsey, etc. God-given categories must be kept separate' (Boyarin, 2007, p. 135). The 'mixing of kinds' is a *divine* prerogative. God's guardians – the cherubim and seraphim – are 'mixed'. The high priest can wear mixed fabrics, and so on, but these are divine exceptions that prove the 'no mixing' rule. The Hebrew word *tebhel*, usually mistranslated as 'abomination' or 'perversion', means a 'mixing' of what should be kept separate. A man having penetrative sex with another man, like a man penetrating an animal, or an animal penetrating a woman (Lev. 18.23), is a similar mixing of kinds.

Cross-dressing is also a mixing of kinds. 'A woman shall not wear a man's apparel, nor shall a man put on a woman's garment; for whoever does such things is abhorrent to the LORD your God' (Deut. 22.5). No self-respecting man would ever appear in public as a woman. There is a strong parallelism between the Hebrew of this verse and Leviticus 18.22, which strengthens the thesis that the wrongness of men having anal sex with men has nothing to do with a particular type of sin; homosexual sin, and everything to do with the mixing of kinds that the Torah forbids:

> The Torah's language is very explicit; it is the 'use' of a male as a female that is *to eba*, the crossing of a body from one God-given category to another, analogous to the wearing of clothes that belong to the other sex, by nature as it were. Moving a male body across the border into 'female' metaphysical space transgresses the categories in the same way as putting on a female garment, for both parties, since both participate (presumably willingly) in the transgressive act. (Boyarin, 2007, p. 136)

There is an interesting corollary arising from this analysis. Yes, anal sex between men is prohibited in Leviticus, but it is the only homosexual sexual 'act' that *is*. Going behind the invention of homosexuality (the word first occurs in 1869), a homoerotic culture may have flourished: 'precisely because biblical and Talmudic cultures did not have, according to my reading, a category of the homosexual, they therefore allowed for much greater normative possibilities for the homoerotic' (Boyarin, 2007, p. 142; and see Olyan, 1996). There is nothing at all in the HB about female–female sexual relations. It is interesting to speculate why this is.

There has been endless discussion over what the Bible is alleged to 'say' about homosexuality. Among most conservative theologians, the Bible 'forbids' homosexuality, a judgement based on seven particular passages of scripture. But there appear to be unresolved difficulties before even getting a conversation started about the interpretation of these texts. Here are three. First, the Bible doesn't 'say' anything. It doesn't have a voice. The Bible lets itself be *read*. It is readers who say what the Bible says.

Anyone who says, 'The Bible says' commits the 'personalistic fallacy' (Thatcher, 2008, pp. 141–5), the fallacy of assuming the Bible is a person, who, moreover, not only speaks but speaks clearly. This simple fallacy bedevils many theological discussions of sexuality, producing 'deceptive rhetoric' (Martin, 2006, p. 2) and bogus claims to divine authority.

Second, conservative treatments of homosexuality in the Bible generally treat 'homosexuality' as if it were one thing, a constant and deviant human condition, 'a singular, established, and identifiable phenomenon across time and culture, as is its inverse, "heterosexuality"' (Dunning, 2019, p. 578). This assumption gives rise, third, to what has been called 'homophobic hermeneutics'; that is, the interpretation of biblical texts that regard it 'as self-evident that biblical literature is characterized by a blanket prohibition of same-sex love' (Jennings, 2015, p. 206). It would be uncharitable and untrue to suggest that these interpreters are all homophobic. Rather, all readers of the Bible run into 'cultural and philosophical constructs' that already govern how appropriate texts are selected and read. But once the homosexuality/heterosexuality divide is set aside as the invention of modernity, and the possibility of entertaining a more complex understanding of sexual relations (in both ancient and late modern times) is allowed, then not only can the usual texts be read differently, but other texts also ignored in the rush to see what the Bible 'says' about homosexuality come into view. Away from the laws of Leviticus, there are several narratives that tell a different story. Here are three.

The story of the destruction of Sodom (Gen. 19) is an obvious victim of homophobic hermeneutics. In it, two angels visit the city of Sodom. Eventually they accept the hospitality offered them by a stranger, Lot. The men of the city demand, 'Bring them out to us, so that we may know them' (19.5). Not content with Lot's offer of his two virgin daughters to the mob, they attempt to enter Lot's house until the angels strike them with blindness. Literally understood, it is a nasty story of menace, potential rape and xenophobia. Its purpose seems to be about something quite different – the failure to observe the Israelite rules governing offering hospitality to strangers. Jesus understood it this way (Matt. 10.15; Luke 10.12). Ezekiel attributed the sin of Sodom to arrogance, violence and greed (Ezek. 16.49). Yet it has been a key text in the condemnation of homosexuality. According to Pope Benedict XVI (in 1986, when he was still known as Cardinal Ratzinger), 'There can be no doubt of the moral judgment made there against homosexual relations' (Congregation for the Doctrine of the Faith, 1986, para. 6). But the moral of the story may be quite different. According to Ezekiel and Jesus, the Sodom story 'warns against the injustice of the wealthy and powerful – injustice especially directed against the vulnerable' (Jennings, 2015, p. 208). Biblical traditions emphasize that the crimes are *social*, not sexual. Such is the usurpation of the story by those who would condemn 'homosexuality', it comes instead 'to license injustice toward the vulnerable on the part of the powerful' (Jennings, 2015, p. 208).

The long narratives describing the relations between David and Jonathan in 1 and 2 Samuel make little sense unless they were lovers (Jennings, 2005, pp. 3–80). A male candidate for ordination in almost any church today, informing his selection committee that his love for another man was 'wonderful, passing the love of women' (2 Sam. 1.26), would likely be told his vocation was mistaken. Yet this is how David described his love for Jonathan when he lamented his death. If the candidate is an Anglican ordinand, he would need (at least until 2023) to provide the (likely dishonest) assurance that his love for another man was 'celibate'.

Then there is the question of David's hidden erection, hidden, that is, by translators who cannot quite believe what they are reading. At one of their meetings, David and Jonathan 'kissed each other, and wept with each other' (1 Sam. 20.41). Then what happens? The King James Bible continues, accurately, with 'until David exceeded'. The Hebrew text reveals that David '"was caused to become big" – in other words, he had an erection'. The Greek translation of the HB (the Septuagint) also 'pushes the meaning towards an orgasm for David' (MacCulloch, 2020, unpaginated). There is an escalation of obfuscation around this verse among more modern translations. The NRSVA, used throughout this book, has 'David wept the more', while the evangelical Good News Translation brings evasion to a new level with 'Both he and Jonathan were crying as they kissed each other; David's grief was even greater than Jonathan's'. These are 'mealy-mouthed and unfeasible modern mis-translations' (MacCulloch, 2020, unpaginated), illustrating homophobic hermeneutics at the level of translation before the great majority of Bible readers even get access to the biblical text.

These, then, are some of the bodies to be found in the HB. We have shared the violent pornographic imagination of biblical prophets. We have seen how ancient physiology and embryology already reflect a gendered understanding of the human infant. Once women are regarded as the property of men, the sense of male entitlement over them becomes unchallengeable. Taboos about menstrual and maternal blood, and the many social disadvantages endured by women as a result of them, still abound. The idea of impurity is a permanent taint imposed by elites who get to define where the boundary with purity lies, thereby excluding countless people in less favoured (impure) groups. It is better to be a man, circumcised and a member of God's covenanted people, than a mere woman. Indeed the capital crime of men having penetrative sex with men is set within a framework of disgust – not the disgust that might be associated with the excretory function of the anus, but the disgust evoked by the thought that a man might consent to taking the place of, or temporarily becoming, a woman. Homophobia turns out to be misogyny in thin disguise. The casual approval of violence, whether genocidal or domestic, reiterated throughout the HB, would be unbelievable were it not already familiar. These are some of the tentacles of misogyny that still cling to late modern minds. We read texts that were later to become foundations for anti-Semitism, racism and the continuation of slavery into the eighteenth century. How did Christians appropriate their biblical legacy?

Notes

1   The Wisdom literature is a type of biblical literature encompassing Job, some of the Psalms, Proverbs, Ecclesiastes, the Song of Songs, Wisdom and Sirach (Ecclesiasticus).

4

Some New Testament Bodies:
Bodies in the Gospels

Bodies Healed and Blessed

For a religion that has often disparaged the human body and developed extreme and controversial teachings about sex, perhaps the first surprise is that little of this was taught by, or can be attributed to, its founder, Jesus of Nazareth. Indeed, even to speak to him as a founder of a religion is to exceed the evidence available. Our knowledge of the historical Jesus is largely confined to the four biblical Gospels. While each is assigned an author's name, we do not know who wrote them. No original manuscripts have survived, and those we have were compiled from earlier sources. There are many discrepancies between them, as well as substantial agreements. The Gospel attributed to Mark is the earliest, probably written around 70 CE. Matthew and Luke both adopted and adapted parts of Mark and must therefore be later. But the Gospels are products of the communities that produced them. They were written to commend the new faith, so they make no modern pretence of historical neutrality. They contain many sayings of Jesus, many memories of him, many accounts of his deeds, lengthy accounts of his arrest and crucifixion, and various stories about his appearances after his resurrection, details of which are difficult to harmonize. While lively debates continue among scholars about what, if anything, happened exactly as the Gospel writers recorded it, they are reliable sources for what some early church communities believed about Jesus at the time they were written.

Nobody, and no body, was regarded as disgusting or vile in the mind of Jesus as the Gospels present him. (I hope a possible exception, when Jesus refers to Gentiles as 'dogs' (Mark 7.27–29), may be taken as a colloquialism. See Collins, 2007, pp. 293–5.) There are many stories in the Synoptic Gospels of Jesus healing people who,

> in terms of purity rules, were blemished, hence either incapable of social relations with the rest of the holy people of Israel (such as lepers, Mark 1.40–5; Luke 17.11–19; the woman with a haemorrhage, Mark 5.25–

34) or barred from the Temple and sacrifice because of some sort of permanent impediment or lack of wholeness (such as those possessed, the paralysed, the lame, the blind). (Malina, 2001, p. 187)

He physically touched people condemned to be ostracized due to their impurity. He renounces by his actions the impurities we considered earlier. Several other stories about him exorcizing demons make sense in modern terms of his intervention in the health of people suffering serious mental ill health. The Gospel of John, describing Jesus as God's Word or self-manifestation, shows no embarrassment in saying: 'The Word became flesh' (John 1.14) (see Chapter 21 below). There is nothing corrupt, tainted or disgusting about real organic flesh. It is what God becomes. It becomes divine.

There is an astonishing event in Luke's Gospel where:

> a woman in the city, who was a sinner, having learned that [Jesus] was eating in the Pharisee's house, brought an alabaster jar of ointment. She stood behind him at his feet, weeping, and began to bathe his feet with her tears and to dry them with her hair. Then she continued kissing his feet and anointing them with the ointment. (Luke 7.37–38)

The narrative is erotic, and the Pharisee is clearly embarrassed about Jesus' close encounter with a 'sinful' woman. Jesus does not stop her kissing his feet, and contrasts the 'great love' (7.47) she has shown him with the disgust of his censorious Pharisaic host. He even told the senior religious leaders of his time, 'Truly I tell you, the tax-collectors and the prostitutes are going into the kingdom of God ahead of you' (Matt. 21.31). Jesus was notorious for his enjoyment of good food and wine and for the company he kept (Matt. 11.19; Luke 7.34), shrugging off the inevitable criticism from his opponents and in stark contrast to the ascetic lifestyles of many later Christian leaders.

Promiscuous Bodies – sex in church

But we are not going to examine Jesus' teaching in the Gospels just yet. That is due to a surprising fact of history. The earliest NT document to discuss such questions regarding the body, race, sex and gender is not one of the Gospels but Paul's First Letter to the Corinthians, written between 53 and 57 CE, well before the consensus date of the first Gospel (Mark, c. 70 CE) and by someone (Paul) who converted to Christianity several years after the death of Jesus and who never knew him. There is a widespread assumption that because the Gospels are placed first in the NT, and are first in importance in relation to the 23 other documents found there, they must have been written first. That is not so. A chronological approach to the sources must begin with Paul, the apostle of Jesus (or so he claimed) rather than with Jesus. So I will begin with Paul, moving to the Gospels (Chapter 5) and then to the later Letters of the NT (Chapter 6). A diversity of beliefs and practices will emerge, not all of them compatible.

The First Letter to the Corinthians opens up the astonishing world of early Christian sex. A church member is having sex with his stepmother (5.1–5), and another with a sex-worker (6.15–20). At the other extreme the church had already asked Paul whether a man should 'touch' a woman at all (7.1), while the disturbing spectacle of unveiled women praying and prophesying during worship gave rise to a mini-discourse on the theological roots of what we might call compulsory gender imbalance (11.2–16), so influential that it would impede the full status of women in the church for two millennia. Reading this early Letter provides startling glimpses into the earliest Christian 'theology of the body'.

The incestuous church member is to be excommunicated, but the rationale for men not having sex with sex workers is elaborately theological. Paul asks, 'Should I therefore take the members of Christ and make them members of a prostitute?' (6.15). It is possible that the question is purely rhetorical, but given the promiscuity in the church and the widespread availability of sex workers at Corinth and throughout Roman society, church members having sex with them would not be surprising. Rhetorical or not, the answer to the question opens up how Paul and those Christians who agreed with him regarded themselves. Christians are in some real material sense said to be the many members of Christ's one body (12.12–28). While the physical body of the crucified Jesus was believed to have been raised, the earliest churches held that the physical presence of Jesus continued, on earth, in the form of his followers, who were members of his body now reconstituted in them. It followed, thought Paul, that when a male believer has sex with a sex worker, Christ also has sex with her (6.15–16). Paul also taught that the Spirit of God or Jesus lived within them again in some material sense. It is likely he also thought that, given the association of male sperm with spirit, ejaculation of sperm amounted to ejaculation of spirit also (Swancutt, 2006). This may explain why it was important for Christians to confine having sex to the baptized, since each person would also be having sex with Christ. On this basis, the problem case of a believing wife having sex with her unbelieving husband (or conversely) demanded a solution, and Paul had one. The unbelieving husband is 'consecrated' through his believing wife. Otherwise 'your children would be unclean, but as it is, they are holy' (7.14).

Paul was horrified by the promiscuous behaviour of some of the early Christians. But he was powerless to stop it spreading. Later writers gave these randy Christians the name 'antinomian' (*anti* = 'against'; *nomos* = 'law'). It persisted into at least the third century CE, and it found its roots in the *emerging orthodox teaching of the churches*. The Jews who became the early Christians had observed the law found in the Jewish scriptures, aided by the rabbis in its interpretation and application. Paul zealously pointed out here that they should no longer follow the law. It is no longer binding on them. They should follow Jesus and his teaching instead. A new age had arrived, rendering Christ's followers exempt from the law. They claimed freedom from the law, with Paul's encouragement, but turned their newly experienced liberty into licence. Non-Jews – that is, Gentiles – would know little or nothing of the Jewish law anyway.

In the absence of a new law, many of the first Christians were happy to exempt themselves from the constraints their former faith imposed. Some would hold that the forgiveness of sins covered not just sins of the past but sins of the future as well. This was not quite as naive as it sounds. It was less of a sense of a carte blanche for believers to indulge in unrestrained carnal activities, and more a sense that forgiveness of sins was a total experience, and by becoming members of a new type of humanity, their actions would be protected from evil consequences. True, Paul opposed them, just as he opposed the Christians who wanted to keep circumcising new male converts. But his doctrinal appeals to notions of faith, grace or justification (key elements of the European Reformation), or his pleas that Christians should subjectively develop a Christian character or cultivate Christian virtues, lacked the specificity and direction of the older religion.

Promiscuity received considerable theological justification, and its extent throughout the NT usually goes unnoticed. It needs to be acknowledged because it helps to explain the growing severity of Christian teaching about sexuality and the body which was raised against it. Paul quotes his opponents, 'All things are lawful for me', and makes the rejoinder against them, 'but not all things are beneficial' (1 Cor. 6.12), adding, 'The body is meant not for fornication but for the Lord, and the Lord for the body.' There are many similar exhortations among the Letters of the NT, early and late, which are likely to be understood today as general imperatives against sexual misconduct or 'fornication', learned and practised in the world of Gentiles and pagans. That would be inaccurate. Promiscuous Christians were *Christians*, not pagans, whose sexual immorality other Christians have always been prone to exaggerate. They had doctrinal reasons for their (mis)conduct. Neither were Christians alone suspicious of desire and promiscuous behaviour.

The Stoic philosopher Gaius Musonius Rufus (*c.* 30–*c.* 101 CE) thought that the failure to control lust was 'a great indictment against humans'. People, he continued, 'should consider sexual pleasures justified only within marriage and when accomplished for the purpose of procreation of children, because this is lawful. But mere pleasure hunting is unjust and unlawful, even if it is within marriage' (Shaw, 2000, p. 409).

Paul is speaking to theologically minded Christians when he confronts them with the rhetorical question, 'Should we continue in sin in order that grace may abound? By no means!' (Rom. 6.1–2). At Philippi, laments Paul, there are 'many' who 'live as enemies of the cross of Christ … their glory is in their shame' (Phil. 3.18–19). In Galatia, a chasm opens up in the churches like the one in Corinth. Some of the believers held that they should keep the law of the HB, including and exemplified by male circumcision. Paul warns them, 'You who want to be justified by the law have cut yourselves off from Christ; you have fallen away from grace' (Gal. 5.4). Others among the believers, right to think they were 'called to freedom', were warned 'only do not use your freedom as an opportunity for self-indulgence' (5.13). The middle way between law and excess, explained Paul, was to 'Live by the Spirit, I say, and do not gratify the desires of the flesh' (5.16). While Paul provided a long list of vices that the Galatians were to avoid (with 'fornication, impurity, licentiousness' at the top), and a long list of virtues that he called the 'fruits' of the Spirit, Christians ever since have found the stark polarity between one or the other difficult to negotiate.

In another Letter attributed to Paul, but generally dated *c.* 85–100 CE, there are Christians who 'make their way into households and captivate silly women, overwhelmed by their sins and swayed by all kinds of desires' (2 Tim. 3.6). Male predatory behaviour was a problem in the churches, just as it is today. The pseudonymous Letter given the name 2 Peter (probably written 80–90 CE) castigates in lurid terms the sexual exploits of false teachers who 'are like irrational animals, mere creatures of instinct, born to be caught and killed'. 'They count it a pleasure to revel in the daytime. They are blots and blemishes, revelling in their dissipation while they feast with you. They have eyes full of adultery, insatiable for sin. They entice unsteady souls' (2 Pet. 2.12, 13–15). Their crime is they liked having sex and could provide justification for their desires:

For they speak bombastic nonsense, and with licentious desires of the flesh they entice people who have just escaped from those who live in error. They *promise them freedom*, but they themselves are slaves of corruption; for people are slaves to whatever masters them. (2.18–19)

Another Letter (which may be as late as 120 CE) is devoted in its entirety to denouncing the 'intruders' who 'have stolen in among you, people who long ago were designated for this condemnation as ungodly, who *pervert the grace of our God into licentiousness*' (Jude 4).

Veiled Bodies – the angelic threat

These references to sexual impropriety (there are plenty of others) are enough to undermine, if not to reverse, the widespread assumption that while pagans were promiscuous, Christians were not. The framework for considering promiscuity was androcentric – about the extent of the sexual freedom and entitlements of free male citizens of the Empire, and of the adult male members of the church community who were experimenting with the religious freedom they claimed in their new faith. The androcentric framework becomes explicit as Paul deals with the freedom Christian women were exercising in the worship of their community.

The lively contributions of some of the women to worship were producing what we might call 'liturgical disorder'. Women could take part until some male leaders started getting jittery about it. The solution to the problem was the imposition of a more basic order – a hierarchical, gendered, order. The order is God – Christ – husband – wife. Paul resorts to repeating the standard gender hierarchy of his time but giving it a new theological twist: 'I want you to understand that Christ is the head of every man, and the husband is the head of his wife, and God is the head of Christ' (1 Cor. 11.3). Centuries before the church stated its doctrine of the Trinity – part of which states that God is three 'Persons' who are co-equal – the *inequality* between women and men in the gender hierarchy is replicated in the *divine* hierarchy where God is the 'head' of Christ. 'Head' (*kephalē*) is a slippery term with several meanings, both in Greek and English. Paul slides from one to another, from 'head' as leader, to 'head' as a body part. Women who pray and teach can do so, provided they cover their heads.

But why should they cover their heads? Clearly the veil is a signifier of something else. But what? The answer Paul gives is responsible for the practice of veil-wearing, or comparable head cover, by women in churches in every century except the present one. And the answers are weird. Veil-wearing is controversial and much discussed in contemporary Europe, partly because it carries a spectrum of meanings, from feminist refusal of the male gaze to abject compliance with patriarchal order. It was much the same at Corinth. Paul takes a familiar text from Genesis: 'So God created humankind in his image, in the image of God he created them; male and female he created them' (Gen. 1.27). Today the text is mistakenly thought to demonstrate the sexual binary or to provide evidence for sexual equality. It was differently read in Paul's day, often as the creation of an androgyne,[1] which subsequently developed into the first man and the first woman. But equality was far from Paul's mind when he puzzled over how to deal with liturgical disorder in Corinth. Only men, he declared, directly image God: 'For a man ought not to have his head veiled, since he is the image and reflection of God; but woman is the reflection of man' (1 Cor. 11.7). The Genesis text of course does not 'say' this, but Paul is convinced it does. He would have considered 'image' and 'reflection' more literally and less metaphorically. Perhaps he thought God the Father *looked* like a man (as much Christian art assumes). Perhaps he thought a veil over a woman's face, like a barrier between an observer and a light source, would remind male observers that when they look at a woman they are not encountering an image of God. Women on this view are still bearers of God's image, but only indirectly, through men – 'woman is the reflection of man' (11.7).

Two further thoughts are quickly added to augment the patriarchal character of his admonition. Seizing on the detail of the second creation myth (in Genesis 2), that the man was created first, he turns the *temporal* priority of the man before the woman (he was made first) into an ontological and axiological priority; that is, he is first in importance and value: 'Man was not made from woman, but woman from man' (11.8). The myth has God creating the woman from the man's side, so Paul notes that the man was created *directly* by God, but the woman *indirectly* by God from pre-existing human materials; that is, a male body. As if that were not enough, another mythical detail is made to do duty. The man is solitary in the Garden and doesn't just want animals for company. The woman in the myth is God's Big Afterthought, created with a purpose – to keep the man company. All this is compressed in the remark: 'Neither was man created for the sake of woman, but woman for the sake of man' (11.9).

And still Paul isn't finished. A woman should have 'a symbol of authority on her head'; that is, a symbol of the man's authority over her. Here credulity is stretched to the limit, for he adds: 'because of the angels'. What? He probably had in mind the myth of the Watchers, the randy angels of Genesis 6 who forced themselves on earthly women and created gigantic offspring. The KJV politely renders the matter 'the sons of God saw the daughters of men that they were fair; and they took them wives of all which they chose' (Gen. 6.2). Perhaps the casual aside about angels was intended as a joke, intended to humour his readers amid patriarchal seriousness. If it was, it is hard to see how macho angels raping earthly

46

women is funny. The scenario conjured up is one where semi-divine male beings, eyeing up 'fit' women in church, are about to fall upon them, but a protecting veil shields them from being noticed. Women are to dress unprovocatively to protect themselves from potential rapists, particularly angelic ones. Finally, an argument from nature is deployed: 'Does not nature itself teach you that if a man wears long hair, it is degrading to him, but if a woman has long hair, it is her glory? For her hair is given to her for a covering' (1 Cor. 11.14–15). But now a further question arises. If a woman's hair is her 'glory', and acts as a 'covering', why does she need a second covering at all? Perhaps she needs double protection from horny angels.

Flying Bodies – on their way up

Paul's teaching about marriage is found here as well. Its influence has held for nearly two millennia. Yet it runs contrary both to other, later, teaching about marriage in the NT, and to its idealization in contemporary Christianities. His advice about marriage can be summed up in a single word: don't.

There are two main reasons for this. The first is the world situation as he understands it. Jesus, the risen and ascended Messiah, will return, *in Paul's lifetime*, and physically remove believers from the world. He had a clear vision of what would happen (although he may have modified it as his life drew to a close):

> For the Lord himself shall descend from heaven with a shout, with the voice of the archangel, and with the trump of God: and the dead in Christ shall rise first. Then we which are alive and remain shall be caught up together with them in the clouds, to meet the Lord in the air: and so shall we ever be with the Lord. (1 Thess. 4.16–17 KJV)

We will meet flying bodies again in Chapter 14 (where in the eyes of Christian misogynists they belong to witches). Paul returns to the theme of a general resurrection in 1 Corinthians (15.51–52), but he is content to call it here, less descriptively, a 'mystery'. But there is more to the vision than the return of Jesus (called the 'parousia'). There is an 'impending crisis': 'The present form of this world is passing away' (1 Cor. 7.26, 31). Perhaps the prospect of the collapse of empire led in his mind to the collapse of the physical structure of the world. Since Christ would rescue believers from the impending denouement, proclaiming the gospel was more important than getting married. Being saved had a strong material dimension to it.

The present climate crisis perhaps enables us to see more clearly the urgency that shaped Paul's thoughts. That crisis is here already, and the deep physical and biological structures that give and support life are already seriously damaged. Human activity has greatly contributed to this, and humans are being summoned to change their ways for the sake of future generations, to stop species depletion and extinction, to make drastic changes to consumer lifestyles, to make ready for global catastrophe and do all they can to prevent it. Inspirational people are already putting the climate crisis before anything else, including marriage. In less patriarchal societies it is possible for married couples to share a 'vocation' towards the saving of the planet. Paul might be read now as summoning people to shape their lives in accordance with priorities higher than marriage and the demands of patriarchal family life.

That was his *extrinsic* reason for discouraging marriage, but there were *intrinsic* reasons as well. He thought marriage was a *distressing* institution to become involved with, as it so often is: 'Those who marry will experience distress in this life, and I would spare you that' (1 Cor. 7.28). It produces both anxiety and divided loyalties (7.33–35). A spouse is a distraction from more important matters. The only justification for marrying, he thought, is doing something positive about lust. There are no justifications of marriage here (or elsewhere in the NT) based on the assumed goodness of having children or benefiting from its sacramental character: 'It is better to marry than to burn' (7.9 KJV); 'If anyone thinks that he is not behaving properly toward his fiancée, if his passions are strong, and so it has to be, let him marry as he wishes; it is no sin. Let them marry' (7.36). Marriage is a concession, a way of life that is second best, very far from accounts of it in the last 50 years suggesting the equality of spouses and mutual devotion.

While students of early Christian origins will be familiar with the unfolding story, twenty-first-century inquirers may be surprised by the extent of promiscuity in the early churches, by the overt and detailed theological justification for the second-class status of women, and by the early disdain for marriage. As we turn, at last, to Jesus and the Gospels, they may continue to be surprised.

Notes

1 'Androgyne' is a compound term, using the Greek for 'man' and 'woman'. It is used here of the first, mythical, human being who had both male and female characteristics.

5

Some More New Testament Bodies:
Bodies in the Gospels

This chapter examines some of the teachings assigned to Jesus in the Gospels about the topics of purity, desire, marriage, divorce, fidelity, celibacy and homoerotic attraction.

It is clear from the Gospels that Jesus said almost nothing about sexuality. That too is a surprise. One might imagine, given the homophobia of contemporary churches, Jesus had said a lot about homosexuality. But there is nothing. There are recorded sayings of Jesus about marriage, divorce, adultery and purity. One of these includes castration. All of them were open to, and were soon to receive, extreme interpretation. There are suggestions of queer bodies too. We will examine these below.

Bodies without Lust?

There is a single saying in the Sermon on the Mount (Matt. 5—7) that appears to forbid men from lusting after women. The author 'Matthew' contrasts the teaching of Jesus with one of the Ten Commandments that forbids adultery. Jesus says:

> You have heard that it was said, 'You shall not commit adultery.' But I say to you that everyone who looks at a woman with lust has already committed adultery with her in his heart. If your right eye causes you to sin, tear it out and throw it away; it is better for you to lose one of your members than for your whole body to be thrown into hell. And if your right hand causes you to sin, cut it off and throw it away; it is better for you to lose one of your members than for your whole body to go into hell. (Matt. 5.27–30)

In Greek the word for 'woman' is the same as the word for 'wife' (*gunē*). The saying may then be referring to the desire of a man to have sex with another man's *wife*, and so not a general condemnation of the tendency to own and to appreciate one's desire for another (Moore, 1992; Loader,

2015). An obvious interpretation of these sayings is that they are examples of hyperbole, often used by Jewish teachers like Jesus for emphasis. But Jesus' saying makes men responsible for their thoughts and desires, and for keeping their wandering minds, and hands, to themselves. It repudiates the assumption that 'the locus of lust was the female body', and puts the onus of sexual restraint firmly back on men (DeConick, 2011, p. 44). Christian men, though, have generally found justifications for guilt and self-punishment in these sayings, worrying that a desiring and approving look directed at the body of another may imperil their eternal destiny.

Jesus was fully aware of scriptural teaching about purity. Along with other rabbis, he teaches that the purity/impurity distinction must be relocated. Rejecting certain interpretations of Torah regulations about impurity contracted through unwashed hands or consumption of forbidden foods, or having sex, the emphasis is instead on *subjective*, inner purity: 'For it is from within, from the human heart, that evil intentions come: fornication, theft, murder, adultery, avarice, wickedness, deceit, licentiousness, envy, slander, pride, folly. All these evil things come from within, and they defile a person' (Mark 7.21–23). Jesus does not negate the obvious insight that many of the evil things people do come from corporate, structural features of humanity that are prior to the actions of individuals, such as racism, sexism and 'casteism' (Wilkerson, 2020). Instead, he teaches that the sources for determining right and wrong are no longer to be found in the minutiae of prescriptions within the scriptures, but more immediately internal, in the human 'heart'; that the actions of people follow from their characters, and they are able to contribute to the characters they come to have. Purity lies in not *wanting* to engage in fornication, theft, murder and so on. Jesus doesn't say anything that we can't also find in other rabbinic texts. Lots of rabbis already thought that way.

Nuptial Bodies – Jesus on marriage, divorce and discipleship

It is widely thought today that Jesus was in favour of marriage. In Protestant churches it has become so commonplace that single people often feel alienated in congregations, arousing suspicions about their sexuality. A consensus of scholarship is that although Jesus regarded marriage as a distraction, he accepted it. The earliest Gospel ('Mark') records an incident where Jesus is asked, 'Is it lawful for a man to divorce his wife?' Jesus offered no criticism of marriage in his reply but forbade divorce absolutely (10.2–12). He, like Paul, was intensely aware of a forthcoming cosmic catastrophe and, like Paul, he thought preparing for it was more important than marrying:

> For as the days of Noah were, so will be the coming of the Son of Man. For as in those days before the flood they were eating and drinking, *marrying and giving in marriage*, until the day Noah entered the ark, and they knew nothing until the flood came and swept them all away, so too will be the coming of the Son of Man. (Matt. 24.37–39; Luke 17.26–27)

Luke's Jesus is more forthright still by dismissing marriage completely, teaching that a man who *separates* from his wife for the sake of the kingdom of God gains rewards both in this age and in the age to come (Luke 18.29). Luke's Jesus also says:

> Those who belong to this age marry and are given in marriage; but those who are considered worthy of a place in that age and in the resurrection from the dead neither marry nor are given in marriage. Indeed they cannot die anymore, because they are like angels and are children of God, being children of the resurrection. (20.34–36)

The context makes clear how radical the rejection is. Jesus is addressing a Jewish group – the Sadducees – who did not believe in the resurrection of the dead. In this saying of Jesus, people who marry are citizens of this world, not of the world to come. They 'belong to this age'. Their married status endangers their partaking in the age to come. These verses are almost entirely overlooked in attempts to arrive at an overall and consistent account of the biblical teaching on marriage. They provide clear evidence for the currently unfashionable view not merely that celibacy is better than marriage but that those unwise enough to marry jeopardize their eternal salvation. Paul allowed marriage as a 'concession'. Here it seems avoidance is the only option.

The growing case for celibacy in the church was made stronger by these words. The conscious avoidance of them in many churches makes their legacy even harder to deal with. Some Protestant theologians find them too hard to treat so leave them alone. A lengthy, well-known and respected study on NT ethics ignores the passage, even in its section on marriage in Luke's Gospel (Burridge, 2007). The comprehensive treatment of Jesus' teaching about marriage in *Living in Love and Faith* avoids treating the passage, and claims (incredibly): 'a clear biblical picture of marriage emerges when you consider Scripture as a whole, and in particular when you read it in the light of the teaching of Jesus on marriage' (House of Bishops, 2020, p. 281). Acknowledging the diversity of teaching about marriage, both in the Gospels and elsewhere in the Bible, would render this hasty and evasive conclusion unnecessary and open the door to acceptance of the diversity of kinship arrangements that already exist in the churches and in the world today. Again, the sense of impending cosmic catastrophe, rather than an antipathy towards sexual relations within marriage, seems to be the main reason for avoiding marriage. In the case of Jesus, the mysterious figure 'the Son of Man' will appear (it may or may not be Jesus), ushering in the Last Days. In the case of Paul, it is Jesus himself who will appear. But such is the urgency of the end times – whatever they were thought to bring – marriage, at least for many of the followers of Jesus, is a distraction from proclaiming the kingdom of God.

There were other more pressing factors that may have led to Jesus' view of marriage. Palestine was under Roman occupation, which was hated and generally cruel. The subjugated people longed for the overthrow of their imperial masters, resented the taxes levied on them, and had to face the constant likelihood of famine. These factors may have made survival and resistance more urgent than raising families. And there is another reason why Jesus may have discouraged marriage: he knew that it was a patriarchal institution in which women often came off poorly. 'Biblical marriage', writes Tal Ilan, was:

> a commercial transaction between the father of the bride and the future husband in which a commodity (the woman) changed hands for a price (e.g., Gen. 34.12; Exod. 2.15–16); biblical society recognized as unquestionable a husband's exclusive rights over his wife's sexual activities. Wives had no equivalent claim on their husband's sexuality; moreover, biblical society, instead of censoring and punishing male sexual aggression, punished the victim by making the raped woman marry the rapist (Deut. 22.29). (Ilan, 2019, p. 222)

Polygamy was allowed and practised in the HB (from Lamech onwards – Gen. 4.19). Childbirth was dangerous. Up to half of all children died before reaching the age of five. A realistic expectation of the *limitations* of marriage for women could possibly have been a factor in Jesus' teaching. The strange words 'they cannot die any more, because they are like angels' may refer to the marital regime of childbearing and rearing as itself a regime of death. Angels, it was thought, don't have sex (they don't reproduce), so not having sex anticipates the angelic state and lives it now – the new age even as the former age passes away. The lecherous angels Paul worried about were exceptions (Chapter 4). There were strong personal and social reasons for avoiding marriage other than the later disparagement of the genital sexual activity that came with it.

Sundered Bodies – Jesus on divorce

Jesus' teaching about divorce certainly conveyed sympathy for women as they suffered under patriarchal arrangements. Two of the Gospels record Jesus being asked the question directly: 'Is it lawful for a man to divorce his wife?' (Mark 10.2; and see Matt. 19.3). As ever, context supplies meaning. The law allowed a man to divorce his wife if 'she does not please him' or 'because he finds something objectionable about her' (Deut. 24.1) and marry someone else. Jesus explains the divorce concession as the result of 'hardness of heart', a lack of empathy for the divorced wife, and (since the heart was understood as a cognitive organ) a lack of sound judgement. Her former husband 'writes her a certificate of divorce, puts it in her hand, and sends her out of his house' (Deut. 24.1). Jesus, objecting to this, quotes from an earlier time, prior to the book of Deuteronomy, to the creation narratives themselves, which say 'God made them male and female.' 'For this reason a man shall leave his father and mother and be joined to his wife, and the two shall become one flesh' (Mark 10.7–8, citing Gen. 2.24). But Jesus adds a comment on these verses. He says, 'For this cause shall a man leave his father and mother, and cleave to his wife; And they twain shall be one flesh: so then they are no more twain, but one flesh. What therefore God hath joined together, let not man put asunder' (Mark 10.8–9 KJV).

The sundered body, then, belongs to an ex-wife, 'sent out' of her former husband's house, with a piece of parchment in her hand, facing an uncertain future, probably stigmatized for ever by failing to please her husband. Jesus does not tolerate this. He teaches instead that in marriage the man and wife become 'one flesh'. The meaning of 'one flesh' has always been contested, though it seems to include sexual union. In marriage *God* joins the couple together, making explicit, and affirming, the implication that no husband has the authority to 'put asunder' his wife. Perhaps a further novelty is the assumption of monogamy. There seems no room for three or more people becoming one flesh (unless of course children are counted within the unity of a family).

So Jesus forbids divorce. But there is a wide exception in one of the Gospels. Matthew has borrowed the narrative from Mark about divorce and altered it. He has Jesus add: 'And I say to you, whoever divorces his wife, *except for unchastity*, and marries another commits adultery' (Matt. 19.9; and also 5.32). The Greek for 'unchastity' is *porneia*, which includes any kind of sexual misconduct (a *pornē* is a female sex worker). Matthew's Jesus allows a man to divorce his wife (and not conversely), whereas the Jesus of Mark and Luke will have none of it. There is a likely reason for this. There were cases of *porneia* in the Christian community from which Matthew wrote, as there were in Corinth and the other churches we know about, and Matthew tries to deal with them sensitively. A wife's sexual misconduct is restored as a reason for putting her asunder: otherwise it is not allowed. A husband who marries a second time is deemed to be still joined by God to his first wife and to be one flesh with her. Hence, sex with a different woman is adultery against his former wife. Mark makes the point more clearly. Yes, adultery is a sin against God, but Mark calls it 'adultery against *her*' (10.11).

The absolute prohibition of divorce was intended to limit the absolute power of men over their wives. It became instead a cruel means of locking women into loveless and violent marriages, as it still does wherever women are denied easy access to it. The force of Jesus' words is to protect 'sent out' wives from stigma and worse. The accusing finger of stigma is directed back to the hands of divorcing husbands. It is timely here to point out the mismatch between the teaching of the contemporary churches about marriage and divorce, and that of Jesus, at least as far as we can construct it from the Gospel records. Only the Roman Catholic Church refuses to acknowledge divorce (although it allows thousands of annulments every year based on the idea that, because of some impediment, God never joined the couple together in the first place). Protestant and Orthodox Churches widely allow it. They are right to do so (I have contributed to their arguments in the past – Thatcher, 1999, pp. 249–88). But their practice involves considerable revision of biblical teaching, which often goes unacknowledged and gives rise to the disturbing question: if the revision of the teaching of Jesus about marriage and divorce is demanded and permitted in some cases, why not in others (like marriage between persons of the same sex)?

Castrated Bodies – Jesus on being a disciple

Both Mark and Matthew record the incredulity of the disciples of Jesus about the permanence of marriage. They tell him forthrightly that if there is no escape from marriage, 'it is better not to marry' (Matt. 19.10). His reply left readers with a conundrum that for some had life-changing physical implications:

But he said to them, 'Not everyone can accept this teaching, but only those to whom it is given. For there are eunuchs who have been so from birth, and there are eunuchs who have been made eunuchs by others, and there are eunuchs who have made themselves eunuchs for the sake of the kingdom of heaven. Let anyone accept this who can.' (19.11–12)

Yes, Jesus accepts their incredulity. Yes, they are right to think they should not marry if they want to keep their sexual freedom, or if they want a way out of their marriage, should it not live up to their expectations. This is in line with his support for the sundered lives of divorced women. Marriage isn't for everyone.

But Matthew *added* to Jesus' reply the further saying about eunuchs. Matthew is using Mark here, but this saying comes from another source. The saying classifies eunuchs into three types. The first type is men born with unusual genitalia, but who can still be recognized or designated as men. The second type is men who have been castrated, whether voluntarily or not. Such men were in demand as trusted servants (de Franza, 2015, pp. 68–106). The third type, becoming a eunuch 'for the sake of the kingdom of heaven' is an exaggerated metaphorical description of the renunciation of polygamy or easy divorce for men. It is a sort of psychic and spiritual castration, but not an actual one. The text 'deals not with the incapacity for marriage or the principled rejection of it (as many readings of this text imply), but *with renouncing adultery*; and hence it has nothing to do with celibacy' (Ranke-Heinemann, 1990, p. 33, emphasis added). It is natural to regard the saying as hyperbole, like the sayings (in the same Gospel) about tearing out your eye or cutting off your hand. Origen (*c.* 184–*c.* 253), a famous theologian, may have taken the saying literally. The practice of actual, physical castration was sufficiently widely practised among Christians for the Council of Nicaea (325) to forbid it. These Christians thought their genitalia vile – physical obstacles to their love of God, better removed. Yet Jesus had no such thing in mind. Orthodoxy condemned castration, but not the theology that endorsed it. A fragment of Matthew's Gospel, probably echoing Jesus' teaching about the renunciation of polygamy and easy divorce, became a proof text for all kinds of ascetic practices associating discipleship with bodily deprivation and mortification.

Contemporary followers of Jesus can still use this text creatively. Perhaps they might want to revert to similar metaphors (i.e. extreme, and painful even to think about) in order to read the text as affirming the value of unwavering and exclusive commitment to their spouse, whatever the consequences might be. Remaining faithful to one's partner cuts off intimacy (if nothing else!) with anyone else. Or they might want to note the new emphasis that has recently been placed on the figure of the eunuch as a powerful counter-cultural icon (Kuefler, 2001). Eunuchs were liminal beings situated ambiguously between male and female. Their very presence in Roman society undermined Roman notions of masculinity as firm, upright and assertive. A eunuch was, and remains, a reminder that alternative masculinities – counter-cultural ways of being a man – are required of Christians in all modern societies, not just the societies of Jesus' time. A crucified Saviour is the very antithesis of popular masculinity, then and now. But the saying was used to endorse celibacy, and to endorse the accelerating range of suspicions about the fallen human body. Superior disciples were deemed, metaphorically or literally, holier without their testicles, so they could proclaim their indifference to the flesh and its demands. But indifference is one step away from loathing.

Queer Bodies – the 'beloved disciple' and other enigmas

The Gospels are generally read as if they belong to a timeless and normative heterosexuality, exemplified by the timeless estate of marriage. But that itself may be due to a long inability to think that Jesus could himself have been the subject of erotic attraction and experience, still less homoerotic experience. When the Bible is used in connexion with same-sex love, there is almost always a concentration on a few 'clobber texts' which are made somehow to forbid it. There is no hint of misogyny in the depictions of him we have in the four Gospels. Indeed, his relations with women were cordial, and he included them among his friends and disciples (Thatcher, 2016, pp. 115–36). But a queer-positive or gay-friendly reading of the Gospel texts may reveal a much closer association between Jesus, homoerotic attraction and same-sex friendships.

The story of the rich young ruler (as it is generally known) contains the sentence, 'Jesus, looking at him, loved him …' (Mark 10.21). Matthew and Luke (borrowing again from Mark) conspicuously omit the reference. The verb 'looking at' is strong, indicating 'an extraordinarily concentrated or focussed gaze' (Jennings, 2003, p. 107). Surprisingly, nowhere else in the Synoptic (i.e. the first three) Gospels is Jesus said to 'love' a particular person. Perhaps 'the homoerotic interpretation of this episode is virtually required if we are to account for the singularity of Jesus' love for just this person' (Jennings, 2003, p. 108).

There is an incident recorded by Matthew (8.5–13), usually announced in church as 'the healing of the centurion's servant'. However, the word used for 'servant' is not the usual *doulos* but *pais* ('boy' or 'lad'). But *pais* is 'a term regularly used in Hellenistic literature to designate the *eromenos* of an *erastes*, the younger beloved of same-sex love' (Jennings, 2015, p. 213). The narrative makes a qualitative distinction between the centurion's lad and his servants, because *doulos* is also used in the story. The lad is very special, and the powerful centurion makes clear his concern for him. The lad 'is lying at home paralyzed, in terrible distress', and Jesus heals him, commending the centurion's great faith. Read in its context, 'the endorsement of at least certain forms of same-sex love on the part of Jesus becomes evident: love that includes unswerving loyalty and the care of lovers for their beloveds' (Jennings, 2015, p. 213).

There is another verse in Mark that might almost have been put there deliberately to generate speculation. Right in the middle of the poignant story of the Last Supper, the betrayal of Jesus, the walk to the Garden of Gethsemane and the wine-assisted slumber of his disciples, the soldiers come for Jesus. Mark alone records: 'A certain young man was following him, wearing nothing but a linen cloth. They caught hold of him, but he left the linen cloth and ran off naked' (Mark 14.51–52). Jesus and the young man are both arrested, but the young man wriggles out of his linen sheet and escapes literally naked. Why was he dressed in just a sheet? What was he doing there? 'The narrative, in effect, undresses him even before the mob does by referring to his nudity first as covered and then as uncovered' (Jennings, 2003, p. 111). Mark is unembarrassed to record his presence and provocative appearance. His unusual and minimal clothing may suggest (as the famous philosopher Jeremy Bentham once did) (see Crompton, 1985, pp. 280–3) that he was a male sex worker. In 2011 I wrote, 'Jesus, we may speculate, was just the sort of company with whom a sexually exploited young man could relax and feel accepted' (Thatcher, 2011, p. 170).

These three incidents are strong hints of homosocial attitudes at the heart of the Jesus story, including those of Jesus himself. But the strongest evidence comes from the character in John's Gospel, aptly known as the beloved disciple. John's Gospel allows symbolic meanings to cover real events, so particular care is needed when reading John as a historical source. Nonetheless, the homoerotic elements of the story are hard to suppress, even among readers (and translators) who would prefer to spiritualize them, or to look away from them altogether. The KJV (1611) records, fairly literally, that at the Last Supper, 'there was leaning on Jesus' bosom one of his disciples, whom Jesus loved' (John 13.23). King James, the most prominent homosexual figure in the early modern period (see Young, 2000), would have delighted in these words. The Revised Version (1881) is even more literal: 'There was at the table reclining in Jesus' bosom one of his disciples, whom Jesus loved.' As translations become more modern, they become more evasive (as in the case of

David's erection – Chapter 3), increasingly anxious to conceal the intimacy between Jesus and the beloved disciple that the text plainly declares (and is repeated later, at 21.20). The Revised Standard Version has the beloved disciple 'lying *close to* the breast of Jesus'. The evangelical Good News Translation (New Testament, 1966) omits all reference to the 'breast' or 'bosom' (*kolpos*) of Jesus and has him '*sitting next to* Jesus', while the NRSV (1989) and the NRSVA has the beloved disciple '*reclining next to* him'. Clearly embarrassment mounts among the translators. There are many cases of 'love lost in translation' (see Lings, 2003), and this is probably one more.

But what cannot be evaded is that there is one particular disciple that Jesus 'loved'. There are four references to this unnamed disciple in John's Gospel (13.22–25; 19.26–27; 21.7; 21.20–23). Jesus loved all his disciples, so why was there a particular disciple for whom Jesus had a particular love? What was this love? One of the other references to the disciple that Jesus loved is the harrowing account of Jesus' crucifixion. Hanging from the cross, and just before he died, he movingly commends his mother to his beloved, and his beloved to this mother. 'And from that hour the disciple took her into his own home' (19.27). The author of a major study, *The Man Jesus Loved*, fairly concludes:

> The singling out of one who is loved by Jesus makes clear that some kind of love is at stake other than the love that unites Jesus to the rest of his disciples. The text itself suggests that we should recognize here some form of love that certainly does not contradict the more general love of Jesus for all, but which does set it apart from this general love. A reasonable conclusion is that this difference points us to a different sphere or dimension of love: love characterized by erotic desire or sexual attraction. (Jennings, 2003, p. 22)

The teaching of Jesus about bodies and sexuality, then, may not be quite as many Christians have been taught to suppose. Sexuality was not prominent in his teaching. He knew that marriage must have been miserable for many women. He knew, as Paul was later to teach, that marriage involves many cares and worries that are best avoided by avoiding marriage altogether. Following him was compared, in one saying, with castration. Perhaps its stark character can be read in our day as a need for men urgently to adopt counter-cultural models of masculinity throughout their lives; that is, to live without the operations of power, dominance, control over women, over less powerful 'others', over nature and much else.

His stark rejection of divorce should be seen as a fierce defence of women jettisoned by their husbands. They cannot be divorced 'for any cause' (Matt. 19.3). The allowing of divorce in Matthew's Gospel may be taken as the writer's own grappling with the exceptionless application of Jesus' teaching forbidding divorce, which in turn may have led to imprisoning women and men in cruel or violent marriages. The willingness of almost all churches to allow divorce (and further marriage) represents a *welcome development* of historical Christian teaching about marriage. But it will inevitably be contrasted with the churches' *un*willingness to countenance another development, namely same-sex marriage, about which there is no teaching attributed to Jesus at all. And there are more than hints in the Gospels that the celibate, heterosexual Jesus, who never experienced erotic attraction in his own body, is more a projection of how later theologians wanted him to be than a picture that the Gospels themselves substantiate.

6

Yet More New Testament Bodies:
More Roots of Sexism and Homophobia

Whatever the reasons for Jesus and for Paul regarding marriage as a distraction, many of the later parts of the NT assume most adult Christians are married. The catastrophe that was the fall of the city of Jerusalem happened in the year 70 CE. The early hope of the return of Christ within the lifetime of believers (1 Thess. 4.13–18; 1 Cor. 15.50–57) was dashed (2 Pet. 3.3–4) and had to be much modified. Roman rule persisted within the province of Judaea and beyond, relentless in the subjugation it required. The Christian communities springing up throughout the Empire began to attract attention. Known for their refusal, with Jews, to acknowledge the emperor as a god, they began to be suspected and persecuted. The presence of slaves as practising members of these communities was seen as subversive of the social order. Christians began to see that this world, and not just the next, was their home, and they began to settle in it. Church order became increasingly important. Their households became scrutinized and they needed rules to govern them, in order to present blameless lives to imperial and pagan critics. There are several of these in the NT, known as Household Codes.[1] It is the time when the Gospels and the later Letters of the NT were written and preserved.

Submissive Bodies – women, marriage and the church

The submissive bodies of this section are the bodies of women married to the free men who control their wives, their slaves and their households. There is a long passage, the only one in the NT, where a first-century *Christian* understanding of the ancient institution of marriage is found, and it is embedded in a Household Code (Eph. 5.21–33). In contrast to the reluctance of Jesus and Paul to commend marriage, here it is assumed. In contrast to the escalating emphasis on asceticism and celibacy by the end of the century, it is positive and affirming. While a positive case for marriage can still be made from it, it also reflects an imperial and Christian patriarchy that continues to influence interpretations today. Wives are dominated by their husbands. He is their master or *dominus*. *Dominus* is Latin for 'master', and 'lord'. It is a title the later Latin Bible (the Vulgate) gives to Jesus. But the dominating husband remains a potential menace to his wife and children. Ideologies that legitimize his domination are responsible for cruelty and sexual abuse on a global scale. To uncover this ideology we need to remain with Ephesians for several pages.

The Code begins with an injunction to 'Be subject to one another out of reverence for Christ.' The hope that the opening verse is about to commend what is usually called 'mutual subjection' is quickly dashed. The verse merely announces how subjection is to be understood. Three times husbands are told to love their wives (5.25, 28, 33b). Three times wives are told to submit to their husbands (5.22, 24b, 33c). There is an uncomfortable implication in this passage (and in parallel ones: Col. 3.18–22; 1 Pet. 2.11—3.6) that rarely surfaces in contemporary theological discussion. Mutuality is not on the agenda. Leading and dominating is what men do, and the Christian husband exercises his leadership by loving his wife. Marital love belongs to the husband only, as a function of his priority or 'headship' in the marriage. The husbands do the loving and the wives do the submitting or 'fearing' – a role on which Augustine insisted (Chapter 12). Wives, the author admonishes, are to 'Be subject to your husbands as you are to the Lord.' Jesus is reported elsewhere as saying, 'No one can serve two masters' (Matt. 6.24). But that is exactly what Christian wives are required to do. In the Household Codes, 'love was a courtesy extended by a superior to his inferiors, not an attribute of an egalitarian romantic attachment' (Knust, 2019, p. 529).

The need for submission is next given a *Christian* rather than a Roman justification. Wives must be subject to their husbands, the author explains, 'For the husband is the head of the wife just as Christ is the head of the church, the body of which he is the Saviour. Just as the church is subject to Christ, so also wives ought to be, in everything, to their husbands' (Eph. 5.23–24). Marriage in the Christian community is directly linked, for the first time, to the death of Christ: 'Husbands, love your wives, just as Christ loved the church and gave himself up for her' (5.25). His life and death are the very embodiment of divine love. This is the only known Household Code in the ancient world that mentions love (see Gombis, 2005). But not all is at it seems. Husbands are to imitate the self-giving love of God. They are to love their wives not because their wives are loveable or valued for themselves (although they may be). They are to love their wives because they are to imitate the God who loves them. Wives are *not* told to love their husbands 'just as Christ loved the church'. Wives are to be passive and submissive. Mutuality is not expected in ancient households, even Christian ones. No one can love in any modern reciprocal sense when the relationship is already governed by obedience and submission 'in everything'.

The mention of sacrificial love in the passage makes it a popular choice for reading at weddings, but – one surmises – there must be millions of bridal couples who have had no idea of the asymmetrical power dynamic lurking just beneath the surface of the text. There are other complications too. If the church is the (feminine) bride of Christ the (masculine) bridegroom, then male Christians are gendered feminine in relation to Christ, yet masculine in relation to their wives, rendering 'Christian sex, in the sense of both gendered identity and sexual practice ... rather queer' (Sanchez, 2019, p. 33). Since all Christians, clerical and lay, male and female, are gendered feminine in relation to their divine bridegroom, is there not a solidarity in the taking on of femininity by the whole church that causes patriarchy to self-destruct?

Unfortunately, there is a lot more to disturb today's readers of this passage, should they inquire further. The imagery employed by the passage invokes the extreme misogynistic imagery of Ezekiel (16.8–14), examined in Chapter 3. Usually overlooked are the details:

> Christ loved the church and gave himself up for her, in order to make her holy by cleansing her with the washing of water by the word, so as to present the church to himself in splendour, without a spot or wrinkle or anything of the kind – yes, so that she may be holy and without blemish. (Eph. 5.25–27)

The church is the bride of Christ, but it is Christ, not her bridesmaids, who gives her a nuptial bath in preparation for the wedding. Christ does it all, and for his own sake. The church is bathed in baptismal water and made clean. Next, Christ puts his bride in her splendid wedding dress, 'to present her to himself as a radiant church, without stain or wrinkle or any other blemish, but holy and blameless'. Since Christ does all this, the process is a further example of male activity and female passivity typical of the ancient gender hierarchy. And that is only part of the difficulty. The strong connection in the HB between ritual pollution and the female body is retained. 'Note how the gendering of dirt is introduced. The gender duality makes the male the active agent: the male brings holiness, cleanness, blamelessness, glory, and spotlessness to the profane, dirty, stained, wrinkled, guilty, *female* principle' (Martin, 2006, p. 113, author's emphasis). She is disgusting, but Jesus makes her clean and acceptable.

In the next verse a different analogy is generated by the flexible core term 'body'. Husbands 'should love their wives as they do their own bodies' (v. 28). Now husbands are no longer exhorted to follow Christ's sacrificial example in giving themselves up in love for their wives. Instead an appeal is made to a different idea, that of self-interest! A husband is to regard his wife's body as an extension of his own. The argument is subtly different too. The writer thinks it natural and right that people should care for their bodies. In general, if we are able, we do: 'For no one ever hates his own body, but he nourishes and tenderly cares for it, just as Christ does for the church' (v. 29). There could hardly be a greater contrast between the body-affirmation of this verse and the treatment of the body by ascetics in later centuries. The idea that a married pair constitute 'one flesh' (v. 31), central to the teaching of Jesus about marriage (which was probably known to the writer), is used to extend the care of the self and its body to the husband's care of his wife's body. The wife does not care for her own body. Her husband cares for it along with his own. The 'one flesh' union soon became an incorporation of the wife's body into her husband's, losing much of her identity in the process. Her bodily autonomy is also lost.

So the building of gender asymmetry gathers pace through the passage. Christ is gendered male. The church, his bride, is gendered female. Human marriage is the metaphor for divine–human unity between Christ and the church. But the long shadow of Ezekiel's misogyny lies over the interpretation of this passage. The Hebrew prophets had used the analogy before, with devastating results for women, masculinizing God, identifying men with deity, feminizing the nation as a whoring, unfaithful, polluted wife. The Code is addressed to husbands only: 'Each of you, however, should love his wife as himself, and a wife should respect her husband' (v. 31).

Degraded Bodies, 'Vile Affections' and Gay Sex

It follows, then, that according to Roman social order and Christian theological order a woman should submit to a man, and a man should never submit to a woman. That is one of the reasons why Paul condemns same-sex love between men. A man should not degrade himself by acting as if he were a woman (Chapter 3). The most quoted proof text purporting to condemn same-sex love is found in Paul's Letter to Christians in Rome. In the course of condemning the behaviour of Gentiles as he, a newly converted Jew, understands them, he asserts, 'God gave them up in the lusts of their hearts to impurity, to the degrading of their bodies among themselves' (Rom. 1.24–25). God also:

> gave them up to degrading passions [or 'vile affections', KJV]. Their women exchanged natural intercourse for unnatural, and in the same

way also the men, giving up natural intercourse with women, were consumed with passion for one another. Men committed shameless acts with men ... (Rom. 1.26–27)

There have been exhaustive (and exhausting) interpretations of Romans 1 (Vasey, 1995; Loader, 2010; Thatcher, 2011; Brownson, 2013; Lings, 2021) that set it in its Roman, Jewish and fledgling Christian contexts. I won't be adding to them here. Paul saw anal intercourse between men as a wilful breach of Levitical law, enacting and embodying the shocking feminization of a male. That is a sufficient explanation for his plain disgust.

What were the 'vile affections' that 'degrade' the men who indulge in them? Paul could not have approved of many instances of men having sex with men or of any sex between men and boys. He knew that powerful men having sex with their male and female slaves was common in the Roman Empire. He knew anal rape was practised as an ultimate act of domination, humiliation or pederasty. They were all common in the Roman Empire. He could find no place for these in any Christian community. Assuming that the meaning of 'natural' coincides with the modern 'heterosexual', he sees same-sex sexual activity as an *excess* of heterosexual desire, a being 'consumed with passion for one another' that exceeds the more 'natural' desire of men for women, and conversely. But same-sex desire is not an intensification of natural and heterosexual desire but a deeply rooted and unalterable orientation. Marriage for same-sex couples would have been unthinkable for Paul, for reasons that are becoming well understood. But it is certainly thinkable now.

What was the 'unnatural' sex that the women were having? If the verse is about women having sex with women, it is the only reference to it in the Bible. But there is good reason to doubt that Paul had lesbian sex in mind at all. 'Unnatural intercourse' (whatever that is) need not be confined to lesbians. The women were subject to men (as the phrase '*their* women' emphasizes), and passive in relation to them. 'Unnatural' might just mean non-coital (Miller, 1995). That was the view of Clement of Alexandria and of Augustine (Allison, 2006). Taking the initiative in sex, having oral or anal sex (Moore, 1995), having sex riding on top of their male partners or in any other position than missionary, might all have counted as 'unnatural'. On this interpretation the women having unnatural sex were not lesbians at all.

Effeminate Bodies

There is a list of 'wrongdoers [who] will not inherit the kingdom of God' in 1 Corinthians 6.9–10, among them 'male prostitutes' and 'sodomites'. Here perhaps the strongest case of homophobic hermeneutics in the entire biblical corpus is to be found. The terms are *malakoi* and *arsenokoitai*, (and they reappear in 1 Timothy 1.10). *Malakos* (the singular form) is a common word in Greek with a root meaning 'soft'. 'When used as a term of moral condemnation, it still refers to something perceived as "soft": laziness, degeneracy, decadence, lack of courage, or, to sum up all these vices in one ancient category, the feminine' (Martin, 2006, p. 44; and see Dunning, 2019, pp. 576–7). The *malakoi* are 'effeminate' men (as the KJV translates). But *arsenokoitai* is much harder to translate. There is no known usage of the word prior to Paul (but each half of the word is used in the Septuagint translation of Lev. 20.13). A brief check-up on the Bible translation data base, Bible Gateway, reveals an apparent certainty among a host of modern translations and their translators that *arsenokoitai* are 'homosexuals', 'perverts' and so on. Perhaps they are. But a trawl of later uses finds other meanings such as 'rape or sex by economic coercion, prostitution, pimping, or something of the sort' (Martin, 2006, p. 41). The meaning is much more open, and once again translators and exegetes may be reading there only what they expect to find. This may be yet another case where modern sex ideology determines ancient meanings.

Classical Bodies

Christian understandings of bodies were rooted not simply in the 'mother-faith' of the Israelites but also in the medical and philosophical views that surrounded and influenced both faiths. The interaction was as much assimilation as opposition. The topic is vast and there is no doubt these views contributed to later Christian misogyny. There are several places in the three previous chapters where wider cultural values are assumed. Paul's hierarchical arrangement of the sexes in 1 Corinthians reflects Roman social mores. Paul adds to it from his use of Jewish sources but leaves it otherwise intact. The long discourse in Ephesians 5 about marriage is a fine example of the then universal assumption that men are active and women passive in relation to men. The difference is that, within the Christian household, dominance and subjection are *heightened*: 'Be subject to one another *out of reverence for Christ*' (Eph. 5.21). Wives now have two masters to serve – their husbands and their husbands' master, Jesus Christ. All the Household Codes reflect a social hierarchy, including the slaves (who at least counted as members of church and household).

Medical knowledge was as important in the early church as it is in the churches today. Two examples must suffice: elements and seeds. In the fourth century CE, this is how John Chrysostom (*c.* 349–407 CE) described the elements of bodies:

> This body of ours, so shortlived, and small, consists of four elements: namely that which is warm, that is, of blood; of what is dry, that is, of yellow bile; of what is moist, that is, of phlegm; of what is cold, that is, of black bile. And someone must not think that this topic is foreign to the spiritual principles we are discussing. (de Wet, 2021, p. 215)

Clearly there were people in Chrysostom's audience who *did* think scientific understanding of the body was irrelevant, and they are reproached. All bodies, inanimate and animate, animal and human, were thought to be composed of elements; all elements have qualities; and in the human case, the qualities are *humours*. The arrangement of these qualities is what makes a being male or female. Everything in the material world was thought to consist, to differing degrees, of the four basic elements: fire, air, water and earth. These elements are known as 'ontological' because ontology is about being, and every being is an arrangement of them.

But the four humours theory is a simplification of earlier Greek views about the body, which often referred more broadly to 'fluids' as well. There were also competing theories of humours (King, 2013). But it is safe to say that blood was reckoned to be hot and wet. It heated the body and kept it moist. The elements and fluids linked human bodies to other bodies in an overall cosmic scheme. Biological difference just is the arrangement of these qualities and humours. Men are hotter and drier than women. Ultimately lack of heat is why women are the 'weaker sex' (1 Pet. 3.7). Fertile men, because of their greater heat, concoct semen, but the very nature of women is to be colder than men. So is their blood. Women are 'half-baked men' (Maier, 2018, p. 189). Women have an excess supply of unconcocted blood, which in males becomes sperm. In women, the excess causes a 'sort of haemorrhage'. In an Aristotelian framework, women are constituted by a series of deficiencies, embarrassing nowadays even to recall. Because they lack sperm and heat, they lack divinity, perfection and reason. Women are less perfect not just because of their lack of heat in relation to men but also because they cannot produce that special substance that conveys the immaterial soul of a person. This was a further reason why men were associated with spirit, women with flesh. Semen bears the immaterial reason that the woman receives, and reason (for Aristotle) is divine. 'Vital heat' makes the semen productive: it works through it. It is 'analogous to the element of the stars' (Aristotle, 2014, Book 2.3). The man's vital heat connects him to God or the gods; to perfection (women lack heat so are imperfect); and to the heavens.

Modern readers are likely to classify these early accounts of sexual difference as 'social constructions' or 'ideological prejudices' (while overlooking the possibility that modern accounts may not be entirely free from similar contaminants). It is easy to see how, once a world view is established that takes polarities such as active/passive, hot/cold, form/matter and soul/body for granted, men and women are made sufficiently pliable to be made to fit within them, and even to confirm them. The weight of these theories pressed deeply into Christian understandings of men and women and the power relations between them. The power relations are confirmed in the NT. There is no ancient theory of conception or account of the human being that even hints at equality between women and men. While early Christians cannot be justly castigated for inheriting, assuming and assimilating theories based on speculative and outdated biology, they can certainly be castigated for maintaining the misogyny that follows from the theory. The influence of such a world view on subsequent generations of women and men can hardly be overestimated.

As misogyny grew in the Christian faith, it was not only fuelled by then contemporary views of human anatomy and embryology. The classical world had definite understandings of everyone's place in society and insisted on the appropriate social signals necessary to retain or express it. There were fixed roles for free men and women, and these too impacted on early Christian attempts to deal appropriately with gender in the fledgling churches of the Empire. 'Males and females are born, but men and women are made through regimes of (self) mastery' (Maier, 2018, p. 10).

Roman men were expected to display 'hardness' (*duritia, robur*) which, while apparently rooted in the body, shaded over into the moral and social realms. Hardness 'referred to the muscularity of the ideal male body; it also symbolized the moral uprightness and self-discipline that men were presumed to embody'. The opposite quality assigned to women was 'softness' or 'delicateness' (*mollitia*), which 'represented not only their delicate bodies, but also their love of luxury, the languor of their minds, the ease with which they gave themselves to their emotions, and their dissolute morals' (Kuefler, 2001, p. 21). Hardness and softness played out obviously in sexual intercourse. The phallus is the penetrator: the softness or *mollitia* of women expressed their role as the penetrated ones. While having sex does not require that either party assume active and passive roles or positions, coitus clearly provided confirmation of the active and passive roles men and women were respectively expected to perform, not just in bed but in all segments of the social order.

Greek and Roman men, writes another historian in similar vein, 'were described with cultural superlatives that reflected their perfect "natural" state: physical and political strength, rationality, spirituality, superiority, activity, dryness, and penetration'. Women, conversely, were thought to embody the negative qualities of 'physical and political weakness, irrationality, fleshliness, inferiority, passivity, wetness, and being penetrated' (Swancutt, 2003, pp. 193–234, 197–8). But without the modern duality of two sexes, Graeco-Roman men and women thought themselves to be made of the same elements and qualities as each other, and constant attention to deportment and self-management were required to maintain or not to exceed the status accorded in the hierarchy. Elite men were imagined as 'hard, rational penetrators' at the top of the social ladder, while 'Women occupied its lowest rungs because they were soft, leaky, and wild – the least perfect male-bodies, their vaginas deemed undescended penises' (Swancutt, 2006, p. 71). Greeks and Romans ranked higher than other peoples; men were ranked higher than women, and women belonged with slaves, foreigners and animals in the requirement of submission to male authority:

> slaves, too, were like animals, women, and foreigners insofar as they lived lives of submission. In short, understanding what it meant to be a man in the Greco-Roman world meant understanding one's place in a rationally ordered cosmos in which free men were placed at the top and what fell beneath could all be classified as 'unmen'. (Conway, 2008, p. 15)

It should be obvious from this chapter that a repetition of biblical verses as if their meanings are eternal will only harm the people who are stigmatized by them. Cultural, historical and gendered assumptions likewise. The Bible is dangerous. We have so far only just begun to appreciate the harm, cruelty, arrogance and prejudice that can be traced to inadequate readings of it. The ideology allowing husbands to dominate their wives (Chapter 17) has persisted for 2,000 years, and remains one of the roots of domestic violence. Ephesians 5 is the high point of the NT's endorsement of marriage. Marriage is assumed in other Letters. This is the version, argued over ever since, requiring an asymmetry of power and the submission of wives. Polygamy is forbidden. Church leaders must have only one wife (1 Tim. 3.2; 3.12). So parlous indeed is the plight of women, due to the sin of Eve, that their very salvation is at risk. Getting married and having babies is their means of salvation provided they also continue in 'faith and love and holiness, with modesty' (1 Tim. 2.15). Modesty of dress is a requirement of Christian wives, and submission to unbelieving husbands is the required tactic for winning them over (1 Pet. 3.1–6). The First Letter of Peter doesn't command husbands to love their wives. They must 'show consideration to your wives … paying honour to the woman as the weaker sex, since they too are also heirs of the gracious gift of life' (3.7).

None of these negative connotations of marriage has a place in contemporary reconstructions of it. The sacrificial love expected of husbands can be extended to include wives 'giving themselves up' for their husbands. It happens anyway. Reciprocal love and devotion *is* a requirement of marriage now. But it is not a requirement of Ephesians 5. How could marriage be commended in the present century unless mutuality was a precondition, assumed in the exchange of consent? Wives can love their husbands as Christ loved the church, even if it never occurred to this first-century author to say so. 'One flesh' can be a wholly positive symbol for sexual and personal union. God is beyond gender, and the church (led, as it has been, by men for nearly as long as it has existed) is hardly exclusively feminine, as the analogy demands. But the arrangements of the Household Codes are 'in the Lord' (Col. 3.18); that is, they don't simply replicate those of Jewish and Roman families. They allow for innovation. And the 'mystery' that is the union between Christ and the church (the Latin translation was *sacramentum*) might provide more than a hint about the potential depth and fulfilment to be found in reciprocal married love.

It is a sad fact of ecclesial life that the loving unions of countless couples of the same sex still lack recognition and generally evoke condemnation, excommunication or worse. 'Affirming' or 'inclusive' churches are exceptions. Standard interpretations ('homophobic hermeneutics') cause incalculable harm to LGBTIQ people (and of course to the moral standing of the churches themselves in the societies they serve). Indeed, it is difficult to see how *any* interpretation of a biblical text can be justified if it inflicts harm while simultaneously claiming to be about a gospel of divine love (see Thatcher, 2021). The visceral tradition of Christian beliefs about 'degraded bodies' and their 'vile affections' has perpetuated itself into every century, including the present one. We return to these themes in later chapters (17—19).

Notes

1 The biblical ones are Ephesians 5.22—6.9; Colossians 3.18—4.1; 1 Timothy 2.8–15; 6.1–2; Titus 2.1–10. Several others exist in second-century Christian writings.

7

A Virginal Body?
Mary Uncovered

One of the strangest elements of Christian thought about the human body is its captivation by the idea of virginity. The HB assigns value to virginity only among brides-to-be and has no place for *perpetual* virginity or virginity as an explicit vocation or example of holiness. We have already met the suggestion that the term *betulim* ('Virginal Bodies', Chapter 2) is more about potential fertility than a lack of penile penetration. The tradition of natural theology demands a positive assessment of the human body and the use of all its organs as made and given by God. Paul had accused the Gentiles of failing to discern God's power and nature, visible 'through the things he has made' (Rom. 1.20). Well, the bodies of women and men are among 'the things he has made', yet the female body became increasingly disparaged by male theologians and church leaders, even within the NT itself, and it is difficult to see how a sound natural theology permitted them to make increasingly vilifying and misogynistic judgements about it. This chapter is an attempt to answer that question.

The 'virginal body' of this chapter is the construct of the patriarchal church as it reflects back on who and what Mary of Nazareth 'must' have been for the growing ideas of the sinlessness and divinity of Jesus to be protected, and the growing fear of women's bodies to be expressed and legitimized. Virginity was an ideal with several roots. It may signal uncompromising devotion to God and God's 'reign' to the exclusion of partnered intimacy. It may be chosen as a conscious avoidance of patriarchal marriage and the dangers of giving birth. It may just happen without being chosen or experienced as a 'calling'. But it may also be rooted in male fear of women's bodies (gynophobia), fuelled by bad theology. Some of that will be described in Chapters 10—12, and its living traces in Chapters 18—20.

The rise and rise of virginity in the early church is entwined with a growing veneration of the mother of Jesus, whose *perpetual* virginity soon became a principal model for women followers of Jesus to adopt. The supernatural conception of Jesus by the Holy Spirit is announced to a young girl, Mary, by an angel (Luke 1.35). But the miraculous conception soon becomes a miraculous *birth*; that is, the near nonsensical belief that during and after the birth of Jesus she remained a virgin, in Latin *virgo intacta* and *virgo postpartum*; that is, intact even after giving birth. The need to explain away the very existence of the brothers and sisters of Jesus, well attested in the Gospels, was already pressing in the second century. Mary begins her theological journey down the centuries as one who, in the words of Elizabeth, is 'Blessed [are you] among women, and blessed is the fruit of your womb' (Luke 1.42). But belief in the virginal conception of Jesus becomes belief in 'the Virgin Birth'. The blessed young girl Mary becomes 'the Virgin Mary'. By the time of the Council of Ephesus (431), the title ascribed to her two centuries earlier, the Mother of God, becomes enshrined in the creed the Council approved. But the process of her elevation from 'Blessed' to 'Virgin', to 'Ever-Virgin', to 'Mother of God' had more to do with the demands of male piety in renouncing sexuality and the company of women than with what the minimal, historical knowledge base concerning Mary ever allowed. Consequently, it is necessary to separate out sharp and necessary criticism of the invention and veneration of the perpetual virginity of Mary from devotional appreciation of her as the mother of Jesus, blessed among women, and commitment to the transformation of the world anticipated in her song of gladness (the Magnificat, Luke 1.46–55). A similar separation is required between the practice of chastity, broadly understood as a contribution to human flourishing, and chastity as abstention from the defilement that sexual contact with the bodies of women inevitably brings. These tensions become acute in this chapter.

There is no trace of any belief about the virginal *conception* of Jesus in the NT, except of course in the legends that became part of the Gospels of Matthew and Luke, and that are endlessly reprised in Christmas cards, carols, paintings, school assemblies, cribs, readings and liturgies. But there is no good reason to think she was not a virgin at the time of her betrothal to Joseph, as Matthew asserts (1.18). For nearly 200 years these legends have been acknowledged to provide little if any historical information about the birth of Jesus. That remains the case: 'The birth and infancy narratives in Matthew and Luke are markedly divergent and, of course, historically unlikely: they are commonly regarded as the evangelists' constructions which show how the Hebrew Scriptures are fulfilled in Jesus' (Maunder, 2019, p. 28). The earliest Gospel, Mark, does not mention the mother of Jesus by name, and she and the Gospel birth narratives seem to be unknown to Paul (who writes of Jesus in Galatians 4.4 that he was 'born of a woman', not that he was 'born of a virgin'). The latest Gospel – John – seems to repudiate any idea of virginal conception, for it twice refers to Jesus as the son of Joseph (1.45; 6.42).

Apart from the Christmas stories, the Gospel narratives proceed as if Joseph was the biological father of Jesus, and that he and Mary were the parents of a large family. Indeed, two of the Gospels appear to insist on the normal paternity of Jesus, perhaps to *repudiate* even the nascent suggestion of a supernatural birth. Mark records that an audience in Jesus' 'hometown' (where there would be local knowledge about his origin) was amazed at his teaching and exclaims: 'Is not this the carpenter, the son of Mary and brother of James and Joses and Judas and Simon, and are not his sisters here with us?' (6.3) The earliest known version of Mark's Gospel, a third-century manuscript called P[45], has the crowd ask not 'Is not this the carpenter?' but 'Is this not the *son* of the carpenter?' (Ehrman, 2005, p. 203). Other manuscripts have 'son of *the carpenter and of* Mary'. Matthew, who uses Mark's version of the incident, also makes Jesus the carpenter's son (Matt. 13.55). There are hundreds of cases in the NT where earlier manuscripts have been altered to reflect later beliefs, and this is one of them. If Mary was a virgin when she conceived Jesus, it is clear from the large family she raised that she could not have refrained from having sex with Joseph after Jesus' birth. Matthew says Joseph 'had no marital relations with her until she had borne a son' (1.25). He clearly thinks they had sex soon afterwards.

Matthew attempts to show throughout his Gospel that the birth of Jesus is the fulfilment of various prophecies in the HB. He makes Isaiah 7.14 ('Look, the young woman [*alma*] is with child and shall bear a son, and shall name him Immanuel'), refer to Jesus' birth, but the Hebrew *alma* (and Matthew's Greek equivalent *parthenos*) is rarely translated 'virgin'. 'Young woman' is more accurate and more frequent. The very first Christians 'spoke Aramaic, and read Hebrew rather than Greek, [so] would not have been aware of it as speaking about a virgin' (Barton, 2020, p. 72). Matthew is unconcerned about the patriarchal status of the mother of Jesus. The supernatural conception of Jesus to a young girl who was probably a virgin is only the beginning of Mary's journey through patriarchal theology. The conception of Jesus is best understood among Christians today as the product of divine agency without rushing into explanations of how the agency was implemented.

Ancestral Bodies

The opening chapter of the NT is, on the face of it, one of the most boring in the whole Bible. Matthew attempts in his opening paragraphs a genealogy of Jesus, deriving him from Abraham through 42 generations. But all is not as it seems. Matthew thinks there is something irregular, as well as supernatural, about this. One might expect a story of complete patrilineal descent, yet that is not what quite happens. He inserts into his line four women from the HB: Tamar, Rahab, Ruth and Bathsheba. This is most unusual, doubly so since 'The one thing they apparently have in common is the dubiety of their sexual liaisons' (Robinson, 1973, p. 59). Tamar seduces her father-in-law pretending to be a sex worker (Gen. 28); Rahab was a sex worker also (Josh. 2); Ruth artfully seduced Boaz (Ruth 3—4); and Bathsheba, 'the wife of Uriah' (Matt. 1.6), was a victim of coercive sex perpetrated by the king, David (2 Sam. 11—12), a circumstance emphasized by the way Matthew names her. Something queer is going on.

The insertion of these women's names into the genealogy is so unusual it must have been done for a theological reason. Matthew knew that 'Those born of an illicit union shall not be admitted to the assembly of the LORD. Even to the tenth generation, none of their descendants shall be admitted to the assembly of the LORD' (Deut. 23.2), yet he overrides the prohibition in his own speculations about the descent of Jesus. The best explanation is that he wanted to counteract rumours about the origin of Jesus, and to state that God is able to accomplish God's purpose as well through extra-marital sexual activity as through the usual patriarchal and patrilineal channels. The genealogy closes with 'Jacob the father of Joseph the husband of Mary, of whom Jesus was born, who is called the Messiah' (1.16). The patrilineal line, from Adam to the Messiah, is subverted not only by Tamar, Rahab, Ruth and Bathsheba but by Mary herself. The implication is not necessarily that Mary stands in the line of women who had extra-marital sexual relations with men (at least three of whom became pregnant). However, the line in which she stands, including the women who were used and abused by famous men, is the line God chooses to bring forth the Messiah. The dubious ancestry of Jesus makes no difference to his divine legitimacy. Mary is located in the company of the victims of patriarchy as well as being descended from its long self-replication from the beginning of time.

Luke attributes the conception of Jesus to the Holy Spirit. The angel Gabriel says to Mary: 'The Holy Spirit will come upon you, and the power of the Most High will overshadow you; therefore the child to be born will be called Son of God' (1.35). There is another long genealogy in Luke, tracing Jesus all the way back to Adam. There is something queer about this too. The genealogy begins with the detail, 'Now Jesus himself was about thirty years old when he began his ministry. He was *the son, so it was thought, of Joseph* ...' (3.23 NIV). There is doubt whether 'so it was thought' *affirms* the natural paternity of Joseph against the growing belief in Jesus' divine origin, or whether it casts doubt upon it; that is, that the opinion that Joseph was Jesus' natural father was mistaken. Elsewhere in Luke it is assumed that Joseph is the child's father (2.33; see also 2.48). The possibility that the Gospel in its present form contains contradictory suggestions about the origin of Jesus is easy to explain: the more mythical-sounding chapters (1 and 2) of Matthew and Luke were added later.

An Intact Body?

Jesus' brothers and sisters, rooted in early Gospel traditions, posed an impossible problem for later assumptions that Mary was *always* virginal. The *Protoevangelium of James*, which some scholars date as early as 145 CE, resolves the problem by making Joseph a widower (*Protoevangelium*, section 8, n.d.), implying thereby that his brothers and sisters are stepbrothers and stepsisters. But even that solution was not radical enough for Jerome (*c.* 345–420), who later rejected it as 'apocryphal nonsense'. No, the ever-Virgin Mary required an ever-virgin husband, and Jerome provided one, conjuring up the idea that the brothers and sisters of Jesus were 'children of the Mary who was the Lord's aunt, who is said to be the mother of James the less, and of Joses and Jude' (Scheck, 1985, p. 151).

Male fear of the defiling properties of intercourse with women already gains ground in the NT. The vision of heaven in Revelation describes 144,000 elite *men* (not men and women). How are the elite identified? 'It is these who have not *defiled themselves with women*' (14.4). In the later NT Letters where marriage is expected, silence in church, modesty in dress, childbearing and rearing is expected of wives. But the ideal of virginity soon comes to eclipse the idea of the Christian patriarchal household, and the *Protoevangelium* assists this development by its almost prurient discussion of Mary's birth-giving body. We will remain with this story for the next few paragraphs for what it suggests about *who* or *what* a 'virgin' was considered to be. Answers to that question are highly significant for modern debates about sexuality and the role 'virginity' is made to perform within them.

Mary's parents, Joachim and Anna, are old and bewailing their lack of children. Anna is told by an angel that she will have a child. Mary is born and at the age of three is made a ward of the Temple, consecrated to the Lord. However, the oncoming of her periods precipitates a gerontological and gynaecological panic:

And when she was twelve years old there was held a council of the priests, saying: 'Behold, Mary has reached the age of twelve years in the temple of the Lord. What then shall we do with her, lest perchance she defile the sanctuary of the Lord?' (*Protoevangelium*, section 8)

They decide to summon all 'the widowers of the people', and they hold a lottery. Mary is the prize and Joseph is the reluctant winner.

The aged Joseph, charged with protecting his new child bride, neglects her and goes off for six months to resume his trade (in this account he is a builder), returning to find Mary pregnant. Both are made to undergo an ordeal akin to the order of bitter water (Num. 5.11–31) (Chapter 3), yet both are found innocent. The biblical story of the journey to Bethlehem follows. Joseph finds a cave, not a stable, for Mary to have her baby while being attended by *two of Joseph's sons*, while Joseph goes into town to find a midwife, not as it happens to assist with the birth but to verify that the birth has happened while leaving the child's mother intact. A luminous cloud fills the cave with light. Animals and birds stand still in anticipation. A midwife attends, with a colleague Salome, who eventually attests the miracle:

Then said Salome: As the Lord my God lives, unless I thrust in my finger, and search the parts, I will not believe that a virgin has brought forth.

And the midwife went in, and said to Mary: Show yourself; for no small controversy has arisen about you. And Salome put in her finger, and cried out, and said: Woe is me for mine iniquity and mine unbelief, because I have tempted the living God; and, behold, my hand is dropping off as if burned with fire. (*Protoevangelium*, sections, 19–20)

The narrative is uninterested in Mary as a person or as a mother. The midwife's remark ('no small controversy …') and her crude examination of Mary's vagina reflects the growing controversies at the time of the book's authorship: the desirability of renouncing of sexual intercourse completely, and the impossibility of the infant Saviour of the world descending down the bloody and defiling birth canal of a young woman.

It seems obvious enough that Salome was performing a virginity test. The test was to discern whether Mary's hymen was still intact. Such a view appears to be endorsed by the (bizarre and barely believable) arrangements in Deuteronomy 22.13–21 whereby the father of a bride can bring his daughter's blood-stained sheets 'before the elders of the town' (Deut. 22.17) as 'evidence' of her virginity prior to having sex with her husband if he complains about her not being a virgin on their wedding night. But the apparent place given to hymens in accounts of virginity and virginity testing in the ancient world, and the particular idea of what or who a virgin is, have recently come under close scrutiny.[1]

To begin with, the hymen is 'the sex myth that's centuries old' (Galer, 2022). It is 'a small, membranous tissue' that doesn't provide a seal over the vagina. Instead,

> most hymens have an annular or crescent-moon shape, and may take many forms of varying thinness and thickness. Few of us would have been told that it can change with age, that some of us aren't born with one, or that it might totally disappear by the time we enter sexual maturity anyway. Or that a wide variety of activity can stretch or tear it, from exercise to masturbation to, yes, penetrative sex. (Galer, 2022)

But millions of women and men still believe an unbroken hymen is satisfactory proof of the virginal status, and Deuteronomy 22 is an undoubted and unwelcome contribution to this cross-cultural yet mistaken assumption. But if Salome's penetrating finger wasn't 'hunting for a hymen' (Lillis, 2016, p. 7), what was she doing with it? There is a plausible answer to the question, but it depends on a prior question: who or what is virginity anyway?

There was a variety of views about 'virgins' in the ancient world. In Greek sources of the second century CE, 'virgin'

> can variously denote all girls of a certain age range, girls characterized by youthful innocence and inexperience (including sexual inexperience), young women who are not yet married and thus not yet 'tamed' and civilized through submission to a husband's authority, and young brides who have not yet produced children. (Lillis, 2016, p. 16)

On a common view of *female* virginity, virgins 'have a closed-off reproductive system until genital penetration opens their bodies' and ends it (Lillis, 2020, p. 259). 'Only in very late antiquity do sources indicate a widespread investment in the idea that sexual virginity and virginity loss can be perceived in women's bodies.' The idea that virginity might be defined by an unbroken hymen is certainly read back into earlier sources, but 'A different set of assumptions about female anatomy can be gleaned from the wealth of medical texts surviving from antiquity … Medical writers assume that normal vaginas are unobstructed passageways' (Lillis, 2020, p. 260).

[P]opular and medical beliefs of the time taught that women's wombs have a mouth that opens and shuts in a natural cycle and in response to sexual, magical, or therapeutic interventions. Womb-opening is not a one-time act performed upon a virgin, but a repeatable process. (Lillis, 2020, p. 265)

The reference here to 'sexual, magical, or therapeutic interventions' gives a clue to what Salome was thought to be doing with her finger. The narrative doesn't tell us what she found inside Mary's body – only that her hand caught fire! But the narrative *does* provide plenty of evidence of signs and wonders that would have been thought in the second century CE to prove a supernatural birth: the survival of the ordeal of bitter waters, the shining light, the burned hand, the enraptured animals. Yes, Salome was looking for confirmation that Mary's birthing of Jesus was supernatural, and she finds it not because of an intact hymen but 'because the ordinary signs of childbirth are absent: her body does not release the usual materials and fluids, her labor and delivery are not painful, and her genitals have not needed to expand, stretch, or tear' (Lillis, 2016, p. 18). Her amazement could be owed to witnessing a bizarrely pristine birthing scene in which Mary, having somehow delivered a child, appears untouched by the bodily effects, painful experience or messy substances that accompany births (Lillis, 2016, p. 19). These are the substances that would have been regarded as polluting, yet no evidence for them existed, further proving Jesus' miraculous birth.

There was a popular genre of narratives in the second century that purported to describe some of the acts of the earlier apostles (see Concannon, 2017). The genre extols the avoidance of sex and marriage in following Jesus. One of the works in the genre is the *Acts of Paul and Thecla*, a tale about a virgin, Thecla (see Cooper, 2013). Thecla renounces her engagement and leaves her home and family in order to follow Paul and practise his brand of ascetic Christianity. Her aggrieved fiancé has Paul imprisoned and flogged. Thecla is miraculously preserved from being burned to death and being eaten by wild beasts. She throws herself into a pool of voracious seals, declares herself baptized and is miraculously saved from being split in two by two bulls charging in different directions. She catches up with Paul, now convinced of her courage and integrity. He tells her, 'Go, and teach the word of the Lord' (*Acts of Paul and Thecla*, n.d., section 10.4). She does, and 'enlightened many in the knowledge of Christ' (section 10.11). She casts out demons and heals so many people that the local doctors can no longer make any money. The story ends with the doctors hiring a group of drunken thugs to gang rape her, believing her violation will arrest her healing powers. Thecla prays, 'Now also deliver me from the hands of these wicked and unreasonable men, nor suffer them to debauch my chastity which I have hitherto preserved for thy honour' (section 11.10), and escapes miraculously through a fissure in a rock that closes after her.

Paul's alleged commissioning of Thecla to teach and preach has attracted much interest among advocates of the ordination of women, and it may be the case that 'actual social circumstances and contestations' (Kraemer, 2019, p. 497) underlie her story. But the book valorizes the ascetic life, which it depicts repeatedly as blessed and miraculously protected by God. The commissioning of Thecla does not really favour women's ministry. Paul at first wanted to have nothing to do with Thecla. Thecla is eventually commissioned by Paul not because she is a woman but because she resembles a man.

> The story does not, actually, propose an alternative system of gender, nor does it challenge the assumptions of feminine weakness and masculine strength. Rather, it continues to map masculine virtues onto those who share its practices and outlook, and feminine deficiencies onto those who do not. (Kraemer, 2019, p. 497)

There is no gender recognition here, only gender transformation, as all or most of the characteristics associated with femininity disappear from her persona. Women can become men by remaining virgins. How?

> A woman whose sexuality is controlled by a man, particularly a man with whom she is liable for sexual intercourse, cannot exercise authority over men; but apparently, a celibate woman could, both because she was not under male authority and because her abstinence from the defining act of female submission and subordination, sexual penetration, perhaps allowed her to be constructed as sufficiently male/masculine. (Kraemer, 2019, p. 498)

A Blessed Body

The diminishing view of women – polluting, defiling, tempting – has eclipsed the positive vision of women of faith, expressed in a positive, explosive joy that bursts into song with the announcements of the miraculous births of John the Baptist and Jesus. 'Blessed are you among women, and blessed is the fruit of your womb', exclaims Elizabeth, with a loud cry (Luke 1.42). Mary's song is by far the longest passage attributed to a woman in the NT. Here she stands in another line of women, not those whose bodies collide with patriarchal systems, but in the long line of Jewish *female singers*, 'from Miriam with her tambourine (Exod. 15.2–21), to Deborah (Judg. 5.1–31), to Hannah (1 Sam. 2.1–10), to Judith (Judith 16.1–17) who also sang songs of salvation, victory songs of the oppressed' (Johnson, 2003, p. 14). Also eclipsed is her real, physical poverty: 'My soul magnifies the Lord, and my spirit rejoices in God my Saviour, for he has *looked with favour on the lowliness of his servant*. Surely, from now on all generations will call me blessed' (Luke 1.46–48). Her 'lowliness' (*tapeinōsis* in Greek) conveys well a sense of class, misery and deprivation. She calls herself a *doule*, signalling her powerlessness. Precisely because of her 'lowliness', God chooses her, and so no male prophet, priest or ruler. The background picture is of one who is 'a poor, first-century Galilean peasant woman living in occupied territory, struggling for survival and dignity, imbued with Jewish faith' (Johnson, 2003, p. 15).

It has taken generations of feminist and womanist scholars to recover and re-commend Mary, rescue her from centuries of passivity, unattainability and quasi-deity, and re-present her as an image of faith for women, and so also for men, a mother of a real (and large) family, not just Mother of the Church and Mother of God. Christian women, meeting in their Bible study groups throughout the world, report their delight in reading the conversations between Mary and Elizabeth, where there is no male intrusion, no apparent influence or control, and the favour she finds is 'with God' and not with men. In her song, she also understands the social, political and economic consequences that the reign of God, instituted by her son, will bring about. Looking back in confidence on what God has yet to do, she rejoices that:

> He has shown strength with his arm;
>   he has scattered the proud in the thoughts of their hearts.
> He has brought down the powerful from their thrones,
>   and lifted up the lowly;
> he has filled the hungry with good things,
>   and sent the rich away empty. (Luke 1.51–53)

Her vision of victory over oppression, liberation from classism and sexism (as we would say) aids women of faith today in churches where they are denied a voice, and where Mary, though revered, remains a stranger to real birth, to the tension of real marriages and real families; where she becomes the visible tool of patriarchy, idealizing a vision of passive, obedient, virginal femininity to the detriment of real women's struggles. Her solidarity with real mothers and real women coping with patriarchal systems; her solidarity with the world's poor, and her faith in God to reverse the world's order of things: these are just some of the liberating features of the story of the young girl Mary of Nazareth, wife of Joseph and mother of Jesus, obscured by centuries of negation of her sex among theologians and Christian leaders. Indeed, a particular view of virginity, that of an unpenetrated woman, has become standard, and weaponized in modern arguments over sexual ethics, not least in *Living in Love and Faith*. I have often asked students what counts as having (straight) sex (Thatcher, 2011, pp. 14–16), and various answers have been given. With lesbian and gay sex, the situation is more complicated still, and with recent attempts to speak of 'spiritual' or 'restored' virginity a tenuous concept of virginity topples over (see King, 2023). As the World Health Organization states, 'The term "virginity" is not a medical or scientific term. Rather, the concept of "virginity" is a social, cultural and religious construct – one that reflects gender discrimination against women and girls', and is a violation of their rights (World Health Organization, 2018).

Notes

1 My thanks to Helen King for her suggestions on this section. The remaining errors are mine.

8

Conceiving Bodies:
The Roots of Contemporary Culture Wars

The very idea of virginity cannot of course be separated from the state of not having sex. Two contentious issues in the early church – contraception and abortion – remain contentious now. Hostility to both may have been due to the fact that the practice of each was evidence of having had *clandestine* sex. The bodies of this chapter belong to straight Christians who had sex and tried to conceal their sins by contraception or abortion; also the bodies of the unborn, whether or not they were aborted. The overturning of the Roe versus Wade decision by the Supreme Court of the United States in June 2022 effectively ended the constitutional right to an abortion for millions of women, and brought the culture wars in that country to new depths of rancour and harm. Although opposed by the majority of Americans, the decision was strongly supported by most Roman Catholic and Evangelical Protestant Christians. These wars have deep roots in some of the sources to be considered in this chapter.

No Christian church sanctioned contraception, even in marriage, until 1930 (Chapter 18). The absolutist position of the Roman Catholic Church on contraception in the time of HIV and AIDS has been scandalous. On abortion, millions of Christians, Catholic and Protestant, take up a position more extreme about the personhood of the embryo than any in the first millennium. Both issues are woven into Christian thinking about the body and sexuality from the second century onwards. It is extremely difficult to bypass the noise of contemporary disagreements in the attempt to understand them in their ancient context, but an attempt will be made in this chapter. Whatever the official teaching of the churches, many women in every generation have needed both.

Contracepting Bodies

Instances of both contraception and abortion cannot be found directly in the Bible although literalists will resort to desperate measures to find proof texts that allegedly support their prohibitions (Jer. 1.4–5 and Psalm

139.13 are often cited). The passage closest to condemning contraception is the story of Onan (Gen. 38.8–10; see Chapter 3). Yes, Onan *was* practising *coitus interruptus*, incurring serious divine displeasure that cost him his life. A man who ejaculates makes himself unclean but commits no crime. A Jewish source calls Onan's sin 'threshing inside, winnowing outside' (Babylonian Talmud, n.d.). There are several sexual practices that are forbidden in the HB, like having sex during menstruation, but contraception, like masturbation, is not one of them. Since men having (anal) sex with men is forbidden one might expect a similar prohibition of contraception if there was a theological reason for one. There wasn't.

Contraception happens when straight, fertile people are physically intimate with each other and try to avoid becoming pregnant. It is intimacy that avoids, is against (*contra*), conception. If the purpose of heterosexual intimacy is narrowly and solely restricted to making babies, then even snogging is a contraceptive act. It is pleasurable (if consensual), but not directed towards conception. But the principal means of the limitation of children for most of history was not contraception but the abandonment or exposure of the newly born, either to certain death or to a perilous fate if the abandoned child was taken and reared by another adult, often a slave owner or brothel keeper. Infanticide had several advantages over contraception. It enabled sexual selection; that is, the removal from families of unwanted girls. It was much safer than abortion, and more reliable than contraception in achieving the aim of limiting family size (Gudorf, 2003, p. 56). Sexual selection continues. In many countries it is still practised, not just by abandonment but by abortion, assisted by the use of ultrasound scanners that indicate the sex of the unborn long before a pregnancy goes to its full term. In India today, 'You will find an ultrasound machine even in a village which has a road over which only a bullock cart can go, and electricity to run the machine and nothing else' (cited in Storkey, 2015, p. 21).

A variety of contraceptive methods was available in the ancient world, including 'the application before coitus of cedar gum, vinegar, brine or olive oil to the vagina or male genitals and a gamut of vaginal plugs and occlusive pessaries, mostly with wool base soaked in honey, alum, white lead or olive oil' (Hopkins, 2017). In Egypt dried crocodile dung was used. Potions were made from herbs, plants, roots, leaves (especially from the willow), and there are references in the NT to 'sorcery' and people who have recourse to it (Gal. 5.20; Rev. 9.21; 18.23; 21.8; 22.15). Sorcery is a synonym for magic, and magic was widely used in the ancient world, with good and evil intent. It is possible that the occurrence of the term in Galatians 5.20 (*pharmakeia*), in a vice list following mention of 'impurity, licentiousness, idolatry', may include the taking of recreational drugs and/or medicines associated with contraception or abortion, but it is tenuous to link sorcery with either.

More Promiscuous Bodies

The promiscuous behaviour of the so-called 'antinomian' Christians did not simply fall away. It continued to be condemned in the later NT. The dubious reputation of some Christians due to their sexual *mores* may have contributed to the repudiation by other Christians of bodily intimacy altogether, placing enormous weight on the scarcely permitted exception of marriage. Contraception is caught up in the concealment of sexual intercourse, and associated with infanticide. The short 'books' of Jude and 2 Peter in the NT are written to Christians whose communities are deemed to have been infiltrated by 'false prophets', by the 'ungodly, who pervert the grace of our God into licentiousness and deny our only Master and Lord, Jesus Christ' (Jude 4). Many believers believed them-selves to be upholding the true faith by eliminating all sexual desire from their lives. Any Christian then, on their view, who admitted to or expressed desire, was already on the wrong side of a moral dividing line and could not be regarded as a 'true' Christian (Knust, 2006). The lurid and slanderous characterization of some Christians, by other Christians, as perversely promiscuous, may be a resort owing more to stereotype than to historical accuracy. But that characterization of fellow Christians persisted, and there was probably more than a kernel of truth to the accusations. It helps to explain why, according to the Roman historians Tacitus and Pliny the Younger, Christians were known only for their 'vices' (see Noonan, 1986, p. 63).

Added to the ambiguity accorded to marriage in the NT was a broader dualism that viewed the body and the created world negatively. It is generally known as Gnosticism (from the Greek *gnōsis* – knowledge), but the borders of Gnosticism are contested, and the word much over-used. Risking generalization, we might say that, for 'Gnostically minded' Christians, having babies only added to the misery of the created world. Knowledge of the spiritual world provided escape from the captivity of creation, but this knowledge did not always exclude or inhibit knowledge of another kind – *carnal* knowledge. There were Christians who were willing to follow their leaders neither into endorsing celibacy, nor prais-ing virginity, nor into marriage with its normal expectation of children. These Christians had a negative valuation of the body and its desires, but their disapproval did not extend to the enjoyment of both. Indulging in sexual intimacy could also find doctrinal support, however tenuous, in for example the teaching of Paul that the law was no longer binding on Christians; or that the forgiveness of sins embraced every sin past or future; or that believers were already made perfect by the salvation Christ had procured for them and could do no wrong; or, since they were the 'elect' of God, chosen by God before time began, their salvation could not be jeopardized: or, still further, if the realm of the flesh was really of no account, why not indulge its desires anyway? While these justifications for promiscuous behaviour may seem specious to us, they were rooted in fragments of emerging doctrine and are evidence of disquiet with the growing asceticism of Christian leaders.

What the Gnostics could not conscientiously do was to procreate (and so to add to the material world), but sexual intimacy can take many forms other than achieving conception. Such activities, which probably included physical or 'medical' contraception (barriers, or herbs and potions) but were not confined to them, became the target of attack under various general headings like 'fornication' that lay to hand. The roots of the church's growing opposition to contraception lay here, in opposing all attempts to engage in bodily pleasures without the intended consequence of conception. It was better not to marry than to marry; and it was better to have no sex within marriage than to indulge in it. There were Christians who could not accept these growing ascetic orthodoxies. It is not difficult to argue that the Christians who attempted to observe them generally had contempt for the Christians who did not.

When Justin Martyr (martyred in 169) wrote to the emperor to give an account of who Christians were and what they believed and did, he reserved his vehemence to condemn the exposure of infants by the Romans, contrasting this practice with the chastity of Christians. 'Whether we marry', he explained, 'it is only that we may bring up children; or whether we decline marriage, we live continently' (Justin, n.d., chapter 29). Exposing children carries the risk that 'We become murderers'. It is a

> sin against God, first, because we see that almost all so exposed (not only the girls, but also the males) are brought up to prostitution. And as the ancients are said to have reared herds of oxen, or goats, or sheep, or grazing horses, so now we see you rear children only for this shameful use; and for this pollution a multitude of females and hermaphrodites, and those who commit unmentionable iniquities, are found in every nation. And you receive the hire of these, and duty and taxes from them, whom you ought to exterminate from your realm. (Justin, n.d., chapter 27)

Justin's indignation opens up the horror of the Christian imagination towards the murder and exploitation of children, adding that men using female sex workers may be unknowingly committing incest, since they might be the unwitting fathers of the prostituted children. It was a short step to make the connection between real child murder as a method of family limitation and the *accusation* of child murder directed against those who practised contraception (and abortion) and so attempted to prevent a potential child from being formed. But Justin also had to defend the Christians against the charge of promiscuity and to affirm resolutely that 'promiscuous intercourse is not one of our mysteries' (Justin, n.d., chapter 27).

Clement of Alexandria (150–215 CE) provides direct evidence that promiscuous intercourse *did* continue and that a religious value was attached to it. He spoke of a Christian leader, a certain Epiphanes, 'whose writings I actually possess', who argued that wives should be held in common (Clement of Alexandria, 1991, p. 258). The justification given was the 'common shared equality' among all created things in their having been created by the one God. It follows from the idea that God has created everything, that people should not own property, especially marital property. Women should be shared around. The androcentrism is too obvious to invite comment. In 1848 the first Oneida Community was established in New York, practising something similar, known as 'Bible communism'. This included the sharing of wives in a practice called 'complex marriage'. Husbands practised *coitus reservatus* (or so they attempted), refraining from ejaculation during intercourse, while Oneida communities later practised 'stirpiculture', pairing couples in order to create spiritually superior children (Wonderley, 2017).

The antinomian roots of the Epiphanians are clear in Clement's explanation of Epiphanes' view: 'He suggests that "mine" and "yours" came into existence *through the laws* [of the HB], so that the earth and possessions were no longer put to common use.' Clement is shocked by Epiphanes. He asks, 'How can this fellow still be listed in our church members' register when he openly does away with the Law and the Gospels alike by these words?' (Clement of Alexandria, 1991, p. 261). But the very question says something about the diversity of sexual morality in the churches. Epiphanes' father was accused of still worse behaviour. He, his followers and 'some other zealots' would gather for 'love-feasts', which quickly became orgies (p. 263).

Murdered and Aborted Bodies

A common view, often repeated in today's sermons, is that while the Empire was promiscuous the churches were not. Revelation 17, where a woman personifies the Empire, has the inscription 'Babylon the great, mother of whores and of earth's abominations' (Rev. 17.5) written on her forehead – a potent symbol of utter decadence against which the churches fought. It is a comforting contrast to repeat (which puts Christians in a 'good' light), but the situation is more complicated. Some Romans, the Stoics in particular, emphasized the control of desire and the suspicion of passions, just as Christians did. Another comforting binary, that the Romans upheld abortion while Christians condemned it, is also more complicated. There is a range of early sources showing that Christians disapproved of *child murder* (it could hardly be otherwise). The earliest is the *Didache* or *Teaching* (of the Apostles), which may be a first-century document. Christians are embarked on the 'way of life', which is contrasted with the 'way of death'. The way of life is based on the Love Commandments of Jesus, which extend the Ten Commandments of the Torah. Based on the commandments that forbid murder, adultery and theft, the *Didache* adds further commandments that associate magic and witchcraft with abortion: 'You shall not practice magic, you shall not practice witchcraft, *you shall not murder a child by abortion nor kill that which is begotten*' (*Didache*, n.d., para. 2.2).

The *Letter of Barnabas*, once considered for inclusion in the canon of scripture, was probably written around 125 CE. Also commenting on the Love Commandment to love one's neighbour as oneself, children are to be included in the category 'neighbour', with clear consequences: 'Thou shalt not murder a child by abortion, nor again shalt thou kill it when it is born' (Barnabas, n.d., para. 19.5). Like the *Didache* both pre-natal and post-natal termination of life are counted as murder. However, the various *Lives* of early Irish saints record abortion miracles in which male and female saints *cause* the unwanted pregnancies of chaste women to disappear (Mistry, 2013). Not surprisingly, later manuscripts gloss or omit these accounts. They may indicate an unusually tolerant attitude to abortion in medieval Ireland, together with a sanguine acceptance of unwanted pregnancies (Callan, 2012). But they also reveal the value to women of chastity, even supernaturally restoring to them the virginal state of which they had been deprived, even at supreme cost to the unborn. Opposition to abortion is constant in Christian traditions, but the popular justification, that the foetus is a person from the moment of conception, is recent.

Hell-bound Bodies

The popular *Apocalypse of Peter* (*c.* 135 CE) describes special places in hell for sexual offenders. There is 'a great lake full of flaming mire'. Women who 'adorned themselves for adultery' were 'hanged by their hair above that mire which boiled up'. The men who used them 'were hanging by their feet, and had their heads hidden in the mire' (James, 1924, sections 24–25). The author then describes the fate of 'the murderers and them that were consenting to them'. They writhe in agony, perpetually eaten by worms. Aborted foetuses are safe and alive, accusing their mothers with vengeful stares:

> And hard by that place I saw another strait place wherein the discharge and the stench of them that were in torment ran down, and there was as it were a lake there. And there sat women up to their necks in that liquor, and over against them many children which were born out of due time sat crying: and from them went forth rays of fire and smote the women in the eyes: and these were they that conceived out of wedlock (?) and caused abortion. (section 26)

Lesbian and gay people are not spared either:

> And other men and women being cast down from a great rock (precipice) fell (came) to the bottom, and again were driven by them that were set over them, to go up upon the rock, and thence were cast down to the bottom and had no rest from this torment. And these were they that did defile their bodies behaving as women: and the women that were with them were they that lay with one another as a man with a woman. (section 32)

Their sin is again characterized in terms of gender infraction. Only women can be penetrated (and by only a penis). Anything else is to engage in feminization or masculinization. It is either to cease to be, or to try to be, a man. The role reversal is patterned in their punishment, endlessly to replicate their infraction of 'top' and 'bottom' positions by being hurled from the top to the bottom of a cliff.

Embryonic Bodies

While resistance to the abandonment of children could be taught on the basis of the Love Commandments or the commandment of the HB not to commit murder (Exod. 20.13), abortion lacked any direct biblical prohibition. The closest reference is the prescription in the book of Exodus about what to do following a miscarriage after a fight:

> When people who are fighting injure a pregnant woman so that there is a miscarriage, and yet no further harm follows, the one responsible shall be fined what the woman's husband demands, paying as much as the judges determine. If any harm follows, then you shall give life for life, eye for eye, tooth for tooth, hand for hand, foot for foot, burn for burn, wound for wound, stripe for stripe. (Exod. 21.22–25)

The barbarous nature of 'eye for eye' is no call for revenge but the placing of a limit on it when it is deemed to be allowable. The woman has no part in determining the punishment of her assailant. He must pay the fine her husband demands, subject to the judges' approval. When the clause 'If any harm follows' refers to the death of the mother, then the 'life for life' principle applies. The offence is a capital one. There is a difference, then, between the valuation of the life of the foetus in the womb and the life of the mother. How this difference is to be understood, in biblical times and in our own, is a key question.

Part of the answer was discussed in Chapter 2. The focus there was on what was believed necessary for a child to be *conceived*. The inquiry unearthed strange beliefs about the superiority of male semen, the influence of heat and cold and so on. But how was a child thought to *develop* in the womb? The answer to that question was confined in the Bible to the requirement that a mother after giving birth had to live out a longer period of uncleanness if her baby was a girl than if he was a boy. These findings told us much about the gender bias underlying ancient theories of conception. But the Greek world had more to say about foetal development, and in particular the development of the *soul*.

The male sperm is the bearer of the soul, but soul develops in stages in the womb. This 'delayed ensoulment' took place in stages. First, the embryo acquired a vegetable soul. Later in gestation it acquired an animal soul, and finally the foetus becomes animated with a human soul. This was the final 'ensoulment' of the foetus. Delayed ensoulment coincided well with the passage in Exodus 21, which gave different values to the lives of the foetus and of its mother. There is no guidance in the Bible regarding *when* the foetus is ensouled: still less can we know directly when the later word 'person' (derived from the Latin word *persona*) can be applied to it. It is a vexed question for Judaism (and Islam as well). In some versions of ancient Jewish law, the foetus 'becomes a full-fledged human being when the head emerges from the womb' (Disney and Poston, 2010, p. 279). There is even in Judaism the principle of doubtful viability, namely that 'an embryo remains an embryo until thirty days after its *birth*, becoming only then a *bar kayyama*, a viable, living being' (Feldman, 1968, cited in Disney and Poston, 2010, pp. 253–4).

The North African theologian Tertullian wrote extensively about conception and held that the soul was a material substance transferred to the embryo by having heterosexual sex (a position known a 'traducianism'). He can therefore be claimed to have taught that life begins at conception, and so is 'sacred' or 'human', or a 'person' from the beginning. But this is to overlook other elements in his work, which indicate that his view was more nuanced. I follow here Margaret Kamitsuka's spirited and convincing attempt to wrest Tertullian from the natalists (Kamitsuka, 2019, pp. 39–47). Tertullian reads the different penalties in the Exodus passage about the miscarrying woman subtly. At one point in his *Treatise on the Soul* he teaches that 'the embryo therefore becomes a human being in the womb from the moment that its form is completed'. Conception is not the completion of its form but only the beginning of it. The law of Moses, he explains, 'punishes with due penalties the man who shall cause abortion, inasmuch as there exists already *the rudiment of a human being*' (Tertullian, n.d., chapter 37). He also shows himself aware of the tools and procedures needed when 'Sometimes by a cruel necessity, whilst yet in the womb, an infant is put to death, when lying awry in the orifice of the womb he impedes parturition, and kills his mother, if he is not to die himself' (chapter 25). In such cases the embryotomy is, in his view, indeed cruel, but also necessary. Tertullian was 'apparently able to see that killing a fetus during an obstructed birth, in order to avoid the gruesome death of both the mother and child, was a tragic but morally justifiable medical action' (Kamitsuka, 2019, p. 47).

Two centuries later, another North African theologian, Augustine (354–430), mused over some of the obvious problems associated with belief in the resurrection of the dead, and wondered whether children who died in the womb would also be raised (Augustine, *Enchiridion*, Book 23, in Outler, 1955, section 85). His answer is a cautious 'yes', as long as they are 'fully formed'. But what of those that are *not* fully formed? He wonders whether they might perish like seeds that do not germinate, or whether perhaps on the day of resurrection God might yet complete their form. The question of course raises another, which he confessed he could not answer, namely: 'When does a human being begin to live in the womb?' (section 86). This leads him to speak of aborted foetuses that are 'undeveloped' and *not* fully formed. He remains undecided. He thinks that to *deny* 'that those fetuses ever lived at all which are cut away limb by limb and cast out of the wombs of pregnant women, lest the mothers die also if the fetuses were left there dead, would seem much too rash'.

It is clear, then, that Augustine's position about the status of the foetus is that it is not already a living human being at conception. At conception it begins the process of formation. His position is similar to that of Tertullian, that a foetus, sufficiently developed to become aborted, can be called 'the rudiment of a human being'. The early church was against the abandonment and murder of children. It placed a high value on the foetus in the womb. And it was opposed to abortion. However, when penances were imposed on women who had abortions, the penance was often 'linked to the condition of the mother. In other words, socioeconomic and other mitigating circumstances were considered' (Kamitsuka, 2019, p. 30). But its reasons for opposition to abortion did not include the recent idea that the foetus is a person from the moment of conception. As the valorization of virginity grew, and the antinomian indulgence in unregulated sexual activity continued, opposition to contraception and abortion was more likely to have been based on attempts by some Christians to stop other Christians having sex, even in marriage. Any sexual pleasure, any non-procreative sex, any delight in one's body or the bodies of others, was for the perishing pagans.

9

Pure Bodies:
Regulating Sex

How were Christians to live in a pagan empire that had crucified their Saviour and was sporadically persecuting and ridiculing them? One answer, repeated in the later Letters of the NT, is by the order and witness of the Christian household (Chapter 6). Sayings of Jesus circulated that showed he accepted marriage (without divorce). Another answer, also recalling sayings of Jesus, moved towards renouncing marriage altogether (Chapter 5). The free-born male Christian appeared to have two alternatives. He would marry and exercise self-control over himself and his household, or he would remain single and remain continent. But the continence option, so common in later centuries, is *angrily rejected* in the NT:

> Now the Spirit expressly says that in later times some will renounce the faith by paying attention to deceitful spirits and teachings of demons, through the hypocrisy of liars whose consciences are seared with a hot iron. They *forbid marriage* and demand abstinence from foods. (1 Tim. 4.1–3)

This is standard Christian polemic, slandering opponents (Knust, 2006) *within the faith* and accusing them of apostasy, gullibility, immorality, hypocrisy and false teaching, in this case all in a couple of sentences.

The pure bodies in this chapter belong in the first instance to all Christians. Their bodies remained pure as long as they came into no sexual contact with other bodies. But there was no agreement about what purity was or how it could be attained. Some Christians required complete abstinence from sex, conflating chastity with continence. Other Christians thought that purity could be maintained within a sexually active marriage ('pure marriage') through which the unity between a woman and a man symbolized the union of the spiritual and carnal realms, and the union of all things at the end of time. Other Christians thought no female body could be pure. In her preparation for the next life, she should repudiate everything feminine and begin her transition to masculine perfection.

Continent Bodies – no sex

But polemic in Letters that later became 'scripture' did not stop the continence option from spreading and gaining influence. Christian men would cultivate a form of manliness that would rival their Roman counterparts. They would control their households or, if unmarried, they would attempt to control their lusts. This too would be thought to impress Roman opinion and indicate the presence of the Spirit in sexually abstinent lives. But the question was always more than one about the witness of the church. It was also about the status of women's bodies, their disturbing presence in the worship of the churches, and their continuing danger to the men who were trying to avoid 'adultery of the heart' (Matt. 5.28). There was 'a broad conflict that gripped the early church, a conflict over women at the altar and in the bed' (DeConick, 2011, p. 38). The same conflict persists into the third millennium.

The Syrian Christian writer Tatian (120–180 CE) was among the first to argue that Christians should have no sex at all, and that married Christians should stop doing it. Baptism was the moment when converts were to abandon their former way of life, which included all sexual relations. He and his followers were soon known as Encratites (from *enkrateia*, 'self-controlled'). Tatian took literally the ruling in the HB that the emission of seed caused the whole body to be impure (Chapter 2) (DeConick, 2011, p. 86). The strands of purity and self-control bind together in his teaching. The perfect God is without flesh (except in the incarnation), yet has made people to be both flesh and spirit. An intense experience of the Holy Spirit was thought to overcome the dichotomy between soul and body. In Syriac the word for spirit is feminine (Brown, 1990, p. 92), and Tatian held that the Christian life was one of marriage, not of a man to a fleshly woman but to the Spirit herself: 'The joining of the existing, insufficient human being to the Holy Spirit formed the center of gravity of his thought. His insistence on sexual abstinence flowed from this overriding preoccupation' (Brown, 1990, p. 90).

Their revulsion towards sex, however, did not extend to the women in their groups, provided they all remained continent. They were criticized for having women among them as travelling companions, assisting with ministry and even living with them. Conspicuous chastity was an intended form of Christian witness, and the chaste women, as honorary men, could be included in the work of evangelism. Since Encratites shunned having sex, they needed plenty of converts. Epiphanius, a fourth-century bishop, gave them short shrift:

if marriage is abominable, all [who] are born of marriage are unclean. And if God's holy church is composed only of those who have renounced marriage, marriage cannot be of God. And if it is not, the whole business of procreation is ungodly. And if the business of procreation is ungodly so are they, since they have been begotten by such behavior. (Williams, 2013, pp. 116–17)

Marcion (85–160 CE) was another influential Christian leader who insisted on continence among believers. If the date of the final composition of the Letter known as 1 Timothy is well into the second century CE, it is possible that he and his followers were the targets of its slander. His despair at the state of the material world and the evil and suffering within it led him to borrow from Plato's thought the idea of the Demiurge. He was the Creator of the material world, but there was a greater God, the God of love that Christ proclaimed. The lesser God was the God of the Jewish scriptures. This God 'had imposed on the human race dull rules and cramping compartmentalizations that cut human beings off from each other. Mankind as a whole, and not merely the Jews, lived "under the Law"' (Brown, 1990, p. 89). A detail from a tirade against Marcion indicates the contrast between the Creator-God and Jesus:

Where the Creator had ordered men to shun lepers, Christ had touched them. Where the Creator had decreed menstruating women to be a source of impurity, Christ had let the woman with an issue of blood lay her hand upon him. (Tertullian, n.d., n.p., 4.9.3 and 4.20.9)

Marcion adopted a plausible interpretation of the saying of Jesus that marriage belonged to 'this age' and that those followers who avoided marriage were already like the angels (Luke 20.34–36). Marriage belonged to the material world with its cycle of birth, death and pain. It was a distraction. Even married converts were expected to renounce their ties to each other and to their children in favour of a different bonding within a different arrangement – the local church. For several centuries Marcion's version of Christianity was equally as popular and widespread as other versions. His aversion to the Jewish scriptures might be paralleled to some extent with the New Atheists of the present century for whom the violence and cruelty of the biblical God is a strong moral reason for denying 'Him'. But their doctrinal scheme was internally flawed, as critics eagerly pointed out. How could there be two gods? If there were, what was the relation between them? If the Creator-God is a lesser god, why did the 'greater' God permit the lesser god to make such a disastrous material world? And yes, there are many parts of the HB where the deity is depicted as vengeful, angry and capricious (as there are in the NT), but these need to be balanced by other parts where the divine love, the demand for justice and the pursuit of wisdom are also clearly manifest.

Pure Bodies – mystical sex

The *Acts of Paul and Thecla* (Chapter 7) belonged to a community that required continence, while others held that marriage was pure. A third contemporary of Tatian and Marcion was Valentinus (100–160 CE), who came to Rome in 138. He and his followers were also Christians, not yet being classed as heretics, although they also maintained separate associations – a church within the church. But they allowed marriage. They used the power of 'Gnostic' myths in their teaching. These myths appear strange to modern readers, but they were thought to have explanatory power and the Valentinians tried to use them to commend Christian teaching. Like more 'orthodox' Christians, they believed in an angelic fall, prior to the fall of Adam and Eve. Instead of horny angels, they 'generally agreed that sin resulted when one of the female aspects of God, an emanation named Sophia or Wisdom, desired to "know" the Father God outside the boundaries of her marriage to the male aeon, Thêletus or Intention' (DeConick, 2011, pp. 96–7). A more straightforward way into their teaching is through their understanding of the familiar text of Genesis 1.27 that the male and female are both made in the image of God. The first human is androgynous. Their separation into a man and a woman reflects the cosmic fall.

The Valentinians emphasized the 'mysteries' of Christian faith. The Letter to the Ephesians had compared the marriage of Christians to the marriage of Christ the bridegroom to the church, his bride. The author called both of these marriages a 'mystery'. The Valentinians saw marriage as a way of overcoming the separation of the sexes at the Fall and anticipating the overcoming of the separation between the true God and the fallen angels at the end of time. An insight into their thought can be gleaned from the following passage from the *Gospel of Philip*, a second-century Gospel associated with them:

The mystery of marriage is great. [Without] it, the world would [not] exist. The existence of [the world depends on] people, and the existence [of people depends on] marriage. Then think of the power of [pure] intercourse, though its image is defiled. (Meyer, n.d., pp. 64–5)

The difference between pure and defiled intercourse is a crucial one. Pure intercourse is not only possible but sacred. It unifies the sexes and anticipates the unification of all things at the end of time. But what exactly is it? The physician Soranus stated the widely held view 'that various states of the soul also produce certain changes in the mold of the fetus' (Soranus, *Gynecology*, 1.39, cited in DeConick, 2011, p. 98). He gave an example of some women who, thinking about monkeys while they were having sex, gave birth to children resembling monkeys! What one was thinking about during sex, along with other misunderstood features of the acts like the mingling of seeds, their quantity and heat, helped to determine the outcome. Pure intercourse belonged to pure marriage. The Holy Spirit, they believed, would honour the holy intention of their couplings in conceiving children who would belong to the Elect. This was part of the mystery of marriage. Intercourse merely for the sake of extinguishing desire was impure and carnal.

The Gnostics accepted that both male and female seed was required to produce an embryo. They also accepted the usual prejudice that male seed was superior to female seed. Pure thoughts would increase the likelihood of the birth of a boy. A girl would need to work harder to achieve her salvation. So while these Christians differed from the Encratites in permitting pure sex within marriage, their 'marital chastity' accrued respect inside and outside their assemblies. Like the Encratites, they allowed women to teach on the basis that chaste women were really men. They were allowed to baptize and perform exorcisms. Known chastity could be empowering for women, as it was among the Encratites, even though its certainty could always be doubted, and perhaps sometimes with good reason.

The *Gospel of Philip* continues with a clear statement of the myth of the first androgyne:

> If the female had not separated from the male, the female and the male would not have died. The separation of male and female was the beginning of death. Christ came to heal the separation that was from the beginning and reunite the two, in order to give life to those who died through separation and unite them …
>
> A woman is united with her husband in the bridal chamber, and those united in the bridal chamber will not be separated again. That is why Eve became separated from Adam, because she had not united with him in the bridal chamber. (Meyer, n.d., p. 70)

Here marriage is no distraction but a mirror of Christ's saving work, as the union of husband and wife becomes a paradigmatic instance of the restored and redeemed creation. It draws attention to the quality of the married relationship and the place of sexual consummation within it, within 'the bridal chamber'. It is an idealized view of marriage, of course, but one that contains the merit of serious theological reflection.

Pure marriage undoes all promiscuity. Evil spirits seize men and women when they lust after each other, yet in pure marriage the same spirits are powerless. Echoing the mystical language of Ephesians 5, the Gospel continues:

> Unclean spirits are male and female in form. Males have sex with souls that are female in form, and females cavort promiscuously with souls that are male in form. Souls cannot escape them if the spirits seize them, unless they receive the male or female power of the bridegroom and the bride. These are received from the mirrored bridal chamber. (in Meyer, n.d., p. 65)

Such is the importance of marriage as a cipher for the overcoming of all separation from God that *even Jesus is depicted as married*: 'The companion of the [savior] is Mary of Magdala. The [savior loved] her more than [all] the disciples, [and he] kissed her often on her [mouth].' Mary is Jesus' 'companion' or *koinonos* (which in its verbal form can mean to have sex with). (DeConick, 2011, p. 139)

> The other [disciples] [64] … said to him, 'Why do you love her more than all of us?' The savior answered and said to them, 'Why do I not love you like her? If a blind person and one who can see are both in darkness, they are the same. When the light comes, one who can see will see the light, and the blind person will stay in darkness.' (Meyer, n.d., pp. 63–4)

The disciples' apparent envy is dismissed. Their question is parried but its premiss is not denied. The saying about light is deliberately opaque. Mystery enshrouds, and is intended to enshroud, the relation between Jesus and Mary of Magdala.

Obsolete Bodies? – no need for sex

The obsolete bodies in this section are the bodies of women, who, in the next life, and as far as possible in this life too, lose their femininity and become men. All that makes them women disappears in their transformation. How so?

We will encounter several further strands to the growing male suspicion of female bodies in later chapters (see also Concannon, 2017,
pp. 122–54). A particular NT verse is widely thought to proclaim the full
equality of women with men (see Martin, 2006, pp. 77–90). The verse
is currently caught up in frenetic and androcentric arguments about the
'place of women' in the churches. Paul, in the context of a long argument,
tells the Christians at Galatia: 'There is no longer Jew or Greek, there is
no longer slave or free, there is no longer male and female; for all of you
are one in Christ Jesus' (Gal. 3.28). Optimistic, liberal readings find in the
verse an end to (in order) racial difference, class difference and sexual difference. All human beings, so the argument runs, 'are one in Christ Jesus'.
Jesus is the leader, the embodiment, of a new humanity in which race,
class and sex count for nothing. The followers of Jesus are perfectly 'one'
because all distinctions between human beings have been broken down.

There are obvious difficulties with this reading. The sad, even deplorable history of relations between Christians and Jews (Chapter 15), the
deplorable history of race relations in the modern period (Chapters 15
and 16), and the exclusion of women from key roles in church and state,
hardly give credence to the liberal reading of the verse either now or in
the history of the church. There was an accelerating trajectory in the
NT that made ever sharper distinctions between women and men. The
liberal interpretation of 'one in Christ Jesus' unfortunately overlooks
that *unity* and *equality* are very different concepts. Unity is more consistent with *hierarchy*. All organizations – churches, hospitals, armies,
businesses, universities, households – have leaders. Good leaders can
unite their organizations in a common purpose. Even organizations like
the Quakers, who take the ideal of equality further than most, are not
entirely exempt.

Another reading of the text finds a return to an ancient *androgyny*,
to the mythical creature of the androgyne who is both male and female,
and who may be hinted at in Genesis 1.27. On this view, 'no longer
male and female' is a future state that mirrors and fulfils the primitive
creation of humankind before the creation of the female sex, described in
Genesis 2 and understood as a separate and subsequent event. Paul was
soon understood to say that the cessation of sexual difference happens
by the elimination, not the transformation, of the female (and he may
have thought this all along). A world of men only is a world where there
is no longer sexual difference. Indeed, there was a strongly held view
that there were *only men*. Women were inferior versions of men, lacking
the arrangement of elements and humours that constitutes the superior,
sexed male (Chapter 6). The transformation of women is the removal of
the imperfections that disqualify them from membership among the more

perfect representatives of humanity. They will become men more fully. The change, sometime in God's future, is 'actually the subsuming of the weaker female into the stronger male, the masculinization of the female body, the supplying of male "presence" (heat, for instance) for the former experience of female "absence" (cold, understood as a lack of fire)' (Martin, 2006, p. 84).

Elsewhere I called the emptying of the human female the prospect of 'feminine obsolescence' (Thatcher, 2016, p. 149). There seems little doubt that by the second century, feminine obsolescence was expected. The *Gospel of Thomas* (usually dated in the early second century CE) suggests this. The last verse of the Gospel, conveying Simon Peter's discomfort at the prominence of Mary Magdalene among the disciples, has him say to Jesus: 'Let Mary leave us, for women are not worthy of life.' This dismissive request receives a dismissive answer from Jesus: 'I myself shall lead her in order to make her male, so that she too may become a living spirit resembling you males. For every woman who will make herself male will enter the kingdom of heaven' (Gnostic Society, n.d., section 114). In the present life women can make themselves male by abandoning their sexual selves, following Jesus, becoming celibate and anticipating the kingdom of heaven (Castelli, 1993). An earlier saying in the *Gospel of Thomas* (section 14) insists on the *unity* of men and women in the resurrected life, no longer male or female. But the new spiritual body remains masculine (McGuire, 2019, p. 381). The idea is, of course, to anticipate the angelic state (which supposedly involves no material bodies, no desire apart from desire for God, and certainly no copulation). The *Gospel of Thomas* would not become a canonical Gospel, but there are many other orthodox expectations of feminine obsolescence, like this one from Jerome (*c.* 345–420):

> as long as woman is for birth and children, she is different from man as body is from soul. But when she wishes to serve Christ more than the world, then she will cease to be a woman and will be called man (*vir*). (Jerome, *Commentary on the Epistle to the Ephesians*, III.5, cited in Armstrong, 1986, p. 129)

The figure of the first man, 'Adam', is contrasted by Paul with Christ: 'for as all die in Adam, so all will be made alive in Christ' (1 Cor. 15.22; and see Rom. 5.12). Adam and Christ are classifications of two types (and so 'typologies'). The first type represents the 'fallen' world, the second the world restored. But both types are headed by male figures. Are women included in the second type? Eve, remember, is said to be responsible for the primal disobedience. The general answer was yes – women are included in the drama of salvation – but how? That further conundrum introduced more uncertainty and ambiguity. And one of the answers was: by becoming men. The question reintroduced itself in different guises. Were women made in the image of God? Was the humanity of Jesus exclusively masculine or inclusively human?

The liberal interpretation of 'no longer male and female' can still be made. The verse does not insist on the incorporation of the female into the male. In the strange thought-experiments that constitute eschatology,[1] males will be 'no longer male'. As the eschatological future for the world is imagined, much about men and masculinities also needs to be changed. The unity envisaged lies beyond the sexual binary. It has been suggested that, for instance, Paul's argument in Galatians should be understood in his invective against those Christians in that community who insisted on circumcising new male converts, as if they, and their converts, remained Jews. Paul's rejection of circumcision is a rejection also of a domineering masculinity that has its locus in the male genitalia (Thatcher, 2020, pp. 133–7). It might still be constructively envisaged that in the new 'type' of humanity, sexual difference remains, but only those troublesome features of it that cause enmity between the sexes fall away and no longer remain. That would be to interpret Paul beyond what history allows, yet it might also be regarded as entirely permissible for Christians to read their scriptures in women-affirming or 'queer' ways. Yes, that is 'revisionist', but why is that a problem? To re-vision is to see afresh, with different eyes, and to promote interpretation that engages with such texts with the sexed and gendered understandings of our own time, and with conscious liberatory intent. In the first centuries CE, however, the gender hierarchy, like the institution of slavery, was insufficiently challenged and the emerging theology served only to reinstate it. The legacy of ancient gender norms still remains and became increasingly misogynistic as the first century drew to its close, the return of Christ a fading hope.

Prominent within the legacy were *the laws governing purity* in the HB (Chapter 2). Leaky, contaminating bodies were to be avoided if personal holiness was to be preserved. Another strand was *the importance of self-control* in all matters to do with the body, including dress, food, public behaviour and so on. Roman society placed a high value on this (at least among free male citizens). Orgasm was the very antithesis of self-control and for many it had to be mainly avoided, even if avoidance required drastic measures (including castration). A third strand was more overtly theological. Eve had brought sin into the world. She was made to associate sexual intercourse directly with the human downfall and cosmic ruin. By avoiding sexual intercourse, so some men thought, one might not only avoid Eve's sin and its transition from one generation to another, but to some extent reverse in the present its perverse effects. A fourth strand was the gendered physiology of the entire period. To be a woman is to be a lesser being. The elements, qualities and humours that comprise the female human body are an inferior arrangement that renders moral and spiritual perfection impossible to achieve.

But these strands in the fabric of continence were matched by alternative strands in the quilt of marriage. The first of these was *divine command*. God had instructed the first human pair to be fruitful and multiply. It was natural and godly to produce children. Another strand was the *regulation and policing of desire*. Was not marriage divine provision for managing sexual urges that would otherwise be uncontrollable? As long as sexual expression was contained within marriage, was it not wrong to restrict it any further? A third strand was the *authorization of biblical households* in the Letters attributed to both Peter and Paul. A fourth strand was the *appeal to divine mystery*. Did not the mystery of the conjugal relation between husband and wife resemble the greater mystery of the conjugal relation between Christ and the church (Chapter 17)?

An astonishing collection of androcentric views about the body and sexuality can be found in the churches of the second century, but common to them all is the suspicion, bordering on fear, of the female body and the dangers of viewing it, listening to it, touching it, desiring it and becoming intimate with it. These fears undoubtedly contributed to the valorization of virginity. The elevation of continent women as honorary men would cause further trouble, and defences of marriage influenced by Gnostic myths were dismissed on other grounds. This was the legacy left for two theological giants – Tertullian and Clement – to sort out as the second century drew to a close.

Notes

1 Eschatology is the study of 'the last things', in Greek *ta eschata*.

10

Regulated Bodies:
Penitent, Plain, Passionless

The plain, unadorned bodies in this chapter are the bodies of Christian women who are required to demonstrate their penitence for the sin of Eve by concealing themselves in penitent – that is, drab and unflattering – clothing ('the garb of penitence') in the churches of North Africa towards the end of the second century. There were also vowed (female) virgins who, because of their vows, were allowed some small ministry within church services. These women ministers are required to be veiled in order to refrain from tempting men (and angels) and causing their ruin. The 'passionless' bodies are the bodies of married men and women who, permitted to have sex in order to have children, were urged to have it only rarely, at particular times (evening is best) and with as little fervour as possible.

Bodies, Penitent and Punished

One of the best-known quotations used by modern writers eager to demonstrate the misogyny of the Christian tradition is Tertullian's accusation that women are 'the devil's gateway'. Developing his instructions to Christian women regarding what to wear in public, he thinks that they and their appearance should reflect the guilt of the first woman. In his *On the Apparel of Women* he insists that the Christian woman is:

> to go about in humble garb, and rather to affect meanness of appearance, walking about as Eve mourning and repentant, in order that by every garb of penitence she might the more fully expiate that which she derives from Eve – the ignominy, I mean, of the first sin, and the odium (attaching to her as the cause) of human perdition. 'In pains and in anxieties dost thou bear (children), woman; and toward thine husband (is) thy inclination, and he lords It over thee.' And do you not know that you are (each) an Eve? The sentence of God on this sex of yours lives in this age: the guilt must of necessity live too. You are the devil's gateway:

you are the unsealer of that (forbidden) tree: you are the first deserter of the divine law: you are she who persuaded him whom the devil was not valiant enough to attack. You destroyed so easily God's image, man. On account of your desert – that is, death – even the Son of God had to die. (Tertullian, *On the Apparel of Women*, Book 1, chapter 1)

There are spirited attempts to limit or deny the clear misogyny in this passage and many others like it. It is fairly said that Tertullian's polemical style of rhetoric takes him to extremes; that what women wore in public in Carthage was controversial, both for its citizens and for church members; and that, by contrast with some other theologians, his views about women were more positive generally. While Tertullian's view of women is less extreme than, say, Jerome's, the developing tradition in which he stands is so deeply androcentric it cannot entertain the possibility that *it is already doing great harm to women*, like many churches today. For this reason we will remain with Tertullian for several pages, for he provides a good example of 'abusive theology' and how it works itself out, and illustrates the strong link explored in Chapter 1 between the church as a patriarchal institution, misogyny as its practice and sexist theology as its justification. It is 'epistemic violence' par excellence, and has had enormous influence. Tertullian demeans women spectacularly, and we should be wary – when weighing the influence of context upon his writings – that patriarchal theology is often unaware of the harm it causes and turns a blind eye towards it when it is pointed out.

Many of the elements of his doctrine of the human person (theologians insist on calling this 'theological anthropology') are present in this passage, which acts like a microcosm of the broader violence-inducing system. It reproduces more harshly the exhortations to women in 1 Peter and 1 Timothy to dress modestly. Modesty is now insufficient. The 'garb of penitence' is now required, a mode of dress that extends the permanent mental and spiritual association between womankind and cosmic ruin (the 'Fall') into the physical manifestation of guilt that the mere self-presentation of a woman in public view is expected to reinforce. The term 'garb of penitence' may help to explain how protesting women in Afghanistan and Iran view the burqa and the hijab. The precarious and painful process of birth is not merely a regrettable fact of nature but must be internalized as a just punishment on all pregnant women just for being women, and belonging to the same sex as Eve. There is more than a hint that the 'gateway' metaphor associates a woman's vagina with the place the devil enters; that the devil had sex with Eve; that a woman's private parts are the downfall of men. Responsibility for the state of the human race (again following 1 Timothy) is *gendered*. Only womankind is gullible enough to let the devil push her into sin. She is *not* made in God's image. Womankind is even responsible for deicide. If she had not sinned, the Son of God would not have been crucified.

Tertullian, following Paul, allows marriage (and was himself married). Christians like Tatian or Marcion who do not allow marriage are 'heretics' and 'alien eunuchs' (Tertullian, *On Monogamy*, chapter 1, in Roberts, et al., 1885). But marriage is second best. Catholic Christianity eventually followed him in valorizing celibacy over marriage while allowing both. I read Tertullian more as one whose legacy heaps on women psychological abuse through what he believes a woman *is*, and how he thinks women should *appear*. In *On the Apparel of Women* just cited, he is concerned about how women appear in public space. In *On the Veiling of Virgins*, he is concerned about how women appear in church. The former combines a scathing critique of consumerism at the end of the second century CE in Carthage and the cupidity and pride that accompanies it, with a scathing critique of women's bodies and his suspicion of all sexual desire.

Made-up Bodies

Perhaps we don't expect, on reading the early 'Fathers' of the church, angry references to the wearing of lipstick, eye liner and eye shadow, wigs, colourful and revealing clothing, jewellery and so on. Tertullian positively revelled in the condemnation of these. Eve, he reasons, even when ejected from Paradise, could not have wanted to wear the cosmetics and the clothing manufactured and made available by pagans, because when she sinned none of those things had then been invented. The clear implication is that nattily dressed Christian women are even worse than the mother of all sin:

> Come, now; if from the beginning of the world the Milesians sheared sheep, and the Serians spun trees, and the Tyrians dyed, and the Phrygians embroidered with the needle, and the Babylonians with the loom, and pearls gleamed, and onyx-stones flashed; if gold itself also had already issued, with the cupidity (which accompanies it), from the ground; if the mirror, too, already had licence to lie so largely, Eve, expelled from paradise, (Eve) already dead, would also have coveted these things, I imagine! (Tertullian, *On the Apparel of Women*, Book 1, chapter 1)

No more, he sternly continues, should Christians want or need to wear them now. The randy angels (Chapter 4) 'who rushed from heaven on the daughters of men' (Tertullian, *On the Apparel of Women*, Book 1, chapter 2) and raped them were not further enticed by their wearing alluring dresses and make-up. No, they were fanciable as they were. Wearing expensive clothes and jewellery now only places women in greater danger of victimhood than the unfortunate women of Genesis 6. The fallen angels were also responsible for teaching humanity other dubious practices, he conjectures, like the smelting of metals and even the making of medicines. They 'laid bare the operations of metallurgy, and had divulged the natural properties of herbs, and had promulgated the powers of enchantments ...', only to confer

> properly and as it were peculiarly upon women that instrumental mean of womanly ostentation, the radiances of jewels wherewith necklaces are variegated, and the circlets of gold wherewith the arms are compressed, and the medicaments of orchil with which wools are coloured, and that black powder itself wherewith the eyelids and eyelashes are made prominent. (Tertullian, *On the Apparel of Women*, Book 1, chapter 5)

Tertullian's reference to the fallen angels is based on the books of Enoch, which were well known as 'scripture' for many Christians, and which he defended as holy and authoritative (Tertullian, *On the Apparel of Women*, Book 1, chapter 3). Like modern evangelicals he even appealed to 2 Timothy 3.16 ('All Scripture is God-breathed', NIV) in support of them, indicating its worthlessness as a proof text (since *what* scriptures are 'God-breathed' is precisely the point at issue, and the books of Enoch never made it into the canon). Tertullian did not separate his attack on the embellishments of conspicuous consumerism from his attack on the women who, in his opinion, were tricked into the desire to purchase them.

Modern readers might praise Tertullian for his critique of excessive wealth, and its many connexions with the flaunting of sexuality, without following him into misogyny. But the positive critique of consumerism and of the wealth that drives it is woven into his negative critique of women and women's appearance. Both the angels in the past and women's husbands now, he continues, found them attractive without further adornment. By renouncing these things women will eventually achieve salvation and so become as angels themselves. Since angels are male, resurrected women will gladly abandon all trace of troublesome womanhood when they are finally saved. Iron and brass are useful materials whereas gold and silver are not, especially when they adorn the bodies of women, like the pearls 'that ambition fishes up from the British or the Indian sea' (Tertullian, *On the Apparel of Women*, Book 1, chapter 6). The dyeing of clothes is contrary to nature. If God had wanted us to wear coloured clothing, God would have made sheep with purple fleeces (Tertullian, *On the Apparel of Women*, Book 1, chapter 8). We met flying bodies in Chapter 4. Here they are again, but what will they be wearing? When female Christians rise to meet the Lord in the air, would they wish to meet him (and the angels) wearing 'ceruse and rouge and saffron, and in all that parade of headgear'? (Tertullian, *On the Apparel of Women*, Book 1, chapter 7). Hair colouration is medically harmful. Disguising a greying head is tantamount to shame for being old. The wearing of wigs is excoriated. God has provided cosmetics to test the continence of women. Christian women don't need to dress up anyway because they don't normally go out. If they do, they should put on their 'armour' of modesty, sobriety and holiness (Tertullian, *On the Apparel of Women*, Book 1, chapter 11). Demeanour and gait must accord with sobriety in case a woman gets noticed by a man (Tertullian, *On the Apparel of Women*, Book 2, chapter 1).

Women's clothing is to be policed by the male gaze. The men guard an important boundary between church and empire, a chosen site of Christian witness – women's bodies and the clothes that cover them. But Tertullian's advocacy of modesty is freighted with the guilt and remorse he is determined to load on to the bodies of all women. It is sinful for a woman to appear in a manner that would let a man think she was desirable, for marriage and fornication each proceed from the same illicit source. Within the midst of his diatribe Tertullian uses an argument that could be positively used by a contemporary Christian account of sexual morality. It consists in obeying the commandment to love one's neighbour as one's self, leading to the inevitable question, at least as old as the parable of the good Samaritan, who one's neighbour is (Luke 10.29). But Tertullian's theological chauvinism redirects the question. Who is the neighbour of a well-dressed woman? It is any man who might entertain desiring thoughts about her, and she would be responsible for his ruin. No woman can love her male neighbour if she dresses attractively. As Tertullian explains, as soon as a man 'has felt concupiscence after your beauty', he has already committed adultery with her in his heart. The man 'perishes; and you have been made the sword which destroys him' (Tertullian, *On the Apparel of Women*, Book 2, chapter 2). Women can be beautiful in form only. Any actual beauty is 'superfluous, you may justly disdain if you have it not, and neglect it if you have. Let a holy woman, if naturally beautiful, give none so great occasion (for carnal appetite)' (Tertullian, *On the Apparel of Women*, Book 2, chapter 3).

It probably never occurred to Tertullian how it is possible for a woman to love herself (equally required by the Great Commandment (Mark 12.28–34; Matt. 22.35–40; Luke 10.25–27) to love one's neighbour as one loves oneself), dressed in the garb of 'shameful penitence'. A similar impossibility occurs when the teaching of the present-day church requires self-loathing from its non-heterosexual and transgender members. His appeal to neighbour love would constitute a sound sexual and gendered ethic for the contemporary church, grounded in a theological account of what love entails. It would emphasize the utmost respect and mutuality required between lovers, and regard for possible children resulting from intimacy. Such an ethic, based on positive regard for the flesh (like John's Gospel), rather than an ethic that sets body and spirit against each other (like Paul's), might see bodies as naturally desiring and desirable, a feature to be expected if bodies are made in the image of a desiring God. Some of the Gnostic Christians understood this. But such an ethic can hardly be found in the early centuries of Christianity. In *On the Veiling of Virgins*, Tertullian addresses a practice that had come to his attention in a neighbouring church. Some women who were ministering in the church were believed to be so holy that they were allowed to remain unveiled during worship. They had transcended their sexuality by renouncing it and had become 'a third gender class, a class that had transcended the first two: man and woman' (DeConick, 2011, p. 111). He responded with a torrent of epistemic and spiritual abuse.

Unveiled bodies

On the Veiling of Virgins only makes sense if there really were women ministers exercising some form of ministry at the time, in North Africa. Tertullian's argument against them being unveiled was based on Paul's instruction that women in church should be veiled (1 Cor. 11.2–16). Their claim to have transcended their femininity and womanhood so that they were no longer women, and so no longer bound by Paul's instruction, gets very short shrift. Virgins are still women! But this argument was driven as much by gynophobia as by theology. Tertullian was aroused by his ire, if not by his lust. Only God needs to know who the virgins are, he thunders. Even wishing to be seen unveiled is a form of lust because there is no innocent motive: the forbidden approval of the male gaze is sought (Tertullian, 1885, chapter 2).

Before leaving Tertullian, a particularly abusive comment of his cannot be overlooked. A troublesome analogy is made between the removal of a virgin's veil before ministering in church and the removal of her clothing as a rapist might when he violently undresses and penetrates his victim.

The spiritual fate of the bare-headed virgin in church is worse than the fate of a woman who has endured a real rape!

> Every public exposure of an honourable virgin is (to her) a suffering of rape: and yet the suffering of carnal violence is the less (evil), because it comes of natural office. But when the very spirit itself is violated in a virgin by the abstraction of her covering, she has learned to lose what she used to keep. O sacrilegious hands, which have had the hardihood to drag off a dress dedicated to God! (Tertullian, 1885, chapter 3)

If angels as far away as heaven can be tempted by the sight of unveiled women, how much more are unveiled Christian women imperilled, he asks. Women don't understand how difficult it is for men to contain their desire, because *women don't have any* (Tertullian, 1885, chapter 10). The fear of any pleasure in seeing a beautiful body, or being seen as one, outweighs every other consideration. In disturbing phallic language, an unveiled woman:

> must necessarily be imperilled by the public exhibition of herself, while she is penetrated by the gaze of untrustworthy and multitudinous eyes, while she is tickled by pointing fingers, while she is too well loved, while she feels a warmth creep over her amid assiduous embraces and kisses. Thus the forehead hardens; thus the sense of shame wears away; thus it relaxes; thus is learned the desire of pleasing in another way! (Tertullian, 1885, chapter 14)

Bodies without Passion

Meanwhile, around 180 CE, 1670 miles along the North African coast to the east, Clement settled in Alexandria, where the church was beset by similar gendered problems. One of his works, the *Paidagogos* or Instructor, contained detailed instructions about how Christians should conduct themselves everywhere – in church, in the marketplace, at the dinner table and particularly in bed. Part of the *Paidagogos* (Book 2 chapter 10) remains untranslated from its original Latin in the two most used online versions of his works[1] – a sure sign that Victorian and Edwardian sensibilities were offended by its directness. Happily English translations of the chapter exist (Clement, in Wood, 1954), and the chapter takes us to the heart of Clement's instructions about the body, sexuality and gender.

Unnatural bodies – of hares and hyenas

Clement gently refutes the marriage resisters on the basis that God has given humanity the charge to procreate, to 'Be fruitful and multiply' (Gen. 1.28):

> Begetting children is the goal of those who wed, and the fulfilment of that goal is a large family, just as hope of a crop drives the farmer to sow his seed, while the fulfilment of his hope is the actual harvesting of the crop. (Wood, 1954, p. 164)

But like the farmer sowing his seed, seed must neither be wasted by being sown 'on rocky ground nor scattered everywhere'. Clement seizes on Moses' instruction to the Israelites to abstain from eating meat from certain animals (Deut. 14.3–8). Among them are hares and hyenas.

Hyenas' genitalia are unusual. All female hyenas have what a contemporary anatomist has called 'intersex plumbing' (Long, Steller and Suh, 2020; and see Gould, 1981). They have a penis containing erectile tissue, and they use their penis to pee. Clement draws on certain, then current, beliefs about the anatomy of each animal and their accompanying behaviour. These beliefs seem to be drawn from three sources: Aristotle, Pliny and an anonymous second-century work, the *Physiologus* ('The Naturalist') (Wilson, 2003). As Clements understands them, hyenas had an extra sexual organ so they could copulate without becoming pregnant. That's why they were always doing it. Males and females were both believed to have an organ that seems to be half clitoris, half vagina:

> Because the hyena is of all animals the most sensual, there is a knob of flesh underneath its tail, in front of the anus, closely resembling the female sex organ in shape. It is not a passage, I mean it serves no useful purpose, opening neither into the womb nor into the intestines. It has only a good-sized opening to permit an ineffective sexual act when the vagina is preparing for childbirth and is impenetrable. (Wood, 1954, p. 166)

But females are preparing for childbirth only rarely. That is because males prefer either to penetrate other males using their own third sexual organ, which 'is large enough for the service of the lusting organs, but its opening is obstructed within', or to use the quasi-vagina of the female.

The 'clear conclusion' that Clement's astonished and embarrassed readers must draw from his description of sowing seed 'contrary to nature' is:

we must condemn sodomy, all fruitless sowing of seed, any unnatural methods of holding intercourse and the reversal of the sexual role in intercourse. We must rather follow the guidance of nature; which obviously disapproves of such practises from the very way she has fashioned the male organ, adapted not for receiving the seed, but for implanting it. (Wood, 1954, p. 167)

Clement thinks that hares too are incurably lustful, leading Moses to forbid eating them. He draws on a legend that a hare develops an extra anus for every year it lives. These too are used contrary to nature. Hares are also fond of rear-entry sex, says Clement. They prefer what today is coarsely referred to as 'doggy-style' (or in this case 'hare-style'?) sex. But he also thinks that female hares have two wombs (which is why they have so many offspring). While one womb is occupied, the other is available. He concludes: 'So the mysterious prohibition [of Moses] in reality is but counsel to restrain violent sexual impulses, and intercourse in too frequent succession, relations with a pregnant woman, pederasty, adultery, and lewdness' (Wood, 1954, p. 168).

Clement also relies on sophisticated philosophical and scriptural arguments to support his behavioural conclusions, but his use of these misunderstood animals serves well to illustrate that all sexual activity whatever outside of procreative intercourse within marriage (in the missionary position) is thought to be contrary to nature and to the will of God. His observations are those of a liberal theologian of his time, undriven by misogyny. But his observations prompt further observations from a different generation of readers. Here are three. First, Clement does not stop to think that the animals he considers are just as much a part of nature as other parts (including people). There is diversity in nature. He might have considered that there is already a precedent in nature for the *human* behaviour he so dislikes.

Second, it provides a strong reminder that many considerations shaping the evolving Christian understanding of sexuality and the body are now forgotten, and indeed baseless. Clement to his credit took philosophy and science seriously and did not create a fissure between scientific and theological thought. Third, he relies on the HB distinction between clean and unclean animals, believing God had declared hyenas and hares unclean because of their unusual genitalia. But we have seen how the NT has little use for such distinctions: they have no place in moral or theological discourse. He utilizes his readers' sense of *disgust* at the conduct of others, a tactic that would be endlessly rehearsed and refined in Catholic Christendom. We also know, as Clement probably did not, that the erect penis of a female hyena is a sign of *submission* to a male (Long, Steller and Suh,

2020). If we are to generalize from what we observe in nature, where would this particular generalization take us?

A man must above all control his passions. Christian believers are 'sages', wise people possessing true 'knowledge', and they are able to summon reason in their internal war against unruly desires. Passions 'are best seen as tendencies built up within the *ego*, which could force the sage to overreact to any situation, to cathect [create emotional energy] it with a charge of personal, egotistic significance that distorted its true meaning' (Brown, 1990, p. 129). Clement knew and agreed with the Stoic ideal of personal freedom from all the passions, believing that Christian witness, assisted by reason and all the other sources available to believers (e.g. scripture, the Holy Spirit) should strive to exceed the Stoics in their determination to pursue *apatheia* – a state of complete passionlessness (Brown, 1990, p. 130).

Clement describes the sexual urge: 'We can see at a glance that the nerves are strained by it as on a loom and, in the intense feeling aroused by intercourse, are stretched to the breaking point. It spreads a mist over the senses and tires the muscles.' We Christians, he insists, have permission to marry if we desire to 'be fruitful', but, he asks, 'how can we possibly permit ourselves to indulge in intercourse each time without restraint, as we would food, as if it were a necessity?' (Wood, 1954, p. 172). Just as 'we must keep a firm control over the pleasures of the stomach', so we must achieve 'an absolutely uncompromising control over the organs beneath the stomach. If, as the Stoics teach, we should not move even a finger on mere impulse how much more necessary is it that they who seek wisdom control the organ of intercourse?' (Wood, 1954, p. 169).

Not only is it wrong to *waste* sperm, it is wrong to '*contaminate*' it. That is why Moses forbade having sex during menstruation. The firm control must extend to the times that sex is permitted. Christians must:

> learn not to celebrate the mystic rites of nature during the day, nor like the rooster copulate at dawn, or after they have come from church, or even from the market, when they should be praying or reading or performing the good works that are best done by day.

After dinner is best, but if it can be delayed it will be more desirable next time. We men must show our wives our self-control 'in the way we avoid every indecency in intimate embraces' (Wood, 1954, p. 174). The 'cover of darkness' must be no excuse for immodesty. Occasional, fully controlled, modest sexual intercourse allows the married Christian to be counted as chaste, 'to practise constant chastity', and to be 'living a life like that of the angels' (Wood, 1954, p. 177).

Dietary bodies

Once celibacy and virginity became established among Christians, they used medical knowledge in their efforts to free themselves from lust. Fasting became not merely a means of controlling the desire for food but for controlling all desire whatsoever. It would lead to extreme practices. Since angels did not eat, the emaciated and haggard bodies of the self-starved were revered and endowed with an honorary angelic hue. Since angels (at least the 'unfallen' ones) did not copulate, the renunciation of sexual activity anticipated the angelic state. And if, by fasting, women and men rendered themselves incapable of producing the fluids necessary for the creation of children – semen, menses, milk – then the new creation had arrived already.

But all foods were thought to contribute, in different ways, to the inflammation or reduction of sexual desire, to better or worse well-being, and to the production of male and female semen (see Grimm, 1996). It was widely held in the ancient world (including in the HB) that women produced semen (Thatcher, 2016). As Christians strove to reduce or eliminate desire, or to avoid pregnancy, what they ate, and in what amounts, became central to their thought and practice. Abstinence from certain foods became a requirement for the attempt to achieve personal holiness.

Heat was the most determining of all the elements. It was responsible for the positioning of the male genitalia outside the male body. But certain foods were thought to heat, and other foods thought to cool, the body. For Galen, 'the four principal humors are products of the process of digestion', and all 'foods can be classified as heating, cooling, drying, moistening, or a combination of these' (Shaw, 1998, p. 54). The historian Teresa Shaw gives some examples:

> [T]he parsnip is classified as heating, thinning, and drying; wheat is heating, while barley is cooling; and wine is heating and moistening. Further, certain foods tend toward the production of certain humors. Thus 'warmer' foods tend to produce bile, while 'cooler' foods produce phlegm. (Shaw, 1998, p. 56)

There are foods that are 'very nourishing and at the same time flatulent'. These are the ones that generate semen (in both sexes), and they include chickpeas, beans, octopus and pinecones. Anyone wanting to reduce their semen generation should eat alternatives such as 'lettuce, the vegetable blite, orach, gourd, black mulberry, melon, cucumber, and rue' (Shaw, 1998, p. 58).

In early Christianity, then, fasting and abstinence from certain foods provide a way to holiness. In this sense, Christians were materialists. What would Tertullian make of a typical Valentine's Day dinner for two in a wealthy capitalist country – oysters or scallops to start, perhaps; next a rare sirloin steak washed down with red wine, and profiteroles to finish? Lovers are still prepared to believe that certain foods have aphrodisiac qualities, in appearance, taste, shape and suggestiveness. Oysters were linked to semen-producing foods. Steak, increasing the amount of blood in the body, was thought to increase lust, like the accompanying wine. The shape of profiteroles? With cream? Imagination has always played its part in relation to the body's reaction to food, but the connection between diet and overall health is better understood today. Concern for what we eat now is increasingly informed by environmental considerations and compassion for animals. Abstinence from certain foods today has become a 'spiritual imperative'. Holiness is re-positioned, found in compassion for creation, but not lost. Perhaps it is the same with sexual desire. Desire is not to be shunned but directed by compassion.

Notes

1 New Advent (www.newadvent.org/fathers/02092.htm, accessed 21.6.23) and Early Christian Writings (www.earlychristianwritings.com/text/clement-instruc tor-book2.html, accessed 21.6.23).

II

Mystical Bodies:
The Flight From Sensuality

The rise and rise of belief in the holy power of the virginal body is considered in this chapter. But virginity is precarious, fragile and shown to be sustained (among the young) by fear. The mystical bodies of this chapter belong to Christian women and men who find meaning in their faith by redirecting all their sensuality and love away from the bodily sites that make sensuality possible and enjoyable, and then relocating them in mystical relations, either in the union of the individual soul with God or by becoming part of the body of Christ's bride the church, as it is embraced by Christ the divine bridegroom. The body is now 'de-eroticized', unable even to entertain the thought of desire for the body of another. Central to this general 'mystification' of the body is the particular body of a black woman, one of the lovers within the biblical book, the Song of Songs. Her body is found to associate blackness with sin generally and sexual sin specifically. Sexism and racism combine in the de-eroticized Song, providing strong encouragement for both during the next millennium and beyond. This 'proto-racist' interpretation is a Christian project, one that should be distinguished from the pre-Christian, and more ancient reading of the female lover's blackness.

Clement of Alexandria died *c.* 215 CE, Tertullian five years later. We know remarkably little about the ordinary lives of Christians in this period: 'The day-to-day life of Christians is a darkened landscape, intermittently lit up for us by the flashes of polemical fireworks that crackled far overhead' (Brown, 1990, p. 142). It was mainly married Christians whose wealth kept churches functioning. It was they who traded with the surrounding Roman world and were influenced by it. Marriage could not be shunned altogether, but it provided children and money. A strict division grew between clergy and laity, and continence was expected of the former. Holiness became associated with *askesis* (ascetic denial), rather than with love. The valorization of virginity, described in earlier chapters, increased further. But the polemical fireworks continued to crackle, casting permanent shadows over women's bodies in their eerie flickering light.

Fearful Bodies – Jerome on women

Methodius (250–311 CE) made the case for virginity in his *Banquet of the Ten Virgins*. 'Virginity is something supernaturally great, wonderful, and glorious,' he begins. It is a 'plant from heaven' that took some time to germinate and flower (Methodius, n.d., chapter 1). With an eye on the sexual cavortings in the HB, he explains how God allowed these, permitting incest and polygamy. Out of polygamy came monogamous marriage, then continent marriage, and now, at the very apex of human development, we have virginity, the flowering plant from heaven, embodied in the incarnate Christ, the 'chief Virgin', who received his uncorrupted flesh from his virgin mother.

The 'fearful bodies' of this section belong to the ascetic Christians, women and men, for whom fear of the devil and of hell is a principal motivation in their struggles to retain their faith. Jerome's Letter is written to encourage Eustochium, a young, wealthy Roman daughter, to continue in her vowed path of virginity. By this time, 'the virginal ideal was spreading like wildfire' (Cooper, 2013, p. 529), yet Jerome could hardly bring himself 'to speak of the many virgins who daily fall and are lost to the bosom of the church' (Jerome, *Letter*, section 13). But he overcomes his reluctance and concludes these lost virgins are insufficiently rigorous in their spiritual practice, even as they are harassed by the devil, or by demons. The Letter is saturated with biblical quotations, as might be expected from the theologian who gave the church its Latin Bible and knew Greek and Hebrew. It is also an attack on affluence. It provides evidence of the great wealth of privileged Roman citizens, many of whom were Christians, and Jerome criticizes them severely, particularly if they were women, enjoying fine food, wine, clothing, the attention of servants and the reputation for supporting the church financially. He exposes the entanglement of the body with affluence (as Tertullian had done), and Roman decadence with sexual excess. On the other hand, he makes the state of virginity the touchstone of difference between true holiness and worldly compromise. He was one of several theologians imposing male authority,

> firming up ... the institutional contours of the virgin's lifestyle as well as a negotiation of her own new social identity in terms of officially defined choices which are 'naturalized', or perhaps we should say 'supernaturalized', by being grounded in the theology of the angelic life and espousal to Christ. (Shaw, 1998, p. 487)

Virgins, he warns, are right to flee from marriage as Lot fled from Sodom, and like Lot's wife they are forbidden to look back. He knows they are subject to constant attack by demons, but believes they are insufficiently prepared to repel them. They are right to fear them; indeed, fear is to be the primary emotion of the alert, wise or 'good' virgin – fear of principalities and powers, fear of the hosts of spiritual foes and enemies on every side; fear even of married and compromised Christians; fear of the flesh and its weaknesses; fear of the corrupted imagination. Virginity can be lost, even by a single impure thought (Jerome, *Letter*, section 3)! But fear is an unpromising basis for advice of any kind, still less for a spiritual quest: 'The weak flesh will soon be ashes: one against many, it fights against tremendous odds' (Jerome, *Letter*, section 3). A virgin is married to Christ. The idea of marriage to Christ started off as a metaphorical state, based on the idea of the church as the bride of Christ, and so every member of it sharing in the church's bridal status. In Origen this becomes an allegorical state. For Jerome, it is an *ontological* state, defining the virgin's very being. If a vowed virgin should, like Lot's wife, look back and become married,

> though God can do all things He cannot raise up a virgin when once she has fallen ... Better had it been for her to have submitted to the yoke of marriage, to have walked in level places, than thus, aspiring to loftier heights, to fall into the deep of hell. (*Letter*, section 5)

Jerome uses his former experience as a hermit to try to convince Eustochium that he understands the pervasive character of lust, and in so doing he lays bare the tortured character of his own soul. He too lived in fear. He tells her he once tried everything he knew to get women out of his mind, and failed:

> Although in my fear of hell I had consigned myself to this prison [the desert], where I had no companions but scorpions and wild beasts, I often found myself amid bevies of girls. My face was pale and my frame chilled with fasting; yet my mind was burning with desire, and the fires of lust kept bubbling up before me when my flesh was as good as dead. Helpless, I cast myself at the feet of Jesus, I watered them with my tears, I wiped them with my hair: and then I subdued my rebellious body with weeks of abstinence. (*Letter*, section 7)

So this is what God apparently wills for some Christians. After Freud we explain such frustrated longings differently. But, Jerome concedes, lust must be an even greater problem for the randier sex: 'If such are the temptations of men who, since their bodies are emaciated with fasting, have only evil thoughts to fear, how must it fare with a girl whose surroundings are those of luxury and ease?' (*Letter*, section 8). They must live in a state of constant emergency. Wine, meat and spicy foods intensify the body's heat, and so its passion. The devil uses these in his attacks on the soul. Virgins should avoid the company of married women (who presumably might be overheard talking about how their husbands are such good lovers). Indeed, they should not go outside at all: 'Let your companions be women pale and thin with fasting, and approved by their years and conduct.' Rejoice instead, urges Jerome, in self-inflicted pain and misery: 'Be like the grasshopper and make night musical. Nightly wash your bed and water your couch with your tears' (*Letter*, section 18).

De-eroticized Bodies – Origen on sex

The 'de-eroticized bodies' of this section are the bodies of men and women, the meaning of whose flesh and bodily loves has been stripped away and discounted to make room for a higher, spiritual 'dis-carnated' (or 'ex-carnated' (see Taylor, 2007, pp. 613–15)) love – a love with all carnality wrung out of it. Human sexual love is exchanged for mystical, spiritual love.

The HB has a book of love poems, traditionally attributed to king Solomon, better known as the Song of Songs. These songs are unquestionably erotic. It is difficult to find anywhere in the long tradition of Christian thought a positive account of eros without the overtones of danger and temptation. The Song of Songs in the HB is a rare exception. It is a remarkable collection of erotic love poetry (where the majority of the poems are attributed by the author, or authors, to a woman). Christians have never known what to do with it. There are no references to it in the NT. Its place in sacred scripture was a puzzle, resolved by making it an implausible allegory illustrating the relationship between Christ and the church, or between the individual soul, characterized as feminine, and the male God. There is an almost universal assumption that the partners are married, or marrying, and so bride and groom, but the text does not support that assumption, which is more the product of disbelief that a biblical text could honestly celebrate human eros and do so without the authorization of matrimony. When the KJV became available (in 1611), the header text of the Song (called here 'The Song of Solomon') struggled to divert the minds of the innocent faithful away from the frank descriptions of the joys of human love towards less inflammatory subjects such as 'The church's love unto Christ', 'The mutual love of Christ and his church' or 'The church professeth her faith in Christ'.

This avoidance of the erotic has never extended to avoiding the enjoyment of condemning it. The opening lines establish a tone of burning and urgent desire:

Let him kiss me with the kisses of his mouth!
For your love is better than wine. (S. of Sol. 1.2)

The place of the book in the Hebrew and Christian Bibles is continually debated. Today it attracts positive feminist affirmation and negative feminist criticism (sometimes in the same book – Brenner and Fontaine, 2000). Leaving such arguments aside, the emphasis here is on what the third-century theologian Origen did with the book.

Origen wrote a famous commentary on the Song that has been hugely influential ever since. He completely de-eroticizes the book, wringing out all the juices of delectability from the text; reigning in the imagination should the reader wish to linger over its pages, until it focuses on the relation between the soul and God (who, it turns out, is not mentioned anywhere among the poems), confining and redirecting every last physical delight to the spiritual, incorporeal world of the soul and its ethereal meanderings. Origen's re-allocation of sensual delight to the soul has inspired countless Christian mystics, male and female. But we will look at some length at Origen's work, in order to understand its *altogether baleful influence* on Christian understandings of sexuality and the body. For whatever mystical flights of the soul may have been inspired by the Song, there were also strong material consequences: the realm of the erotic, the enjoyment of it, the recognition of bodily pleasure; these are to be permanently turned off by all Christians seeking perfection. Thus, from the third century onwards, a veil was placed over the delights of erotic love in which this biblical work manifestly indulges. Worse than the veil, which merely conceals what is underneath it, much Christian theology, following Origen, *misrepresents* and disparages the body, negating it in order to find elusive delight elsewhere.

Origen was the master of allegory. Every physical detail in the Song must be understood by its imagined spiritual counterpart. The physical details of the poems are many, for the lovers' love is beautifully integrated into the natural world which models it. The lovers adore each other's bodies – their eyes, ears, hair, teeth, cheeks, lips, necks, breasts, feet, thighs, bellies, navels. These are sensuously compared with the rest of nature – flowers, fruit, fruit trees, honey, spices, wild animals, perfumes, ointments, jewellery. 'I advise and counsel everyone', Origen writes, 'who is not yet rid of the vexations of flesh and blood and has not ceased to feel the passion of his bodily nature, to refrain completely from reading this little book and the things that will be said about it' (Origen, 1957, p. 22). 'If any man who lives only after the flesh should approach it [the Song]', he warns,

> to such a one the reading of this Scripture will be the occasion of no small hazard and danger. For he, not knowing how to hear love's language in purity and with chaste ears, will twist the whole manner of his hearing of it away from the inner spiritual man and on to the outward and carnal; and he will be turned away from the spirit to the flesh, and will foster carnal desires in himself, and it will seem to be the Divine Scriptures that are thus urging and egging him on to fleshly lust! (Origen, 1957, p. 22)

One wonders who is twisting meanings here. How *can* the language work mystically if its carnal settings and experiences must first be denied? Origen insists on his 'spiritual interpretation' of the Song. He brings to the text the assumption that the lovers are related to each other as bridegroom and bride, and so he allows himself to invoke the familiar biblical imagery of Christ being related to the church. Bridal love becomes a 'type', an allegory or partial representation, of the greater love of Christ for his bride, the church. Bride and bridegroom, he explains, 'denote either the Church in her relation to Christ, or the soul in her union with the Word of God' (Origen, 1957, p. 58). The church and the soul are thus rendered feminine, and each must render to her Lord or husband the deference due to each. The soul is not united to its own body, but to Christ in a one-to-one relationship that avoids the body altogether.

An insightful example of how allegory destroys the warmth of human love and connection occurs in Origen's treatment of Song 2.6. The Song in its original Hebrew is notoriously difficult to translate, and Jerome translated it into his language of Latin. Translating Origen's Latin back into English is a further headache. Nonetheless, there appear to be few difficulties with this particular text: 'His left hand is under my head, and his right hand shall embrace me is the English translation' (Origen, 1957, p. 204). The verse invites the reader into a scene where the woman enjoys her lover exploring her body. Not for Origen. Hands and head are immediately spiritualized. 'Turn with all speed', he admonishes,

> to the life-giving Spirit and, eschewing physical terms, consider carefully what is the left hand of the Word of God, what the right; also what his Bride's head – the head, that is to say, of the perfect soul or of the Church; and do not suffer an interpretation that has to do with the flesh and the passions to carry you away. (Origen, 1957, p. 204)

This loving physical embrace is given a complex spiritual anatomy. It is Christ caressing the church. His right hand represents the revelation of God prior to God's incarnation in Christ. His left hand represents the incarnate Christ embracing the church, supporting her drooping head. Alternatively, suggests Origen, it is the soul of the believer, male or female, in mystical union with her lover Christ himself.

Thus is every last sensual detail, every longing, every intoxicating odour, every poetic link with the beauty and diversity of the created world, emptied of its material significance, its meaning transferred to a different, invisible world, one especially accessible to a castrated male theologian, whose body becomes an impediment to his faith even as it is plundered to express faith's substance. 'All these things were, then, as spices and perfumes, cosmetics as it were of the soul' (Origen, 1957, p. 73), he writes. Countless Christians ever since Origen, embarrassed by the pleasure they know their bodies can give them, have looked past erotic delight towards a different, ethereal delight beyond their undoubted struggles with their desires. The delights of nature and the human body are *affirmed* in Origen, but only to bring about their greater denigration both in this life and the next. They give the soul a language, no more, for the expression of a greater spiritual love. The love we have for one another, and for particular others, is dangerous, even forbidden. Demons lurk within it to tear us away from the only bosom where there is true solace: the bosom of Christ, or the bosom of the church that he caresses. We must somehow overcome the flesh and channel all our erotic thoughts and desires into being brides of Christ and being embraced by him.

Black, Stigmatized Bodies – racism emerges

The black bodies of this section belong to all black-skinned persons as they begin to be perceived by white-skinned male Christian theologians. Sexuate human bodies are somehow to be renounced for the believer to achieve union not with other human bodies but with God. But if the sexuate human body happens to be black, then another set of renunciations also applies. We are now entering even more distressing territory, finding here some of the seeds of what was to become theologically grounded racism (Chapters 12, 15, 16). One of the lovers (the woman) is black, and emerging from Origen's spiritualization of this body further damaging assumptions about the association between femaleness and blackness take shape.

The woman in the text clearly rejoices in her blackness:

I am black and beautiful,
   O daughters of Jerusalem,
like the tents of Kedar,
   like the curtains of Solomon.
Do not gaze at me because I am dark,
   because the sun has gazed on me. (S. of Sol. 1.5–6)

It is possible 'black and beautiful' be translated 'black *but* beautiful', though a positive reading ('and') is more likely. Origen reminds his readers that Moses was praised for marrying a black (Ethiopian) woman, and that God inflicted his sister Miriam with leprosy for criticizing the match (the male Aaron, also criticizes the match, but he escapes punishment – Num. 12.1–16). She is a Gentile, a Cushite. There is, in her, 'an abundance of natural beauty' (Origen, 1957, p. 128), which directly derives from having been made in God's image (Gen. 1.27). Here lies a thought that might have lightened the burden attaching to femaleness and blackness in later Christian understanding, but once 'black' and 'beautiful' become allegories for characteristics of the spiritual world, the light is obscured. And light (or rather the absence of it) is precisely the problem. Her darkness is associated with her being a Gentile, welcome in the church like all Gentiles, but a Gentile nonetheless. How did this black woman become black? The natural interpretation is given by the woman herself ('the sun has gazed on me'), and Origen doesn't disagree with it. But the allegorical interpretation renders her dark 'by reason of her former sins' (Origen, 1957, p. 113). Her soul is stained with blackness, and her beauty, once found in her young desiring and desired body, is to be replaced by a different beauty brought about 'through faith and change of heart' (Origen, 1957, p. 113).

And blackness turns out not to be such a natural condition after all. It is 'something that she has suffered through force of circumstance' (Origen, 1957, p. 107). It introduces unresolvable questions about what used to be called 'natural evil'. Blackness provides a potent description for what is wrong with the soul, requiring the radiance of light to remove it. 'Light' and 'dark' are core metaphors of faith. 'God is light and in him there is no darkness at all' (1 John 1.5). What happens here is a double association with sin. A woman's body is blackened by it, and her whole being disfigured by Eve's disobedience. There is an obvious need for a fundamental examination of the use of light and dark, white and black, in Christian theology. Darkness is the precondition of light, not its negation.

But blackness had been associated with the devil since the *Letter of Barnabas* (*c.* 125 CE). There the devil is already called 'the Black One', 'crooked and full of a curse', whose 'way' leads to 'eternal death' via a comprehensive list of sins (Barnabas, n.d., 20.1). But in the famous *Life of Antony* written by Athanasius (293–373 CE), the devil, blackness, women's bodies and men's desires are brought together in a visceral, kaleidoscopic nightmare. Intended as a tribute to Antony (a monk who moved into the Egyptian desert in 270 CE and was later made a saint), the Devil is said to have attacked him, 'disturbing him by night and harassing him by day' (Athanasius, 1892, section 5). There is a contest between them: 'one would suggest foul thoughts and the other counter them with prayers: the one fire him with lust the other, as one who seemed to blush, fortify his body with faith, prayers, and fasting.' Anthony is winning the battle, so the devil turns up the heat:

> And the devil, unhappy wretch, one night even took upon him the shape of a woman and imitated all her acts simply to beguile Antony. But he, his mind filled with Christ and the nobility inspired by Him, and considering the spirituality of the soul, quenched the coal of the other's deceit. Again the enemy suggested the ease of pleasure. But he like a man filled with rage and grief turned his thoughts to the threatened fire and the gnawing worm. (Athanasius, 1892, section 5)

Women's bodies are the devil's principal means for bringing about the downfall of holy men. But defeated, the devil's next ruse is to appear in a different guise – 'like a black boy, taking a visible shape in accordance with the color of his mind'. Antony remains unmoved, and Athanasius concludes the conversation with these words:

> But Antony having given thanks to the Lord, with good courage said to him [the devil], 'You are very despicable then, for you are black-hearted and weak as a child. Henceforth I shall have no trouble from you, for the Lord is my helper, and I shall look down on mine enemies.' Having heard this, the black one straightway fled, shuddering at the words and dreading any longer even to come near the man. (Athanasius, 1892, section 6)

Jerome makes many allusions to Origen's *Commentary* in his *Letter to Eustochium*, written in Rome in 384. He agrees with Origen's assessment of the reason for the blackness of the female lover in the Song: it is due to the human race being tempted by the Devil (assumed to be black). In John's Gospel there are Jews who say, in a dispute with Jesus, 'Abraham is our father' (8.39). Jesus gives a different account of their origins: 'You are from your father the devil' (8.44). That verse occurs countless times in later Christian anti-Jewish polemic (see Chapter 15), but here

Jerome extends the idea of demonic parentage to all black people as well. He applies the verse first to all humans: 'Born, in the first instance of such parentage we are naturally black ... even when we have repented' (Jerome, *Letter*, section 1). But while all humanity is sinful, black people are present, visible tokens of primal sinfulness. In his *Homily 18* the meaning of 'Ethiopia' is said to be 'black and cloaked in the filth of sin'.

> At one time we were Ethiopians in our vices and sins. How so? Because our sins had blackened us. But afterwards we heard the words: 'Wash yourselves clean!', and we said: 'Wash me, and I shall be whiter than snow.' We are Ethiopians, therefore, who have been transformed from blackness into whiteness. (Jerome, 1964, p. 140)

Jerome begins the long association of black as the colour of sin and death (Devisse, 1979, p. 59). Sincere Christian men (Origen was not canonized) were seeking moral and spiritual perfection and urging others to follow them. Francesca Stavrakopoulou speaks for many when she finds there 'the demonization of black people, dressed in tropes of eroticized danger and sinful deviancy'. 'Something of this', she continues,

> can be attributed to the colour-coded dualism inherent within early Christian theology, which lent itself as easily to the whitening of divinity as it did to the blackening of evil. In the iconography of Western Christendom in particular, divine brightness and lightness would morph into corporeal whiteness ... Across early medieval Europe, on the walls of churches, in illustrated Bibles and prayer books, and in the pictures conjured in sermons, Jesus was made in the image of his light-skinned, wealthier worshippers – and increasingly contrasted with black demons. (2021, p. 186)

More of this later.

12

Enslaved Bodies:
Slavery Affirmed and Justified

The hierarchical bodies of this chapter are bodies that are arranged in order of superiority over other bodies. This is the *ordo* that was thought to operate throughout the whole universe. Hierarchical bodies may be ranked in an order of sex, class, nationality, race or religious affiliation, but the gender hierarchy is the basis that allows powerful men to devise and to enforce all the others. There is a particular concern in the chapter with husbands and wives, and slaves and slave owners. Our earlier analysis of ancient thought revealed that in the elemental scheme of things everything, animate and inanimate, had a sex, so it is no surprise that 'the biological differences between male and female bodies become symbolic of other cultural boundaries and categories' (Power, 1995, p. 8).[1] But these orderings are now reinforced by theological considerations that become settled in the fourth and fifth centuries CE. The effects of these considerations remain plain to see even today. Slavery was always seen as a natural (as well as a social) institution, but in Christian theology it began to be regarded as a result of the Fall, a just punishment falling on some, provided by a just God, and so unquestionable. More than this, slavery was hard-wired into theology on the basis that all Christians are the slaves of their Lord and Master, Jesus Christ. This familiar model of the Christian's relationship to God blurred the boundary between metaphorical and real slavery, at the expense of real slaves themselves (Chapter 15).

Jerome's ranking of virginity is expressed in his oft-quoted statement 'I praise wedlock, I praise marriage, but it is because they give me virgins' (Jerome, *Letter*, paras 19, 20). He dismissed, or rather reinterpreted, numerous biblical statements supporting marriage, along with several NT narratives that are plainly false if Mary was and remains *virgo perpetua* (Chapter 7). His polemical attacks on theologians who disagreed with him grate on contemporary ears. Helvidius (*c.* 393 CE), in a lost work, had drawn attention to the references to Jesus' brothers and sisters in the Gospels (Mark 6.3; Matt. 13.55), more or less proving that Jesus belonged in a large family headed by Joseph and Mary. He is slandered as an 'ignorant boor', a blasphemer and a madman, and the references are dismissed contemptuously as a 'chorus of the Jews', prattling on about 'a team of four brethren and a heap of sisters' (Jerome, *Letter*, para. 18). Mary and Joseph never married, he retorts, shaping scripture to enforce his riposte. Jovinian had argued, in another lost work, that marriage and virginity were equal in the sight of God, and that the birth of Jesus was a real birth, thus attacking the orthodox view that 'the infant Jesus passed through the walls of Mary's womb as easily as his Resurrection body passed through the tomb in which he had been laid, and through the closed doors behind which the bereaved disciples were meeting (Anon., 1893). Jovinian was peddling 'nauseating trash', exploded Jerome, even as he compared virginity and marriage with a hungry person eating barley instead of cow shit (Jerome, *Against Jovinianus*, 4, 7).

Ruling and Ruled Bodies – Augustine on women and marriage

To modern-day Protestants, Jerome's view about virginity will surely sound extreme. It indicates his fear of women's bodies and his determination to make them honorary men by insisting on their removing every trace of their femininity, and especially by the permanent closure of their wombs. His gross dislike even of the thought of having sex is a very different kind of celibacy from those modern vowed sisters and brothers who know and appreciate their sexuality, and whose renunciation of it is a costly, self-sacrificial act, motivated by a greater love for God. We have already seen that a considerable effort is required to understand the theological roots of classical Christian misogyny. These become more deeply embedded in the thought of Augustine.

Augustine's sexual history is well known. He lived with an unnamed concubine for 15 years, had a son with her and ended the relationship because it was detrimental to a forthcoming marriage. His marriage was delayed (his bride was not old enough to marry), so he procured a second concubine, before renouncing her, his forthcoming marriage and sex altogether. He had a dramatic conversion (famously described in his *Confessions*, Book 8) and adopted an ascetic faith thereafter, deeply influenced by the shame and guilt resulting from his previous sex life. 'Ruling' and 'ruled' bodies in Augustine's context belonged to a wider discussion about 'headship' (deriving from 1 Cor. 11), and rumble on in evangelical churches today. Kim Power reminds us that 'head' was a euphemism for penis (Power, 1995, p. 132), so the nuanced connection between masculine leadership and male genitalia, obvious to ancient thought, is lost to us (unless the colloquial 'giving head' is bringing it back). According to

Augustine, if women wish to see themselves in the image of God, 'they must look not in a mirror but at their husbands' (Power, 1995, p. 154). However, how Augustine gets here is far from obvious.

Men should rule over women. That, for Augustine, *is* obvious, a fact of the natural and the revealed order of things. But men also have to rule themselves, to control the very 'un-ruly' elements and passions within them. Ruing his past sexual excesses, he confessed a failure of self-control over his own libidinous desires, a failure that persisted even after his conversion, and manifested itself in his inability to control his erections. Adam before the Fall knew no concupiscence. There is no reason, wrote Augustine, 'why we should not believe that before the sin of disobedience and its punishment of corruptibility, the members of a man's body could have been the servants of man's will without any lust' (Augustine, 1984, p. 589). People can manage to perform all kinds of unnecessary physical actions if they want to, he averred, like waggling their ears or moving their scalps up and down. They can 'produce at will such musical sounds from their behind (without any stink) that they seem to be singing from that region'. But it is not possible not to have an unwanted erection. Here psychology, mythology and theology combine, to devastating effect. He could not differentiate between his persistent tumescence and his previous sex life now considered desperately sinful. Arousal and the sense of sin became permanently combined. Augustine was the first theologian to take the opening chapters of Genesis entirely literally, and he associated the cosmic Fall of those chapters with the primal corruption of sexuality. The original sin of the first human pair became the doctrine of Original Sin, transmitted from one generation to the next, the original STD (sexually transmitted disease).

Body and mind are to be regarded, following Plato, separately. The image of God is to be found in the mind, or soul. But every human soul itself has masculine and feminine aspects. The masculine aspect of the soul is rational and contemplates the eternal truths of reason and God. The feminine aspect of the soul is directed towards the body. Different names are given to these different aspects of the soul: wisdom, or *sapientia*, to the male part of the soul; *scientia* to the female part. Men have more of the male part of the soul, and this is where the image of God is reflected. Following Genesis 1.27 that men and women *both* share the image of God, and mindful of Paul's claim that man 'is the image and reflection of God; but woman is the reflection of man' (1 Cor. 11.7), Augustine attempts a compromise between these two positions. Human beings collectively are known as *homo*, and *homo* is in the image of God. But human beings are man (*homo, vir*) and woman (*femina, mulier*). The bodies of women and men apart from their souls do not share the divine image. Women as *homo* are in the image of God, but women as *femina* or *mulier* have the image of God compromised because their souls are turned to the demands of the body and the material world. Men are characterized by *sapientia* – the realm of reason, intellect, contemplation. *Sapientia* achieves union with the eternal God. Women are characterized by *scientia* – the realm of appetite, of practicalities, of caring for others, of temporal busy-ness, of corporeality.

Women thus characterized can only participate in God's image when they are ruled by men. Augustine sees the domain of *scientia* as the domain of desire. The whole domain is rendered feminine, even when it is manifest in men. The feminine domain acts as an

> intermediary between the world of the senses and the reason of wisdom. When the feminine is appropriately ruled, then the gaze of the inner being remains focused on eternal things. However, if the inner being does not restrain the feminine, the demonic will seize control. (Power, 1995, p. 144)

A man must control the feminine within him. If he is a married man, he must control the feminine both within himself and his wife. Because women are more feminine than men, women are the locus of sexual temptation – an authoritative Christian example of slut-shaming. Wearing the veil is necessary since it symbolizes and enacts the corporeal control of real women by real men and is given overwhelming theological justification.

While Augustine's derogation of women's bodies does not match the nightmarish and obscene vitriol of the prophet Ezekiel (Chapter 3), it inflicts greater damage upon them. Their bodies, along with those of men, cannot reflect God's image. Their souls *can* reflect God's image if the feminine within them is ruled not just by themselves but also by the male rulers who, in accordance with nature and God, rule them. Adding to the influence of Tertullian and other writers, a permanent blow to women's self-esteem was struck. They are required to be ruled by men and carry with them the internalized masculine view that they are responsible for sexual temptation and men's ruination. The notion that women's bodies are intrinsically dangerous to men also damages men by the way they look at (or look away from) women, and it damages women by requiring them to internalize a demeaning view of themselves. The idea that women need men to control and protect them is responsible for untold and unfathomable unhappiness and violence against them, while the belief that women cannot image God in their bodies reduces their bodies to objects – the very basis of the growing modern menace of internet pornography. Yes, theology is implicated in that revolting 'industry', fuelling its appeal:

There is irony in the fact that the institution which has continually proclaimed that women are not to be exploited as sex objects has done so
much to sexualize women's bodies as entities divorced from their essential human being. (Power, 1995, p. 154)

Yes, Augustine's teaching about the female body is an appalling act of
epistemic, spiritual and emotional violence (Chapter 1). Yet Augustine
attempted a positive doctrine of marriage, around its 'three goods'
– children, fidelity and sacrament. The first two goods, he observed,
Christians share with pagans. The third is unique to the faith – a bond
that, due to the clear teaching of Jesus forbidding divorce, could not
be broken. Augustine could accept neither Jovinian's acceptance of the
equality of marriage with virginity nor Jerome's disparagement of it.
The three goods have been used ever since as a convenient summary of
Christian marriage. There is a sound method at work here, inquiring what
values couples bring to and receive from marriage, and emphasizing these
as goods, but the context of Augustine's compromise is hugely different
from ours, and there are several reasons why his synthesis cannot command support today.

First, Augustine taught that husbands and wives could be friends.
There is 'a certain friendly and true union of the one ruling, and the other
obeying' (Augustine, *On the Good of Marriage*, section 1). That doesn't
sound like friendship. Mutuality and equality are missing. The ruler/ruled
framework is endorsed. Second, although marriage contains goods, *it is
never itself a good*. Or, more precisely, Augustine distinguishes between
intrinsic and *extrinsic* goods; that is, things that are good in themselves
or self-evidently and things that only *produce* goods without being self-
evidently good in themselves. While wisdom, health and friendship are
examples of ends in themselves, marriage is not. It is an end towards
other things (its three goods). However good wisdom and friendship are,
marriage and sexual intercourse are not necessary to produce either, for
'such is the state of the human race now ... there fails not numerous
progeny, and abundant succession, out of which procure holy friendships'
(section 9). And since marriage and sex are not necessary for producing
the extrinsic good of friendship, it is better not to choose them: 'It is good
to marry, because it is good to beget children, to be a mother of a family:
but it is better not to marry.'

Having sex, then, is a definite no-no: doomed, like the desire that initi-
ates it. Paul's concession that married couples are not to deny one another
(the so-called 'marital debt' – 1 Cor. 7.3–4) is reluctantly turned into an
occasion for encouraging fidelity. But marriage dampens sexual ardour
by converting it into desire for children. There is 'a certain gravity of

glowing pleasure, when in that wherein husband and wife cleave to one another, they have in mind that they be father and mother' (Augustine, *On the Good of Marriage*, section 3). John Chrysostom called marriage a 'medicine against fornication', and a later meaning given to *sacramentum*, 'sacrament', was *medicinum*, the medicine that turns the sickness of desire into the desire for offspring. By the time of Augustine the damage to the experience of having sex had been done. It is hard to imagine the anxiety, the fear of demons, the sense of inevitable sin or the guilt attaching to any pleasurable sensation, for which these and similar strictures were responsible.

Enslaved Bodies – a blessed state!

The hierarchical ordering of bodies is nowhere more obvious than in the institution of slavery, which unfortunately was supported by almost all theologians. The Greek word for body, *sōma*, functioned as a synonym for *doulos*, 'slave' (Glancy, 2003, p. 9). This section indicates how the master–slave relationship was internalized even in marriage. It indicates how Christian slave masters treated their slaves, and how slavery as a metaphor for the human relationship to God excused slavery and endowed it with divine legitimation.

It is widely held that a lone voice against slavery belonged to Gregory of Nyssa (*c.* 335–*c.* 394 CE), who in an explosive sermon on a text clearly assuming slavery (Eccles. 2.7) exclaimed:

> You condemn a person to slavery whose nature is free and independent, and you make laws opposed to God and contrary to His natural law. For you have subjected one who was made precisely to be lord of the earth, and whom the Creator intended to be a ruler, to the yoke of slavery, in resistance to and rejection of His divine precept ... How is it that you disregard the animals which have been subjected to you as slaves under your hand, and that you should act against a free nature, bringing down one who is of the same nature of yourself, to the level of four-footed beasts or inferior creatures ...? (Gregory of Nyssa, *Homilies on Ecclesiastes*, in Maxwell, 1975, pp. 33–4)

Gregory held there was a single human nature created and redeemed by God, which Christ had assumed, and in which there were no hierarchical divisions. Owning another person, he thought, amounted to gross human pride and even theft, since God is the rightful 'owner' of all human beings. God created people free, and slavery robbed slaves of their freedom. Yet even this lone voice may be conveying a different message. A detailed study of the church's slaves concludes that Gregory's target was not the institution of slavery but the ostentatious and wealthy slave masters in his congregation. The sermon was on the text 'All is vanity', and Gregory was explaining 'why riches are ultimately worthless. And an overabundance of slaves was simply a good example of excessive wealth' (Sommar, 2020). Yes, he thought all people were intended by God to be free, as long as freedom was confined to their souls not their bodies.

Augustine took slavery for granted and emphasized that while God had made people free, slavery was a consequence of sin having entered the world. The presence of slaves throughout the world was evidence of God's primeval curse on humanity, as just punishment for the Fall. Slavery afflicted the body but not, he maintained, the mind. Indeed, being a slave was an opportunity for learning certain virtues, especially humility, obedience, patience, forgiveness and submission. He was certainly no abolitionist. The First Letter to Timothy contained the exhortation to all 'under the yoke of slavery' to 'regard their masters as worthy of all honour', especially if they were church members (1 Tim. 6.1–2). There were many Bible passages that assumed and supported slavery, and no passage urging its abolition. For Augustine, slavery, 'though in itself a wretched state, yet, being conducive to the development of important elements of moral life, it is itself a way to blessedness' (Mary, 1954, p. 367).

In the Roman Empire, masters having sex with slaves was common. 'For many slaves, rape was a fact of daily life' (de Wet, 2019, p. 3). The practice was frequently condemned by Christian preachers, showing that it was not absent from Christian households. Indeed, Salvian of Marseilles (c. 400–490 CE), a Christian priest, attributed the sack of Rome (410 CE) and other imperial cities to God's punishment on the *Christian* slaveholders of the Christian Empire for having sex with their slaves. Salvian was in no doubt that the practice was widespread among rich Christian landowners and slaveholders. Upholding Augustine's insistence on mastery (including self-mastery), Salvian inveighed not against slavery as such, nor the violation suffered by victims, but against the masters' own failure at *self*-mastery. They were accused of becoming slaves to their own lusts, and were therefore unfit to exercise mastery over others. Like runaway slaves they too had run away, but from their divine Master and 'His laws': 'There is a sense of great irony and shame because these slaveholders expect their own slaves to be obedient, yet they fail in their obedience to their heavenly Master' (de Wet, 2019, p. 2). Whereas Roman law did not regard the sexual exploitation of slaves as a crime, or even misconduct (slaves had no rights), Christian leaders regarded the sin of sex with slaves as adulterous. Salvian thought the sexual behaviour of the conquerors of Rome was *better* than that of Christians:

> Among the Goths no one is permitted to indulge in fornication ... Yet we wonder that the lands of the Aquitanians and of us all have been given by God to the barbarians, though those same barbarians are now purifying by their chastity the places polluted by the fornication of the Romans. (de Wet, 2019, p. 6)

Salvian's accusations cannot be rejected as an exaggeration or as applicable to only a tiny minority of slaveholders (like bad apples in a barrel). Classical scholarship suffers an 'overt perspective of disregard' for slaves (duBois, 2008, p. 6), due to their very ubiquity and invisibility, and it is too easy for modern readers to dismiss as slanderous or impossible the sex crimes of Christian masters. Slaves are bodies, at the extremity of the body/soul dichotomy, and as such could easily be regarded as non-persons (even though they were inevitably involved in the intimacies of personal care of their masters and mistresses and perhaps education of their children). Once powerful human beings fail to treat other human beings as persons, or treat them as inferior persons, demeaning attitudes towards them inevitably result. If a human being is placed outside the moral community, that community can persuade itself that its own moral rules need not apply beyond its own boundaries. A useful term for this process is 'alterization' – the rendering of some people as 'other', accompanied by a negative attitude like contempt, mistrust or objectification. These Christians, inheriting ample precedent from the mores of Empire, may well have indulged themselves with the bodies of the powerless. Perhaps they stand as another frightening reminder that the fulfilment of vile desires requires other bodies to be vilified, or at any rate viewed as disposable or with contempt.

Many ascetic Christians practised what is often called 'spiritual marriage', but even this unofficial practice was tainted with the abuse of slavery. They lived together with commitment and without having sex – 'friends with benefits', but without sexual ones. It was called *suneisaktism* ('companionship'), and the female companions were the *subintroductae* or *agapetae* (beloved women). These Christian men and women rejected marriage, but also the more extreme forms of asceticism. Chrysostom had warned his congregation that they should keep few slaves, and slaves who were dismissed from service sometimes joined in households where they would meet and live together often with other women and men of higher status. Its commonality is evidenced by condemnation from church leaders, East and West, such as Irenaeus, Tertullian, Cyprian, Eusebius of Emesa, and the Cappadocians. Jerome, in his *Letter to Eustochium*, called them 'unwedded wives', 'novel concubines' and 'whores'. The brothers and their companion sisters profess to find 'spiritual consolation from those not of their kin', but 'their real aim is to indulge in sexual intercourse' (Jerome, *Letter*, section 14).

But something else was going on. Slavery was also a link between real marriage and spiritual marriage, since Chrysostom and many others *regarded real marriage as a form of slavery*. He quoted Paul on the anxious cares of married life, and queried why the *subintroductae* would abandon the limited benefits of marriage while incurring all its chores. Within these households or communities, tasks once performed by slaves still had to be performed, whether by men or women, with the result that 'syneisaktism became a substitute not only for marriage, but also for slave-holding and slave management' (de Wet, 2017, p. 64). These Christian social experiments were condemned not only for the opportunities for sex that undoubtedly occurred but for the very disruption to the social hierarchy of master and mastered that these novel domestic arrangements clearly represented. Free men who did the work of slaves were no longer rulers of their domains but in danger of being ruled by women. The ideological framework of master and mastered was endangered, yet this was the framework basic to the church's self-understanding – Christ as Lord and Master (*Dominus*), dominating his faithful servants (slaves) who, as an expression of faith, submit to him completely. The Christian household was intended to reflect this pattern, not to controvert it.

Metaphorized Bodies – everyone a slave

Earlier we saw how Origen had turned the bodies of the lovers of the Song of Songs into a comprehensive metaphorical scheme standing for something else – the love of the soul for God or Christ's love for the church. Real bodies and their languid delights are dismissed. A similar process occurs with the bodies of slaves, with equally damaging results. The church had another metaphorical scheme for denying the deprivations of real bodies. It enabled it to blank out the indignities and lack of personal status of real slaves, and turn a blind eye towards the moral evil of slave ownership for a further 1,300 years. In this scheme, Christians regardless of rank are all slaves, slaves of the one Master, the Lord Jesus Christ. Powerful people, by imagining themselves as the slaves of their divine Master, enabled themselves to make light of the institution of slavery:

the church not only accepted slavery as a social institution, but it used the slave model of behavior and mode of existence as a metaphor for the practice of Christian religion, the composition of Christian theology, and the formation of Christian subjectivity, and the metaphor of slavery also played an important role in Christian leadership formulations. (de Wet, 2015, p. 9)

Christian slave owners may generally have treated their slaves well. It was often possible for slaves to be 'upwardly mobile' and to benefit from their masters' patronage. Some Christian leaders had a bad conscience about slavery (for example, Chrysostom), yet even the lowly place of slaves in households seemed to confirm their *natal* and ontological status as 'other', and rendered slavery as an institution ever more normal and inevitable. Why reform the institution when the author of Ephesians had enjoined Christian slaves to:

obey your earthly masters with fear and trembling, in singleness of heart, as you obey Christ; not only while being watched, and in order to please them, but as slaves of Christ, doing the will of God from the heart. Render service with enthusiasm, as to the Lord and not to men and women, knowing that whatever good we do, we will receive the same again from the Lord, whether we are slaves or free.

And, masters, do the same to them. Stop threatening them, for you know that both of you have the same Master in heaven, and with him there is no partiality. (Eph. 6.5–9)

Recently writers have drawn attention to the interiorization of the status of slaves by the slaves themselves, *as a consequence of faith*. This is a process similar to the one we found among Tertullian's and Jerome's female readers, expected to internalize his demeaning view of them. Using terms made popular by the French philosopher Michel Foucault, Chris de Wet speaks of the 'surveillance' of slaves and of a 'Christic panopticon' (2015). The 'panopticon' is the point inside a prison from which all cells are viewable. Slavery and imprisonment are similar: they both deny freedom. But the Christic panopticon requires slaves to internalize their unfree status twice over. Christ is watching them too, observing their souls and their bodies, their thoughts and their actions. Slaves have two masters to obey (whatever Jesus may have said about that being impossible – Matt. 6.24). 'Being watched' is a sinister synonym for 'surveillance' (an invasion of private space), and the Christian slave is being watched twice over. The double yoke of slavery is to be internalized. Service must be 'from the heart'. Surveyed by everyone in the household, a slave of Christ must be an exemplary slave, serving his earthly lord as if he were his heavenly Lord, who watches and knows all dispositions and motivations. In the same hierarchical scheme, slave owners are cast as Christ-like. Mention of fear and threat perhaps reveals more about slavery than the author intended. The Mastery of the heavenly Christ or his Kyriarchy ('lordly rule') endows slavery with holy legitimacy. The earthly master saw himself as representing the heavenly Master in the Christian family, just as the earthly priest represented the heavenly Priest in the Christian church.

Indeed, the more slavery was thought about from a Christological perspective, the worse the position of the slave became. This is hard for contemporary Christians to understand. We perhaps respond well to the reverse idea of Christ becoming *our* servant, One who 'emptied himself, taking the form of a slave' (Phil. 2.7) and who washed the feet of his disciples. This idea of self-emptying is called (from the Greek) *kenōsis*, and has been popular since the nineteenth century. But the incarnate One who becomes a servant and the heavenly Master demanding obedience from his slaves do not play well together. Indeed, they seem irreconcilable. The Latin for 'lord' or 'master' is *dominus*, and the Dominus *dominates*. He exercises dominion. Everywhere the Dominus requires obedience and deference. However Christ's suffering came to be understood, Christian slaves' understanding of it was prescribed for them. Slaves, says the author of 1 Peter, addressing them directly, must 'accept the authority of your masters with all deference not only those who are kind and gentle but also those who are harsh'. Why? '[B]ecause Christ also suffered for you, leaving you an example so that you should follow in his steps' (1 Pet. 2.18, 21).

Yes, the suffering Christ is the example that all Christians, not just slaves, should in their own way follow. Yet how was that 'kenotic' model compatible with the expansion and defence of Christendom, and the naked exercise of real dominion, sovereignty and authority? If Christ is for us a slave, how is he any more a master? Does not the fashion of regarding Jesus today as a servant rather function to mask the damage done by Christians in the name of their absolute Master and Lord? We return to those difficult questions in Chapters 15—16.

Notes

1 I have followed Power closely in her careful and balanced unpacking of Augustine's thinking about women and the image of God.

13

Disgusting Male Bodies:
Leaky and Loathsome

The bodies of this chapter belong to monks who ejaculate in their sleep, and men who have sex with men, in particular, priests. But the discourse surrounding these bodies and their activities incorporates and intensifies body negativity, masculine embarrassment and moral disgust, which unfortunately cannot be left behind in the Middle Ages. Since priests and monks were exemplars of spiritual perfection, their struggles with their bodies were held to be normative for lesser Christian men. The baleful influence of this discourse is everywhere apparent in the churches.

Wet, Dreaming Bodies

Wet dreams, the involuntary emission of semen while asleep, are universal among men. They are less frequent among men who have regular sex with a partner or who masturbate (i.e. nearly all of us at various times in our lives). Sexually active men may go for years without a wet dream and may be astonished to learn that the natural occurrence of a seminal discharge could have caused such agonized soul-searching among Christian men, throughout every century since the first, and especially among priests and monks committed to a vow of celibacy. Most of the church's theologians over 2,000 years have been celibate (or married and committed to minimal sexual contact with their wives), and their struggles over wet dreams contributed to shaping and reinforcing body-negative and sex-negative attitudes that remain undislodged today. These struggles need to be 'excavated' in order to be understood and overcome.

Wet dreams, unusually, allowed the *male* body to be scrutinized and pollution to be detected. The problems associated with wet dreams were many (see Elliott, 1999, for a full account; also Stewart, 2002). We noted (in Chapter 2) that according to Leviticus 15.16–18 a man always 'pollutes' himself when he ejaculates, whether by himself or with a partner. Did the impurity of a man who had just ejaculated (like a woman with her period) bar him from officiating at, or receiving, the holy Eucharist?

Or was the devil tricking him into abstention in order to deprive him of the grace the Eucharist provided? But attention soon focused on the *dreams* accompanying emissions, and on the causes of them. Were they enjoyed? Why had they arisen? Could they have been prevented? The introspection required by obtaining answers to these questions raised even deeper questions about the struggle between soul and body. The questions were ontological, driving down into the depths of a man's being. The unwanted discharge of semen in sleep (a trivial matter in the HB) became an overwhelming problem in the monastic life. The wet dream seemed to be evidence against the priest and monk ever achieving the purity to which he aspired. The introspection required demonstrated 'the extent to which masculine identity was overinvested in the will and its exercise of reason' (Elliott, 1999, p. 27).

Before examining some torturous thoughts about emissions, questions for us must arise about how we read them. Monks then and now seek purity of life and devote their lives to attaining it. They do this for God and believe themselves to be called by God to a life of perfection. They deserve respect, even admiration. Yet reading and imitating John Cassian or John Climacus on the struggle against wet dreams as part of their drive towards spiritual purity makes following Christ for most modern readers deeply unattractive, a recipe for misery, failure, self-absorption, discomfort towards their bodies, and the missing out of the simple enjoyment of the good material things of life provided by God, including orgasms. Their theology is best left in the desert where it originated. It is not enough for the church to battle against the world. Holy (heterosexual!) men must not only battle against the charms of women, real or imagined. They must be at constant war *with themselves*, for their desires for women go deeper than their explanations for them. That is only the beginning of their miseries. For in the arousal, as in the emission, Satan himself, or any of an army of evil spirits, present themselves as foes, to be resisted even in sleep. It is a forlorn life, inviting the judgement that it is also very far from the openness and uncloseted compassion of Jesus. The shadow side of monastic life, exemplified by the problem of the wet dream, must lead to a profound suspicion of the ancient theological framework that gave rise to it. And the framework includes the masculine God who has a prurient interest in his followers' fantasies, and expects his closer followers to endure acute physical and psychological discomfort in acquiring their salvation.

The Teaching of the Twelve Apostles or *Didascalia Apostolorum* (a third-century (*c.* 230 CE) Syrian document) considered whether the male body in its leaky state provided an opportunity for an evil spirit to enter it; whether menstrual and seminal discharges prevented a person from receiving the Eucharist; and whether Christians who considered themselves polluted by seminal discharges were applying Jewish practices and laws to themselves, contrary to the gospel (Brakke, 1995). The answers given are easily and helpfully applicable to today's arguments about sex because they have real and enduring theological weight. 'Through baptism,' the author retorts, Christians 'receive the Holy Spirit, who is ever with those that work righteousness, and does not depart from them by reason of natural issues and the intercourse of marriage, but is ever and always with those who possess Him' (Homer, 1929, chapter 26). The Spirit does not depart when the male body leaks.

But in answer to the question whether Christians mistakenly impose the Jewish law upon themselves, the author applies a rule that exposes a fault line in modern biblicisms. The rule is: don't quote scripture when it is no longer applicable. He distinguishes between the law of Moses and the further legislation occurring after the erection of the Golden Calf (Exod. 32.1–4), which he calls the 'Second Legislation', and leaves his readers in no doubt that obedience to this part of the scriptures is not only wrong but outrageous:

> But if there be any who are precise and desire, after the Second Legislation, to observe the *wonted courses of nature and issues* and marriage intercourse: first let them know that, as we have already said, together with the Second Legislation they affirm the curse against our Saviour and condemn themselves to no purpose. And again, let them tell us, in what days or in what hours they keep themselves from prayer and from receiving the Eucharist, or from reading the Scriptures – let them tell us whether they are void of the Holy Spirit. (Homer, 1929, chapter 26, emphasis added)

Reset in a contemporary context, this anonymous author still warns Christians in no uncertain terms not to use the HB in matters of morality where they are no longer applicable. They should be looking to Christ and not the HB for their salvation. At a time when homosexuality is still condemned by many Christians on the basis of verses from Leviticus, he warns against attempts to obey laws that are no longer applicable to Christians.

Anthony the Great (251–356 CE), writing in Coptic to various monasteries in Egypt, was in no doubt that nocturnal emissions could be and should be stopped. There is, he records, a process of purification, 'by much fasting, by many vigils and prayers', which begins to enable the Spirit to teach the mind how to purify both soul and body (Anon., 2018). While there are motions of the body 'implanted by nature', an apparently involuntary ejaculation is still 'a kind of sickness', evidence of resistance to the Spirit's testimony. Contrary to the *Didascalia*, Anthony affirms evil spirits can take over the mind, as it struggles against its own body and soul, enacting an internal tripartite warfare within the person. Evagrius (345–399 CE), a fellow monk, was more interested in the fantasies accompanying the emissions. Demons use these to attack the sleeping monk who, even in his sleeping state, can consent to them. Monks, he insisted, can expect to have emissions because they are 'natural movements of the body'. But it is important to attempt to train the soul so that when an emission occurs, it happens *without any sexual images or urges:*

> When the natural movements of the body during sleep are free of images, they reveal that the soul is healthy to a certain extent. The formation of images is an indication of ill health. If it is a matter of indistinct faces, consider this a sign of an old passion; if the faces are distinct, it is a sign of a current wound. We shall recognize the proofs of impassibility in the thoughts by day and in the dreams by night. (Sinkewicz, 2011, p. 107)

Monks must attempt the complete elimination of passion, and in this they will more perfectly resemble the complete impassibility of God.

Augustine acknowledged that emissions were involuntary, and so technically without sin. He confesses a vivid wet dream is intensely pleasurable – almost as pleasurable as having good sex. 'While I am awake they [sexual images] have no power into my thoughts, but in sleep they not only arouse pleasure but even elicit consent, and are very like the actual act' (Wei, 2012, p. 364). He should know. But the very pleasure of them is an index of the soul's sickness, requiring prayer to God that he not consent to 'those disgraceful and corrupt acts in which sensual images provoke carnal emissions' (Wei, 2012, p. 364). The monk John Cassian (*c.* 360– *c.* 435) attributed regular emissions to any of three causes: a gluttonous diet that required humours to be expelled; 'a lack of vigilance during the daytime over one's thoughts and images'; or a Satanic attack intended to keep the monk away from the Eucharist (Brakke, 1995, p. 448). The Latin of chapter 12 of his *Conferences* was too embarrassing for the 1894 translator (Gibson, 1894) to include in his English edition. Perfect purity was exemplified by an absence both of erotic dreams and of an accusatory wet patch in his sleeping attire: 'The culmination and perfect proof of purity is if while we are asleep, no pleasurable titillation creeps up on us, and, while we are unconscious, there is no filthy product [seminal emission]' (Wei, 2012, p. 368). Monks were advised to:

> cover their loins with lead plates, lest perchance a nocturnal emission caused by a dream diminish the strength which they have acquired over

a long period, so that the contact of the cold metal on their genitals may inhibit the shameful liquid. (Wei, 2012, p. 370)

It is difficult to believe the agony and consternation caused to perfection-seeking monks by wet dreams over centuries. The same agonies would be directed towards masturbation in the modern period. John Climacus (d. 649 CE) advised novices that dreams of *all* kinds were inspired by demons. Never have a full stomach, he warns, for 'when the stomach is full … , with a smile the spirit of fornication comes, and having bound us hand and foot by sleep, does with us all he pleases, *defiling soul and body with its impurities, dreams, and emissions*' (Gibson, 1894, p. 55, emphasis added). 'He is chaste who even during sleep feels no movement or change of any kind [never has an erection] in his constitution' (Gibson, 1894, p. 57). If you are 'seriously ill', an emission is more likely, he explains, because a demon is more likely to attack you when you are physically weak. Pride is another source of pollution: 'when we pride ourselves that we have not been subject to these effluxes for a long time', the demon strikes (Gibson, 1894, p. 61).

Some success in controlling wet dreams itself seems to have become an issue in twelfth-century Byzantium, where monks were imposing severe penances on other monks, less successful in avoiding accidents between their legs. John Zonaras, a fellow monk, was surprisingly liberal about the matter. He simply regarded them as a fact of nature, for which God rather than sinful human nature was responsible:

For tell me, beloved, what sin or uncleanness is there in a natural secretion, as if anyone wants to make a crime out of the mucus expelled from the nostrils, and the sputum of the mouth, and also the secretions of the belly? (Perisanidi, 2018, p. 46)

Zonaras' opponents, he averred, like those criticized in the *Didascalia*, were also using the ritual anxieties of the HB about semen being in the wrong place, in a manner that pointed away from, instead of towards, Jesus Christ. 'Are you not even aware', he asked, 'that in this particular opinion you are following Judaic customs and renewing the orders of the Old Testament, which the Saviour has abolished by becoming human?' (Perisanidi, 2018, p. 47). If, in the imagination only, a man found himself in bed with a woman and climaxed, he was still guilty of no sin, *unless* he 'had a preexisting passion, nourished desire for a woman in his thoughts, turned this over in his mind, and hence the visions followed in his sleep' (Perisanidi, 2018, p. 48).

In the next century, Thomas Aquinas sealed the church's teaching about wet dreams, giving a scholarly summary of earlier teaching about the matter, which lasted until the twentieth century and is still accepted by some. 'In itself', nocturnal pollution, he wrote, is no sin because it happens when a man is asleep and so unable to exercise his powers of reason. An involuntary ejaculation is to be understood medically as the discharge of an 'excess of seminal humor'. But if the excess of humours is caused by excessive eating or drinking, or some other known cause, then it is preceded by sin, and so is sinful. In company with Augustine a wet dream is sinful if it is caused by an unguarded moment or a casual disposition; that is, if it occurs 'from thinking about carnal sins with concupiscence for such pleasures, because this leaves its trace and inclination in the soul'. And third, an emission might occur 'through the wickedness of the devil alone'. It is then a sin if there has been a 'neglect to guard against the devil's wiles' (Aquinas, 1974, 154.5).

The worry about wet dreams continues to this very day in the church's liturgies. A traditional Anglican compline service (available in *Common Worship*, the Church of England's current liturgical suite) includes a hymn containing a verse in which worry about wet dreams and their associated thoughts could hardly be more evident:

From all ill dreams defend our eyes,
From nightly fears and fantasies;
Tread underfoot our ghostly foe,
That no pollution we may know.
(Church of England, *Common Worship*, 'An Order for Night Prayer')

I have been dismissive of the theology of wet dreams, its scarring of the soul and its contempt for the natural functions of the body, its insistence on the need for constant introspection, its unceasing generation of anxiety and failure. I think it deserves no place whatever in contemporary Christian thought. But that does not mean its lengthy and agonizing discussion has no value in our own context. A lesson from these stalwarts of continence may lie in their discovery that some sexual fantasies may be, if not literally demonic, harmful both to fantasizers and ultimately to the people who are the object of their fantasies. There are at least four ways in which its heritage may yet speak to people with a penis. First, male sexual fantasies are multiplied a millionfold by ubiquitous pornography, some of which contains shocking scenes of violence, humiliation, degradation, loathing, objectification and misogynistic contempt for women and their bodies. It is right to protect oneself from the corrupting effects of such displays, and to do so vigorously. Second, it is wrong to contribute to the social devaluation of women that many pornographic images bring about. Third, there is an obvious place for vigilance and struggle, not against the devil and malevolent demons but against the many social and cultural tendencies that devalue and objectify human bodies, especially those of women. Male fantasies about women will be appropriately modified or 'purified' not by treating them as objects or temptresses or by building institutions, with or without walls, that exclude or demean them, but by gaining an enhanced respect for them, which patriarchy has never been able to provide.

Fourth, the monastic and celibate traditions set an example to sexually active Christians today not to refrain from sex (or even thinking about it – if that were possible) but to have 'just' sex (Farley, 2006, pp. 207–44) within an enlarged vision for what chastity comprises (Thatcher, 2011, pp. 191–211). 'Just sex' does not mean 'only sex (and nothing more)', but sex informed by 'just' principles like respect, mutuality, equality, empathy and so on (Farley's title is *Just Love*). And fifth, these traditions testify to a paradoxical self-knowledge where we do *not* fully know ourselves and are to some extent impervious to what lies 'deep down'. They understand deep failure in loving oneself and one's neighbour, a failure that confession cannot eradicate (Sanchez, 2019, p. 127). They require us to seek and to practise an ethic that knows its unknowing, and recognizes the frailty of all human loves including the love of one's 'bodyself'.

Sodomitic Bodies

Sodomy, or *sodomia*, was a term first used by Hincmar of Reims (806– 882 CE) (Olsen, 2011, pp. 33–6). Modern usage confines it to anal intercourse, but in Hincmar's time it covered any sexual aberration apart from non-reproductive sex between married couples. For St Peter Damian (1007–72) the term encompassed 'four classes of unnatural vice': masturbation, mutual masturbation, inter-crural intercourse (a penis between the thighs of another person) and, most serious of all (in his view), anal penetration. He wrote a letter (Letter 31) to Pope Leo IX that became known as the *Liber Gomorrhianus*, a work that treated of anal sex with visceral disgust and laced the disgust with theological interpretation. The popularity of this work in subsequent centuries may have contributed to the intense and generalized loathing of anal sex and of people who are thought to practise it, even today. Calling it the 'unmentionable sin' may spare the blushes of those who wish to condemn it, but it's very 'unmentionability' (except obliquely) in church documents about sexuality needs to be called out, however uncomfortably. Disgust can never by itself be a reason for condemnation of behaviour (Chapter 1), and disgust also requires analysis since it is an emotion that inevitably leads to violence. Remnants of the term 'sodomy' persist in modern invective.

Consequently the 'sodomitic bodies' of this section belong to people who are intimate with each other, wherever a penis goes, or explodes. There is an important caveat. They are viewed through a particular theological filter that finds them, and their actions, vile. The filter, of course, will also require analysis. It is not assumed that in the eleventh century Damian's estimate of same-sex relations was the only or majority view. Neither is it forgotten there was also a thriving homosocial culture that serves as a contrast to it. This culture may be more relevant to late-modern concerns about homosexuality than Damian's execrations of the sodomite.

Damian's principal concern was the sexual immorality of the clergy. The tenth and eleventh centuries were the most scandal-plagued in the church's history, until the ongoing abuse scandals now. Many bishops and priests were living with their wives and concubines even though such liaisons had been forbidden since the fourth century. The papacy itself was mired in intrigue, murder and adultery (for a brief torrid summary, see Allen, 2018). Pope Leo IX, as soon as he was installed in 1049, sought to reform the clergy, and it was to Pope Leo that the anguished Damian wrote. Damian was a self-flagellant who insisted that clergy should lead pure, blameless lives. He believed sodomy was rife among them. The ordination of clergy, he held, is akin to a second baptism, guaranteeing that they enter a new or higher spiritual life, beyond the expectations of lay Christians. Priests through their ministry, he begins, produce spiritual sons and daughters. Next, he compares the wrongfulness of three irregular sexual relationships: a priest raping a woman he has just baptized; a father having sex with his daughter; and a bishop having sex with another priest whom he has ordained. Which is worse? The first is *spiritual* incest (the woman is his spiritual daughter). The second is actual, physical incest. The first is worse than the second (spiritual incest is said to be graver), but the third is worst of all. Why? Because the first two cases are in accord with nature (!), while the third is not. The third *is* incestuous (the victim is the bishop's spiritual son), but contrary to nature as well, and so worst of all. The incestuous father has sinned, but he has 'done so naturally with a woman, while he who engages in turpitude with a cleric has committed sacrilege against his son, incurring the crime of incest and dissolving, with a male, the laws of nature' (in Rollo, 2022, p. 15).

A man having sex with a man, he continues, is worse than having sex with an animal. That is because the man who penetrates an animal brings about his eternal perdition only, whereas the man who penetrates another man brings about their joint ruin. Suppose a man just has sex with himself? Well, that's as bad as bestiality, because a single act of private pleasure, unconfessed and unabsolved, also brings about the man's eternal punishment:

Consider, then, the terms bartered in this dangerous exchange: for a momentary delight whereby semen is in an instant ejaculated, the penalty that follows does not end over the course of millennia. Think how wretched it is that, for one member, its yearning now gratified, the whole body along with the soul is afterwards perpetually tortured in the flames of the most atrocious fire. (in Rollo, 2022, p. 20)

The flames of hell burn yet more fiercely for priests who have sex with each other, and then *grant each other absolution* from their crimes. Their impact on the morals of the flock of Christ is profound. 'What fruit is now to be found in the flocks', he asks, 'while the shepherd is plunged to so profound a depth into the belly of the devil?' (in Rollo, 2022, p. 21).

Damian's choice of words has been sharply analysed. The very act of anal penetration is subjected to a visceral theological condemnation. Plunging into the belly of the devil is a theological description that skilfully uses choice metaphors to associate anal sex with the demonic. The penetrated rectum is already demonic space. 'Falling' into the rear of another (another phrase used) echoes the fall of Genesis 3. Falling into the anus of another is falling into hell already. Even the opening or gaping of the anus during intercourse is enlisted into theological service:

The body of the receptive partner thereby becomes a site of diabolical depravity that metaphorically anticipates the place of infernal punishment both parties in intercourse will eventually inhabit. Anally to penetrate another man, 'to fall into the posterior of another' is also 'to fall into the abyss of sodomy,' which is in turn 'to fall into the pit of gaping ruin'. (Rollo, 2022, p. 22)

All four types of sodomy involve messy ejaculation. This too is described theologically. With Leviticus 15.16 in the background, Damian refers to 'sodomites' as those 'who befoul themselves with the ejaculated contagion of semen'. The choice of words is more than simple vitriol. It combines 'themes of fluid, infection and discharge that resonate with particularly damning effect' (Rollo, 2022, p. 24).

I have dwelt on these disconcerting scatological details for several reasons. They belong to the historical record, and they have surfaced as the result of careful scholarship. But the strongest reason is that Damian's 'book' is another example of loathing and hate speech in a religious context, and, as with the *Malleus Maleficarum* (Chapter 14), it comes with strong theological vindication. I suspect the work has strongly contributed to Christian homophobia throughout the world ever since. There is a Roman Catholic organization, the *League of Saint Peter Damian*, which affirms unaltered the teaching of the *Liber Gomorrhianus* and inveighs against 'liberals' like Pope Francis who dare to speak, off the record, less judgementally and more compassionately about gay people. The League advocates Damian's solutions also: top down, the purging of gay bishops and priests. It leaves unqualified the assumption that all non-procreative sexual contact is sodomitic. It draws strong and severely misleading parallels between the abuse crisis of the eleventh century and the abuse crises of today. Yes, contemporary churches have long concentrated on homosexuality in order to deflect from the state of heterosexual sexual morality among them, and its associated violence. There may be a parallel here. But the problem of concubinage, rife in the Middle Ages, was itself the product of the unrealistic and unenforceable expectation that priests should not marry. Priests who turned to each other in their search for intimacy may have been 'same-sex attracted', but are more likely to have found women repulsive from the account of women that the church provided for them. Given the teaching that friendship between men was superior to relationships with women, it is hardly surprising that some of these friendships became physically intimate ones. If there is a way of preventing a continuation or resumption of the present crisis (Chapter 22), the key is a different sexual theology and anthropology, and the serious, unqualified and unambiguous acceptance of the modern scientific finding that homosexuality is part of nature and so in accordance with nature, and not contrary to it.

Fortunately, there are other sources from which theology can draw, apart from this self-mortifying saint. His letter initially was not well received, and Leo IX agreed only that those clergy who owned up to anal sex should be kicked out of the priesthood. Appropriate penance could save the others. Neither was Damian's explicitness immediately popular. A different tone towards homosocial friendships, rather than a concentration on sexual acts between men, was adopted a century later by Aelred (1110–67), the Cistercian monk and abbot of Rievaulx, in Yorkshire, from 1147 until his death. Although Aelred does not concentrate on the physical side of relationships in his profound and influential work *Spiritual Friendship*, he does not shun physical contact between monks. He controversially allows the spiritual kiss between friends to be physical (the derivation is from the Song of Songs). He describes 'how physical kisses can be used for good and can be honest: kisses can be signs of reconciliation, peace, love, and unity in that kisses join people physically' (Bennett, 2017, p. 119). He saw all 'friendship love' or *philia* as being rooted in God: 'God is friendship' (Aelred, 1977, I.69–70).

Friendship *between men and women* was scarcely comprehensible in Aelred's day, since it necessarily lacked equality and would be based on the usual gendered dualities of superior/inferior. What mutuality could there be? Yet same-sex friendships within monasteries (and convents too) were also dangerous, since friendships tend towards the exclusion of others and may lead to concealment and growing intimacy (Summers 2015, pp. 692–5). Aelred dismissed both difficulties. He offered a novel interpretation of Genesis 2.21–22. The making of the woman from the side of the man is no argument for her subordinate status, he thought, but evidence of her equality with the man. They can therefore be friends. In friendship there is neither superior nor inferior (Aelred, 1977, I.57), so friendships between women and men are possible. The danger of over-development within particular friendships, common in monastic settings, can be overcome, he thought, by 'allowing nothing which is unbecoming and refusing nothing which is profitable' (Aelred, 1977, III.129–30). He took for granted that these friendships were enabled and nourished by the monastic community itself, and that individual monks should be capable of forming lasting bonds between one another, finding God within these relationships and simultaneously remaining open to the spiritual ambience and demands of the wider community.

Despite Damian's strictures about immorality among clergy, it is generally agreed among medievalists that the eleventh and twelfth centuries saw a vibrant homoerotic culture throughout Europe (Puff, 2013; Rollo, 2022). Aelred's community in Rievaulx was a Christian reflection of it. Attitudes towards same-sex love were complicated, and sometimes contradictory. 'Medieval culture accommodated uncensored, at times unquestioned, and at other times celebrated expressions of same-sex love – sexual and nonsexual' (Puff, 2013, p. 379). Single burial sites for same-sex couples throughout the Middle Ages have been found and documented. John Boswell, in an erudite and famous work in 1995, published his discovery of nearly 80 manuscript versions of what may fairly be called prayers for establishing 'same sex unions' or 'the making of brothers' (Boswell, 1995). The vehement abhorrence of sodomy, imprinted in ecclesiastical discourse since the time of Damian, eventually gained ground, but this existed in acute tension with a variety of social arrangements throughout Europe wherein men (and to a lesser extent women too) formed friendships, shared beds, swore oaths of allegiance and, like Cardinal Newman (1801–90) and his friend Ambrose St John, whom Newman described as the great love of his life, were buried (in 1890) in the same grave.

Damian and Aelred cannot be strictly compared. Damian wanted to root out corruption, as he saw it. Aelred wanted to praise friendship between people (whatever their sex). But the tone of each writer could hardly be more contrasted. The contrast continues today.

14

Tortured and Enclosed Bodies: Misogyny Erupts

The tortured and murdered bodies of this chapter belong to the women who were arrested and tried as witches in the name of the Christian religion and as an explicit result of its teachings. The enclosed bodies of the second half of the chapter belong to those saintly women of northern Europe whose good works, humility and poverty could not be allowed to expose by example the medieval church for its wealth, arrogance, corruption and cruelty. They needed to be literally shut up.

Reading, teaching, preaching and researching theology for more than 60 years, two historical books stand out from all the rest in their impact upon me. They were not books that confirmed the faith I had sought to commend and defend. Neither were they biographies of famous people of faith. The first was *The Hammer of Witches* (1486); the second, Martin Luther's *On the Jews and Their Lies* (1543). My reaction to each was, first, disbelief that such virulent misogyny and racism could ever have been penned by Christians; second, mounting horror as the plausible theological bases for these books were uncovered; and third, that the systems of theology producing these appalling results have never been 'owned' by the churches, in order for them to be 'disowned' subsequently. How naive I was! Deep soul-searching and repentance is a prescription for the spiritual lives of individuals, yet the collective soul of the church seems to prefer a willed amnesia to a full confession. Fourth, I became aware that my own theological education, and indeed theological education even now, consciously avoids the shadow side of Christian history altogether. Church history itself is barely taught and, when it is found, it is usually a highly selective and sanitized version, generally ignoring the unimaginable horrors that also belong to it. Finally, it has taken nearly a lifetime for me to conclude that the misogyny of *The Hammer of Witches* continues in the twenty-first century in more subtle forms, and the racism of Luther, the very 'father' of Protestantism, is very much alive. This chapter is about misogyny; the next about anti-Semitism and racism.

The Bodies of Witches

The number of women who lost their lives in witch hunts and trials is contested. A respected estimate from the Statista archive, covering Europe (but not the Americas), is that between 1300 and 1850, 42,215 people were tried and 26,063 of these were executed (McCarthy, 2019), often after prolonged torture, encouraging them to confess to their 'crimes' (Levack, 2013, pp. 5–6), and many more died awaiting trial. Other estimates are far higher. In Scotland alone, a small, underpopulated country, the Protestant Kirk ensured the death of over 1,000 victims between 1590 and 1670. This section grapples with the misogyny of the authors – more akin to the contemptuous resentment of the online incel ('involuntary celibates') subculture than to the disciples of Jesus. It then describes some of their beliefs and assumptions about demons, along with other antecedent causes deriving from earlier centuries. Witches were believed to be in league with demons, while on another reading it is their persecutors who may more justly be described as demonic.

In 1486, Heinrich Kramer, a Catholic clergyman and witch hunter, published *Malleus Maleficarum* (*The Hammer of Witches*). There is an early section titled 'Concerning Witches who copulate with Devils' (Part 1, Question 6). The authors set themselves a prior question: 'why a greater number of witches is found in the fragile feminine sex than among men' (Kramer and Sprenger, 1948, p. 41; subsequent quotes from pp. 42–7). They begin their answer with a proof text from Ecclesiasticus 25: 'There is no head above the head of a serpent: and there is no wrath above the wrath of a woman. I had rather dwell with a lion and a dragon than to keep house with a wicked woman' (25.15–16). 'All wickedness is but little to the wickedness of a woman' (25.19). The members of the 'fragile, feminine sex' are 'more credulous', and 'since the chief aim of the devil is to corrupt faith, therefore he rather attacks them'. They are 'more impressionable', and so 'more ready to receive the influence of a disembodied spirit'. And they have 'slippery tongues', which they use to influence other women and to talk themselves out of the accusation of witchcraft. They are 'unable to conceal from their fellow-women those things which by evil arts they know' (Kramer and Sprenger, 1948, pp. 43–4).

Women are 'feebler both in mind and body'. With regard to the intellect, and to 'the understanding of spiritual things', women 'seem to be of a different nature from men'. The Bible confirms they are 'intellectually like children'. There is a decisive 'natural reason' why women are as they are and why most consorters with evil spirits are women. The reason is a woman 'is more carnal than a man, as is clear from her many carnal abominations'. Even before the Fall, the first woman was created imperfect, deceiving, doubting and weak. The detail that God made the first woman from one of Adam's ribs (Gen. 2.21) is made to support the further belief that the first woman 'was formed from a bent rib, that is, a rib of the breast, which is bent as it were in a contrary direction'. God made a big mistake, because 'through this defect she is an imperfect animal, she always deceives'. Samson's wife deceived him by her tears (Judg. 14) (never mind that she was being blackmailed, by men – Judg. 14.15). Her example shows that all women are by nature deceitful. A woman is also a natural doubter, a fact allegedly confirmed by the derivation of the Latin *femina*. It comes from *fe* and *minus*. *Minus* means in Latin roughly what it means in English, a 'lack'. And that is why womankind is 'ever weaker to hold and preserve the faith'. Devils seduce more women than men, because women are a pushover. Easy prey: easy lay.

Scripture is made to show that the emotions of women are as equally defective as their understanding. The anger of women is 'as the tides of the sea' – 'always heaving and boiling'. Women are jealous and envious: Sarah of Hagar (Gen. 21), Rachel of Leah (Gen. 30), Hannah of Peninnah (1 Kings 1), Miriam of Moses' unnamed Ethiopian wife (Num. 12), and Martha of Mary (Luke 10.38–42). The calumnies mount up. Defective intelligence makes them gullible to temptation. They have 'weak memories' and cannot learn from experience. They have no sense of discipline. They are emotionally immature (the 'defect of inordinate affections and passions'). If they are given political power they cause havoc and disaster with it (Jezebel, Helen of Troy and Cleopatra are adduced as examples). Because men can find the voice of a woman dangerously attractive to them, a woman is said to be 'a liar by nature'. A woman's 'gait, posture, and habit' is 'vanity of vanities' (Kramer and Sprenger, 1948, pp. 45–6).

The cumulative, slut-shaming case against women now reaches its climax: 'To conclude. All witchcraft comes from carnal lust, which is in women insatiable.' Women have a ravenous demand for penetrative sex, if not with obliging men, then with eager demons ('Wherefore for the sake of fulfilling their lusts they consort even with devils'). Men are spared the desire of having kinky sex with demons, because Jesus was a man: 'And blessed be the Highest Who has so far preserved the male sex from so great a crime: for since He was willing to be born and to suffer for us, therefore He has granted to men this privilege' (Kramer and Sprenger, 1948, p. 47).

The *Malleus* provides an eternal warning about the misuse of the Bible and the human misery it causes (Thatcher, 2008). It creates a *moral* problem for today's Christians. What does it say about our traditions that it exists at all? Why is it there? These calumnies about women were fairly standard in the medieval period, and the work itself at the time was regarded as extreme. Nonetheless its theology led (in the same work and in the wider church) to the trial and execution of countless women. While most contemporary societies do not prosecute witches, misogyny and the inevitable violence against women it produces remain. The familiar excuse that we now live in more civilized or modern times cuts no ice. Christianity was stronger (in Europe) then than it is now.

Demonic Bodies

So far we have sampled only the misogyny that fuelled the practice of the prosecution and execution of witches. But what or who is a witch? How can anyone have sex with a spirit that lacks a body? What sort of sex did they have? What were the crimes of which witches were guilty?

There was a medium or diviner at Endor (1 Sam. 28) whom King Saul consulted about the outcome of his battle the next day with the Philistines. This person is sometimes assumed to be a 'witch' (the NRSVA calls her a 'medium'). She conjures up the spirit of the dead Samuel ('Whom shall I bring up for you?' – 28.11). Such persons were necromancers – they communed with the dead. Witches featured in many pagan legends, and not all of them were malevolent. Often their knowledge of the natural world enabled them to be respected as healers. God had commanded through Moses, 'Thou shalt not suffer a witch to live' (Exod. 22.18 KJV, also Deut. 18.10–11) – a key driver in the insistence on their judicial murder. Witches were found in the Bible. That was enough to verify their existence and root them out. Angels had sex with women (Gen. 6.1–3). The supernatural world was crowded with spiritual beings. Incubi were evil spirits who visited women at night to have sex with them. Succubi visited men (evil spirits were all straight – they were gendered constructs). What happened over the long medieval period was the gradual materialization of demons. Augustine had classified all pagan gods as demons, justifying the destruction of thousands of statues and works of art, and the burning of whole libraries (Nixey, 2017). 'Demons were simply a part of the Judeo-Christian worldview. Medieval Christian theologians, however, gave new life to succubi/incubi by reviving the belief that they were actual beings' (Young, 2018, p. 159). The vividness of sexual dreams, at a time when anything sexual was associated with sin, was itself partly sufficient to guarantee the imagined external reality of the images. But the persistence of the *wet* dream (Chapter 13) was to enhance even further the imagined solidification of the fantasy-turned-reality. Dyan Elliott explains, almost incredibly, how the *Malleus* surmises what happens after an unwanted ejaculation:

> Thus a demon would first pose as a succubus, garnering the unsuspecting human male's seed, next would transport it at dizzying speed (so none of the heat of its generative virtue would be lost), and then would shapeshift into a male-seeming incubus. In this form it would impregnate a woman. (Elliott, 1999, p. 33)

The demons of course are fantasies, dangerous phantasmagoria, belief in whom cost many innocent women their lives. They are the product of a crazed, clerical imagination that cannot begin to cope with its natural, God-given, erotic attraction towards women:

> The occasion of involuntary ejaculation, and its phantasmic accompaniments, opens the way to anxious acknowledgment of gender turmoil held at bay by original and inadequate acts of stabilization and exclusion. The clergy had attempted to create a female-free zone premised on a body that was hermetically sealed by ascendant male reason. Women reentered through the fissures in body and soul. The fantasy women that return to our sleeping clerics are masculinized monsters that lure the clerical world toward the witch hunts. (Elliott, 1999, p. 34)

Some of the fantasies in the book are clearly to do with fear of castration. In one report the inquisitors ask, 'What is to be thought of those witches … who sometimes collect male organs in great numbers, as many as twenty or thirty members together, and put them in a bird's nest, or shut them up in a box … ?' One such victim reported that:

> When he had lost his member, he approached a known witch to ask her to restore it to him. She told the afflicted man to climb a certain tree, and that he might take which he liked out of a nest in which there were several members. And when he tried to take a big one, the witch said: You must not take that one; adding, because it belonged to a parish priest. (Kramer and Sprenger, 1948, p. 121)

The answer to the question of how such an incredible story could ever have been entertained by two of the most intelligent Christians of the time is partly provided by the authors themselves: 'that it is all done by devil's (*sic*) work and illusion', both the sight of a nest of penises and the physical loss of one. Who would believe, in advance of the facts, that in the Italian town of Massa Marittima there remains a fresco of a penis tree, dating back probably to 1265 (see King, 2017, for its reproduction and comments)? A modern reader, confronted with such fantasies, may be exasperated by the lack of *any* adequate explanation for them. The fantasy is, of course, an illusion, as the inquisitors themselves say, but it is they who are being deceived by their misogynistic beliefs. Whereas we assume the inquisitors are deluded, they believed they were establishing the truth. What they thought of as an illusion and the devil's trickery still required real, malevolent women, and the witch hunters produced them in their thousands. These women could viciously attack male genitalia. And there were also malevolent men, the anxiety of whose state of mind led them to attribute their penile dysfunction, and even loss, to the *maleficia* of the devil's women.

One of the 'key transformations' that contributed to the witch craze around 1430 was the growing suspicion attached to the practice of magic (Stokes, 2013). Augustine had taught that magic was associated with demons, and a growing scholarly interest in magic led to a determined attempt to reassert the older fear of it: 'The writers of the 1430s attached the simple if diabolic practice of magic to a chthonic ["relating to the underworld"] nexus of evil, an amalgamation of dark stereotypes that had been applied to the early Christians by their persecutors in ancient Rome' (Stokes, 2013, p. 580). The amalgamation included 'most disturbing perversions: child murder, cannibalism, deviant sex, and the worship of evil', and these accusations were directed at heretics and Jews, as well as witches. The common notion of a witches' 'sabbath', and of their meeting in 'synagogues' carried a notable and deliberate anti-Semitic inflection. A parallel transformation took place within the criminal justice system. Justice began to be administered by an inquisitorial process, replacing an accusatory process where complainants accused wrongdoers directly. The confession of sin to a priest was already an inquisitorial process, and this transformation, already used by the church, was supported by it. It made torture, as an additional tool in the process, more morally acceptable and outsiders much more vulnerable. People of some social standing were still able to swear an oath in court and be believed, but 'without the honor and reputation sufficient to use the protection of oaths, outsiders were subjected to much harsher criminal justice, including torture and a much higher incidence of mutilation and execution' (Stokes, 2013, p. 583). Widows and people living on their own, especially if they were poor or lived remotely, were particularly likely to fall under suspicion. Once again, the poor and the vulnerable suffer most.

Other contextual elements combine in contributing to a possible explanation for the belief in witches to have taken hold. Dyan Elliott, in *Fallen Bodies: Pollution, Sexuality, and Demonology in the Middle Ages*, looks to the collective *psyche* of male religious leaders. Belief in demons or evil spirits was widespread, an ever-present reality in ordinary life. Menstruating women continued to be regarded as disgusting. Through Eve, womankind was regarded as a temptress through whom the Devil attacked beleaguered masculine souls. Holy men, being men, desired women no less for being holy, and themselves felt disgust at their insistent bodily promptings and imaginings. Randy clerics had always been able to have sex with concubines (often tolerated by their congregations) and, if Peter Damian is to be believed (Chapter 13), with each other. But in the eleventh century (the time of the Gregorian reforms), the requirement of celibacy was more strictly enforced. The expectation of increased devotion to Mary to compensate for the material loss of close female companionship was unsuccessful. The belief that the bread and wine at holy communion was transformed into the real body and blood of Christ required that any priest handling God's very body was himself expected to be pure in body and soul. The elevation of clergy as a veritable 'third sex', defined against the laity as sexually abstinent, created a burden that many of them found impossible to bear. That burden continues today. The role of imagination clearly played a major part in fantasies about witches: 'The advent of the witch provided unprecedented and unintended corroboration for the images that spawned her' (Elliott, 1999, p. 160). Women, banished from the clerical imagination, returned in gross forms to torment their detractors.

Elliott makes an uncomfortable charge that Christian theology needs to take seriously. It is that the faith uses words in such a way that the materialization of *spoken* objects becomes actual, just by the speaking of them. The three examples she gives demonstrate what is at stake. God *speaks*: the world is brought into being. God *speaks* God's own Word: it becomes 'flesh' (John 1.14). The priest *speaks* the words of consecration over bread and wine: they become God's body. A similar transformation happens with the materialization of the witch. The evil women of the clerical imagination 'were transformed into the conviction that these women, who were so perversely allied with the devil, actually existed'. They are spoken into existence over centuries:

> The repressed sexual desires and thoughts of the clergy do not stay repressed. They re-emerge in the form of the witch. The requirements of clerical celibacy entailed a repression of libidinal instincts, particularly heterosexual ones. Gathering force in the unconscious, the banished instincts broke through into the conscious mind as hideous and predatory fantasy women. (Elliott, 1999, p. 8)

Elliott's work sheds light on how images of pollution, sexuality and demonology – subject to repetition in shifting contexts – made the materialization of the witch 'canonical and compulsory for a people'. Belief in witches, moreover, did not remain simply a matter of dogma but was the motor behind deliberate collective actions that resulted in widespread persecution and murder (Elliott, 1999, p. 161).

The persecution of witches was 'a giant collective fantasy of Western Christians, expressive of their deepest fears. It was an international sickness inspired by a religion of love' (Armstrong, 1986, p. 90). It caused many women to internalize and believe they were guilty of the absurd charges made against them. Even the brooms on which they were alleged to fly may be a product of the male fear of women. As Serinity Young explains, in *Women Who Fly*:

> Traditionally, women are the preservers of orderliness: they keep the cave, hut, house, or apartment separated from the dirt (nature) that drifts in from outside. The witch who turns her broom into a source of freedom rather than domestic drudgery turns the patriarchal social system upside down. (Young, 2018, p. 8)

It is often said, especially in controversies about sex, that the sources of theology are scripture, tradition and reason. The *Malleus* shows us that these worthy sources by themselves are completely useless for doing theology. They may be necessary but they are never sufficient. The work is packed with extensive quotations from the Bible, and from many theologians and philosophers, yet the wisdom found there did not begin to soften its death-dealing impact. All three sources are weaponized. They became the hammer designed to go to work on the anvil of Christian misogyny. Beware! The sources of theology can easily become a hammer to smash inconvenient others. Or they can be hammered into any shape that justifies prejudice and violence.

Enclosed Bodies

The bodies in this section belong to intensely devout women in the Middle and Later Middle Ages who were enclosed in communities because they were thought too dangerous to the reputation of the church to be allowed into the world. They saw visions, heard voices, prophesied, performed great acts of charity and humility, went to gruelling and intrusive sessions with their confessors, but were nonetheless often accused of witchcraft and persecuted, like Margaret Porete, who was burned to death in Paris in 1310 for her 'errors'. Outstanding Christians, who wished always to remain within the Catholic Church and to affirm its teachings, even about women, were never free of suspicion and often became victims of the horrifying misogyny described in the previous section. Inevitably Christian women, whether vowed or not, internalized the gendered estimation of themselves as inferior to men in every way – 'spirit is to flesh as male is to female' (Bynum, 1992, p. 98).

We saw (Chapter 11) that Origen's brand of mysticism spiritualized the very language of desire, emptying it of its sensual qualities. Erotic love, channelled into the relation between God and the soul, or between the divine bridegroom and his bride, flourished in this period. The 'male-stream' (Schüssler Fiorenza, 1985) of Christian mysticism continued the trend. It has been compellingly analysed by the late Grace Jantzen (Jantzen, 1995). Three of her examples are Dionysius (or Pseudo-Dionysius – dates unknown, roughly early sixth century CE), Meister Eckhart (c. 1260–c. 1328) and Bernard of Clairvaux (1090–1153). All of them remain popular today. Dionysius had a huge influence on the Catholic Church, but he is noted here for the gaping lacuna in his works. *Women are never mentioned in all his writings.* His mystical theology proceeded via a hierarchy of being and knowing – indeed he introduced the word 'hierarchy' to theology (Jantzen, 1995, p. 97). Emphasizing the mysterious character of the sacraments and the 'true' meaning of scripture, Dionysius taught that the spiritual path to God passed through the three steps of purification, illumination and perfection. He taught the unknowability of God beyond all the names ascribed to God. The path of the mind to God was a negative one – the *via negativa*. The angels too were believed to exist in a hierarchy of power. So was the church, with its various orders of bishops, priests, deacons and lay men and women. The cognitive path of the mind or soul to God ascended through all things to the One beyond all names who, at the apex of the hierarchy, could be known as the author (the *archè* of the hier*archy*) of all that descended from its source.

It is clear that women were placed at a disadvantage in this system. They were associated with bodies, not minds. They had less access to education, and so to literacy. They 'lacked' the superior minds of men more attuned to the job of illumination or meditation on the scriptures. The orders of the church were closed to them. They were not allowed to teach, and in the hierarchy of being they were for ever inferior to men. Eckhart and Bernard scarcely hold a better record. A feminist defender of Eckhart might point to his willingness to preach, often in the vernacular, to women's communities, and in his surmise that being a woman did not after all preclude a human being from holiness. He recognized their intellectual and spiritual capabilities. But when he speaks *about* women it is always 'in sexualized terms, as either virgins or fruitful wives: that is, in terms of their relationship to men' (Jantzen, 1995, p. 113). His biblical exegesis is filtered through the usual assumptions. Through reason, people share in the image of God, but women's reason is inferior. In opposition to women's mysticism developing in Rhineland in his time, Eckhart insisted that women were too associated with their sensory faculties, their bodiliness, their dimmed reason and their responsibility for original sin for them to venture far on the mystical path. Their visionary experiences were of no importance. Bernard, nearly 200 years earlier, had provided a mystical theology in a different tone: love. God is love. The aim of the Christian and the mystic is to seek union with God through love, and to express their love for Christ in acts of love. What could possibly be wrong with that? Only that Bernard replicates the de-eroticized love we found in Origen. Love for God is spiritual. Whereas both women and men are trapped in bodiliness, women are more trapped in it, and having inferior reason are less able to transcend it.

A different style of mysticism is found among the women (though many differences remain between them): 'There is no intellectualising or spiritualising, no climbing up into the head, or using the erotic as an allegory hedged about with warnings' (Jantzen, 1995, p. 133). Using the poems of Hadewijch of Antwerp (born 1200) and others, Jantzen shows:

> The difference goes deeper than genre. Rather, the genre reveals a different perspective on what mystical union is. It is not a mysticism of reason or spirit, not even of an affective spirit, however loving and passionate that spirit might be. Rather, 'fruition' ["a concept of union with God in direct experience"] involves a union of the whole being, eating and drinking and consuming Love, having her enter one's whole self, in a union so complete and intimate that it is natural to describe it in sexual terms. (Jantzen, 1995, pp. 136–7)

Julian of Norwich (born 1343) spoke of a union of sensuality and substance within the human being, an integration of body and soul in preference to a duality of conflict. Union with God proceeds not by an abandonment of the body and its desires in asceticism or mortification, 'but bringing the whole of the self, sensuality included, into the unity of the love of God in which she believes we are enfolded' (Jantzen, 1995, p. 149). It is sin that produces the binary of mind and body, she thought, and participation in Christ that brings them back together. Just as Jesus had brought God and humanity into a perfect unity (as the Chalcedonian creed teaches), so he unites or reintegrates the person, male or female.

If a woman did not marry, what was she expected to do with her life? She might remain single and live as a relative or a servant in a wealthy household. She would be required to be chaste. A common option was the convent. Many women began their lives there as oblates, donated or relinquished by impoverished parents at a young age. By the twelfth century there was a need for more convents to be built, but these could not contain the number of women who wished to serve God by serving the poor and the sick and living lives of remarkable austerity. Some of these women would join itinerant preachers, the simplicity of whose lives and clothing drew attention to their sincerity and to the contrasting *lack* of poverty within the institutional church. Clare of Assisi (1194–1253), founder of the Poor Clares, ever eager to minister directly to the poor, was forbidden by St Francis to do so outside the convent house. A growing number of women – 'beguines' they began to be called (an old Middle French term for 'member of a lay order') – lived in independent houses where they had more freedom. The beguines and their (fewer) male counterparts, the 'beghards', were orthodox Christians living according to the apostolic model of chastity, poverty and simplicity (Deane, 2011, p. 82). Typically they took care of widows, unmarried women, and wives left at home by their husbands fighting in the Crusades (Liberman, 2014). Their spirituality was impressive – too impressive to be tolerated. Probably 15 per cent of women in the mid-fourteenth century in Cologne were beguines (Southern, 1970, p. 240). The women were not bound by a rule, and from 1215 the creation of new religious orders was forbidden. They were often suspected of heresy. They presented a formidable challenge to the patriarchal church, which ultimately ensured their obedience, tried some of them for heresy or witchcraft, and insisted on their enclosure. In 1421, Pope Martin V required that any remaining groups of women outside of enclosure be destroyed (Jantzen, 1995, p. 207).

These women were also well known for their severe austerity with regard to food. Food would normally be scarce, so frugality in relation to it had a moral and spiritual purpose. But prolonged fasting led to emaciation and amenorrhea, and some women would choose this route (like the women surrounding Jerome) for several reasons. By setting aside their sexuality they made known their lack of interest in marriage or the attention of men. They often exceeded expectations governing the vow of chastity. The reception of bread and wine in the Eucharist was fundamental to the spirituality of them all. They would ingest the very body of God in Christ, and their very receptivity of 'divine food' was itself a source of visionary, poetic and prophetic experiences and utterances. The several works of Caroline Walker Bynum have shown that what seems to be a practice both peculiar and bizarre was for these women actually *not* a determination to mortify their bodies in order to soar above them into the realm of the spirit. Rather, it was a means of identification with Christ, sharing his pain and suffering through their own pain and suffering, while also finding and ministering to Christ as they found him in the pain and suffering of others. But as Jantzen insists, their holiness is also predicated on the internalization of themselves as inferior, subservient and fleshly. It was

> bought at a price which no man would ever be expected to pay ... The identification of women with the flesh, and with the suffering humanity of Christ, meant that the religious symbolism which went most deeply into the psyche was a symbolism which placed women to men in the role of the suffering servant. (Jantzen, 1995, p. 223)

The distinction is important for the theme of this book. There is a real difference between self-denial for the sake of achieving personal spiritual perfection, and self-denial as a form of identification with and devotion to other people. Such women did not regard their bodies as *vile*, as sin-laden and potentially disgusting objects beyond the control of the will. Their bodies were a drastic means of solidarity with the crucified Christ and the suffering poor, and so a union with him of body as well as soul. But their spirituality and their fund of good works, known over most of Europe, did not soften the hyper-suspicion of the church authorities towards them. They had supporters in the hierarchy, and the distinction made there between good and bad beguines (those accused of 'false seeming') (Deane, 2011) was increasingly difficult to make. Some of them, like Hildegard of Bingen (1098–1179) and Catherine of Siena (1347–80), were canonized as saints. But the worse betrayal of these women was for many of them to be identified with their mirror image, the witch, and exterminated. As Bynum explains:

> By 1500, indeed, the model of the female saint, expressed both in popular veneration and in official canonizations, was in many ways the mirror image of society's notion of the witch. Each was thought to be possessed, whether by God or by Satan; each seemed able to read the minds and hearts of others with uncanny shrewdness; each was suspected of flying through the air, whether in saintly levitations or bilocation, or in a witches' Sabbath. Moreover, each bore mysterious wounds, whether stigmata or the marks of incubi, on her body. The similarity of witch and saint – at least in the eyes of the theologians, canon lawyers, inquisitors, and male hagiographers who are, by the fifteenth century, almost our only sources for their lives – suggests how

threatening both were to clerical authorities. Woman's religious role as inspired vessel had come to seem utterly different from man's role as priest, preacher, and leader by virtue of clerical office. And because it seemed so different, it titillated – and was both encouraged and feared. (Bynum, 1988, p. 23)

If you were a pious woman who had visions, you were in danger. But if you were poor, or lived alone, or in the country, you were in greater danger. The degree of your 'otherness' would be greater. As we would say today, you would be queer. As Serinity Young explains in *Women Who Fly*:

The social reality of the women accused of witchcraft was that they were mostly single (either unmarried or widowed), rural (and thus less influenced by elite religious and social views), poor (and thus power-less), and often older. In short, they were women free of male super-vision in an age that had no way of conceptualizing such women; they had to be disorderly because they were 'out of order', that is, outside the hierarchy of God over man and man over woman. If they were not under the rule of a man, they must be under the rule of the devil. It was inconceivable that they could be autonomous. (Young, 2018, pp. 164–5)

But women suspected of witchcraft were by no means the only victims of abusive, discriminatory theology. Jews and Muslims, non-Caucasian people, slaves – there are more horrors to come in the next few chapters.

15

Perpetually Inferior Bodies:
Jews and Muslims

The bodies of this chapter belong to the millions of Jewish and Muslim people who fell victims to Christian interpretations of Jewish and Christian scriptures. They were rendered servile, subjects of calumny and gross misrepresentations; hated, persecuted, exiled, robbed and murdered. The hatred of Jews reached its zenith in the death camps of the Second World War. Relations with Muslim countries remain deeply affected by the atrocities of a millennium ago, and the systematic distortion of the Islamic faith in Christian propaganda.

Chapter 12 noted how the institution of slavery was 'baked in' to Christian doctrine. The Christian life was modelled and lived as a state of slavery – Christians were slaves to their Master, Jesus Christ. Slavery was assumed and scripture supported it. The canopy of metaphor spread over slavery enabled slave owners to blank out the real, servile conditions of actual slaves, while slaves, consciously or not, internalized their enslaved condition as wretched. The sense of social superiority that slavery accorded to slave owners was matched by the sense of inferiority attaching to slaves. This sense of inferiority was not only psychological, but even deeper – an *ontological* state that defined and affected human beings at their deepest level. This chapter shows how a similar process occurred with regard to the status of Jews and Muslims.

Servile Bodies (1) – Jews

A major study of racism in medieval Christianity (Kaplan, 2019) emphasizes that the sense of ontological superiority over others lies at the basis of racism too, and that theology creates and supports it. The study identifies the assumed *inferiority* of one group in relation to another as 'a primary category of analysis', and asserts that 'the creation of a hierarchy in which one group represents itself as superior to another constitutes a necessary element of racism' (Kaplan, 2019, p. 1). Medieval theologians constructed, from scripture, the doctrine of *servitus Judaeorum* (the idea that Jews too were slaves and were to be treated as such). A *servile* body (from the Latin *servilis*) is already half way to being a *vile* body, a body defined by activities considered unsuitable or demeaning for a free person to undertake. The uncomfortable charge to be investigated is that this sense of *hereditary* inferiority, persisting through time, increased in gravity and effect during the period, leading to pogroms against Jewish people during the later Middle Ages. Ontological inferiority, the state endured by women and slaves in Christendom, was not confined to them, but reproduced with regard to Muslims, and later on (as we will see in the next chapter) to the peoples of Africa. It is a heritage almost too distressing to explore.

The development of anti-Judaism, like the development of misogyny and the invention of the witch, is based (at least in part) on biblical texts. It will be necessary to introduce briefly several of these, to understand how they were later interpreted and applied, catastrophically, by Christians to Jews. The first is the story of Cain's murder of his brother Abel (Gen. 4.1–16). God curses Cain, who is forced to be 'a fugitive and a wanderer on the earth' (4.12). Nonetheless 'the LORD put a mark on Cain, so that no one who came upon him would kill him' (4.15).

The second passage is the puzzling and fragmented story (described in Chapter 2) where Canaan, Noah's grandson, is cursed with the status of slavery because his father Ham accidentally found his grandfather (Noah) naked and drunk (Gen. 9.18–27). The third passage is Genesis 21 regarding the fate of Abraham's two sons – Ishmael, whom he had with his slave Hagar the Egyptian, and Isaac, whom he had with his wife Sarah. Hagar and Ishmael are cruelly sent into the wilderness (to die?). God's blessing will be channelled through Sarah's 'legitimate' son, Isaac, and his descendants. Paul refers to this story in his Letter to the Galatians. Consciously treating it as an 'allegory', he associates the *new* faith with Sarah; the older faith with Hagar:

> Now this is an allegory: these women are two covenants. One woman, in fact, is Hagar, from Mount Sinai, bearing children for slavery. Now Hagar is Mount Sinai in Arabia and corresponds to the present Jerusalem, for she is in slavery with her children. (Gal. 4.24–25)

There are several clear references here (and in Romans) to the people of the old covenant being slaves. Paul assures his readers 'we are children, not of the slave but of the free woman' (Gal. 4.31).

The fourth passage is the story of Esau and Jacob. Rebekah, wife of the patriarch Isaac, has given birth to twins, Esau and Jacob. Their rivalry is said to have begun while they were still inside Rebekah's body. The Lord said to Rebekah:

Two nations are in your womb,
    and two peoples born of you shall be divided;
one shall be stronger than the other,
    the elder shall serve the younger. (Gen. 25.23)

The narrative moves quickly on to a famous tale of deception. Esau is the elder brother of the twins, but Jacob connives with Rebekah their mother to deceive their dying father into giving him the father's blessing and inheritance instead. In Romans 9.12 Paul refers to this story. He takes sides between Christian converts from Judaism who believed they were still required to keep the law of Moses, and those converts (influenced by Paul) who regarded themselves as freed from its obligations. He interprets the Jewish scriptures in a way that has been called figural ('allegorical', 'typological' or just 'Christological' will do equally well), finding everything there as pointing in some way to Jesus Christ as its fulfilment. And he does this when appealing to the story in Genesis 25. The new faith, he declares, is the 'younger', and as the text indicates, 'the elder shall serve the younger'. The older faith will 'serve' the younger one. Jews must serve Christians. Paul remained a Jew, but once Christianity had split from Judaism, the text was assumed to imply that Jews must serve Christians.

Two incidents in the Gospels must be added to the list. So the fifth passage is the detail, recorded (only) in Matthew's Gospel, that the Roman governor, Pilate, in order to appease a mob on the verge of a riot, 'washed his hands' of the responsibility for sentencing Jesus and handed him over to the crowd. Matthew records: 'Then the people as a whole answered, "His blood be on us and on our children!" So he released Barabbas for them; and after flogging Jesus, he handed him over to be crucified' (Matt. 27.25–26). The sixth passage is John 8.21–59, where Jesus is depicted as having a conversation with some Jews. In the course of this, Jesus tells them they are slaves to sin. When they say to Jesus, 'Abraham is our father', Jesus replies:

You are from your father the devil, and you choose to do your father's desires. He was a murderer from the beginning and does not stand in the truth, because there is no truth in him. When he lies, he speaks according to his own nature, for he is a liar and the father of lies. (John 8.44)

So far the category 'slave' is only used metaphorically. Jews were not materially slaves, but the *Christian* Jews who wanted to remain obedient to the Jewish law were accused by Paul of being metaphorically enslaved or 'held captive' by it, of living according to 'the flesh' instead of living 'in the Spirit' (Rom. 8). By the time of Augustine, it was widely believed that all Jews, not simply those Jews who, according to Matthew, had bayed for Jesus' death ('His blood be on us and on our children!'), inherited guilt for his crucifixion. God had punished them by allowing Jerusalem to be destroyed, and by dispersing them throughout the world.

Augustine used the Cain and Abel story ostensibly to *protect* Jews. Cain figuratively stands for the Jewish people, and the 'mark of Cain' stands for God's protection of them. But the *identification* of Jews with Cain bore a terrible price: to be cursed, dispersed, punished and made for ever servile in Christian lands. The curse of Canaan was also interpreted allegorically. Canaan came to represent all Jews. Following Paul, Esau (the elder brother) is also made to represent all Jews, who are to serve 'Jacob' (the Christians who came to rule the Roman world). Their servile status within the Empire is confirmed. This is not real slavery, but a heavily theological vilification of Jewish identity that ensures their hereditary inferiority in the eyes of Christians. The figures of Cain, Ham, Esau and Sarah would feature prominently in subsequent supersessionist theologies (theologies that assume the Christian church has superseded the Jewish people as the people of God), and this biblically derived inferiority would cost Jews dear when the canon lawyers started to codify the theology and put it into practice.

The mark of Cain continued to afford some protection to Jewish people while their status as inferior and servile in the lands of Christendom was codified. Even in the twelfth century, and mindful of their subservience, 'Jews flourished in the lands under Christian control, enabling them in various contexts to occupy positions of authority over Christians' (Kaplan, 2019, p. 37). Unlike Muslims they offered no perceived threat to the Christian order. The protection of the mark of Cain became toleration, and such toleration became increasingly limited. Secular authorities were ordered to ensure Jews return to their servile role, and their ensuing privations were considered to be a gracious incentive to convert to Christianity. A Christian may own a Jew. A Jew may not own a Christian.

An undoubted incentive to the justification of slavery in the High Middle Ages was provided by Thomas Aquinas. He taught that there were two legitimate forms of slavery: one entered into human life after the 'Fall'; but the other *existed in the pristine state* prior to that cosmic calamity ('prelapsarian'). He called this economic or civil subjection, and could find no moral argument against it. Superiority and inferiority, domination and subjection, are not only the consequences of original sin, manifested in the sinful world that Jesus redeemed. They belong in paradise, apart from and prior to sin, and so they require no redemption. Calumnies circulated about Jews, stoking anger and resentment – for example that Christian nursemaids were forced to express their milk into latrines if they had taken communion; that Christian slaves, and their sons, owned by Jews were forcibly circumcised; that Jewish men had a mysterious disease of bleeding which marked their inferiority both as Jews and as men (because it mimicked menstruation or was a haemorrhoidal affliction); that Jews used the blood of Christians in religious rituals. Similar absurd and malevolent imaginings were directed against witches. Jews were required to wear clothing that distinguished them from Christians. Should Jews have their children taken away from them? And forcibly baptized? These questions were widely raised, greatly adding to Jewish insecurity. The status of slaves gave them no rights over their children, and Aquinas held it would be no injustice to baptize Jewish children against their parents' wishes. He did not advocate it though, relying only on the precedent that the church had never done such a thing.

But in the twelfth century Jews began to be caricatured in European art with gargantuan hooked noses and other grotesque features. In 1190 in York, 150 Jews were murdered by a Christian mob who had promised them safety in exchange for forced baptism. Many more died at their own hands, besieged in Clifford's Tower, believing suicide a lesser fate than surrendering to Christians. An author from Singapore, herself no stranger to British colonization and racism, asks:

> How often do standard ('mainstream') histories of England discuss as constitutive to the formation of English identity, or to the nation of England, the mass expulsion of Jews in 1290, the marking of the Jewish population with badges for three-quarters of a century, decimations of Jewish communities by mob violence, statutory laws ruling over where Jews were allowed to live, monitory apparatuses such as the Jewish Exchequer and the network of registries created by England to track the behavior and lives of Jews, or popular lies and rumors like stories of ritual murder, which facilitated the legal execution of Jews by the state? (Heng, 2018, pp. 4–5)

The circumstances of Jews throughout Europe were little different from those in England. In the later Middle Ages,

> virtually all adversities in society were blamed on the Jews, who figured as the embodiment of all that was uncanny or subversive of the established order in society. Sorcery, virtually all magic, poisoning of wells, blighting of crops, desecration of the host, and the ritual murder of

Christian boys – these and all other sorts of evils were charged against them. (Hillerbrand, 2017, p. 449)

And the great Protestant reformer, Martin Luther, chose to believe them all. Indeed, he wrote: 'I firmly believe that they say and practice far worse things secretly than the histories and others record about them, meanwhile relying on their denials and on their money' (Hillerbrand, 2017, p. 592). His *About the Jews and Their Lies* (1543) is as distressing to read now as the *Malleus Maleficarum* late in the previous century. It is the starkest example I know of earnest biblical interpretation gone horribly, terribly wrong, with disastrous results for millions of people. His 'advice' to the secular authorities was fourfold: 'First, that their synagogues be burned down, and that all who are able toss in sulphur and pitch; it would be good if someone could also throw in some hellfire' (Hillerbrand, 2017, pp. 588–9).

> Second, that all their books – their prayer books, their Talmudic writings, also the entire Bible – be taken from them, not leaving them one leaf, and that these be preserved for those who may be converted. For they use all of these books to blaspheme the Son of God ...' (p. 589)

Third, they should be 'forbidden on pain of death' to worship and teach, or (fourth) even to mention the name of God within the hearing of a Christian:

> We must not consider the mouth of the Jews as worthy within our hearing. He who hears this name from a Jew must inform the authorities, or else throw sow dung at him when he sees him and chase him away. (p. 590)

But, Luther observed, Christians would still be left with a 'problem', that Jews would still practise their faith in secret. This was his solution:

> We have to part company with them. They must be driven from our country. Let them think of their fatherland; then they need no longer wail and lie before God against us that we are holding them captive, nor need we then any longer complain that they are burdening us with their blasphemy and their usury. This is the most natural and the best course of action, which will safeguard the interest of both parties. (pp. 590–1)

For all his reforming Protestant zeal, Luther did not depart from Catholic theological and social repudiation of the first people of God. Instead, he drove it into new depths of hatred – using vitriol, sarcasm, much biblical learning and gross misrepresentation to produce what must be the classic Christian racist text. His book dismayed most of his fellow reformers and was initially ignored. But the damage done to Jews would become much worse. The racism expressed in this text, with little alteration, would reproduce itself with devastating results for colonized people in the following centuries.

Servile Bodies (2) – Muslims

If Christian racism begins with our treatment of Jews, an equally virulent form of racism was soon to explode with the arrival of the 'Saracens' or Muslims in the seventh century. There was no direct reference to them in either biblical testament, so no biblical understanding of who they were. While Jews were accused collectively and perpetually for the crime of deicide, no such accusation could be made against Muslims, who were unquestionably expansionist and who threatened the governments of Christian lands. Having established to the church's satisfaction the perpetual servitude of Jews, the same scriptures would be used to extend their slave status (in Christian eyes) to Muslims. Ishmael was a key figure in this interpretation. Sent into the desert, and dismissed from the elect line of God's chosen, Muslims must be descended from Ishmael. Did not Paul himself say that Hagar, Abraham's 'slave-wife' and Ishmael's mother, had born 'children for slavery'? Jews and Muslims do not dispute the origin of the peoples who became Muslims in the expulsion of Ishmael and his mother in Genesis 21. Christians from the time of the early church regarded Jewish people (who rejected the 'new covenant') as prefigured by Hagar and Ishmael, children of an old covenant. The status of hereditary slavery is extended to Hagar's additional children, the Muslims. A legal ruling from the early fourteenth century states:

> Sarah signifies the Holy Catholic Church, the handmaiden Hagar, the accursed sect of Muhammad which took its origins from her. Therefore, the Holy Church, symbolized by Sarah, may use that accursed handmaiden as the blessed Sarah had used her, by beating her. She may use her as her Lord commands, by driving her out and depriving her children of inheritance and possession ... For ... they are the offspring of a slave woman, and are therefore themselves slaves. (quoted in Kaplan, 2019, p. 144)

It followed from an exegesis of this kind that just as Sarah turned on Hagar and Ishmael and had them expelled into the desert, so Christians could wage war against Muslims, Hagar's children, and expel them from Spain and other former Christian lands. Since Muslims like Jews are to be regarded as slaves, they too must be in perpetual servitude to Christians. We saw in Chapter 12 how Western Christians came to regard real physical slavery as a consequence of sin having entered the world, a wretched but inevitable state. Augustine's doctrine of the just war recognized that conquered peoples could be turned into slaves. He also defined 'legitimate combat as one which avenges injuries' (Kaplan, 2019, p. 148). But Augustine broadened the definition of what could count as just to include Christian theological pronouncements about God's justice. The way was open, and quickly travelled, from the idea of a just war to the practice of a *holy* war: 'Augustine's notion of justice included respect for divine rights ... [A]ny violation of God's laws, and, by easy extension, any violation of Christian doctrine, could be seen as an injustice warranting unlimited violent punishment.' His permission to avenge, and his broader analysis of justice, 'paved the way for later justifications of holy wars and crusades that punished all manner of wickedness and vice' (Kaplan, 2019, p. 148).

Yes, in doctrine the just war becomes the *religious* just war (against enemies of the faith); that is, a *holy* war. A holy war was already well attested in the HB. A just war required a legitimate authority to authorize it. Pope Innocent IV (pope from 1243 to 1254) declared that he, the pope, *was* such an authority. He is 'the vicar of Jesus Christ', who 'has power over all men. Both infidels and the faithful belong to Christ's flock by virtue of their creation.' If infidels do not obey the pope, 'they ought to be compelled by the secular arm and war may be declared against them by the pope and not by anyone else' (quoted in Kaplan, 2019, p. 150). Christ is Lord over Christian 'sheep' and Muslim 'cattle' alike. When King Duarte of Portugal (1391–1438) sought papal permission to seize the Canary Islands from Spanish control, it was given, and given in terms scarcely to be expected from the vicar of Christ:

By Apostolic authority uninterrupted to the present we concede to you the full and free power, that the Saracens and pagans and other infidels and all enemies of Christ whatsoever, and wheresoever established, the kingdoms, dukedoms, royal courts, principalities and other realms, lands, places, villages, fortresses and whatever other possessions, movable and immovable goods ... might be invaded, conquered, plundered, and subjugated, and their persons reduced to perpetual slavery, besides the kingdoms, dukedoms, royal courts, principalities and other realms, possessions and goods of this kind, be brought and made over to you and your successors, and also be converted forever to your use and advantage and the same successors the kings of Portugal. (quoted in Kaplan, 2019, pp. 156–7)

The generalization 'Saracens' was already to impose an essentializing unity on diverse Arabs and people of the Near East. Jerome had been the first to suggest that Arab peoples called themselves *Sara*cens in order to pass themselves off as descendants from *Sara*h, in order to conceal their 'real' heritage as descendants from Hagar, the mother of Ishmael. Muslim Arabs were accused, falsely, of using the name Saracen in order to portray themselves as legitimate descendants from Sarah, Abraham's wife, not from Abraham's slave and concubine, Hagar: 'Attributing the invention of the name Saracens *to* the enemy, as a sly act of self-naming *by* the enemy, is thus not only a brilliant lie, but one that brilliantly names the enemy as liars in the very act of naming them as enemies' (Heng, 2018, p. 112, author's emphases).

Jerusalem had been under Islamic occupation for over 400 years when local Christian populations, fearing persecution, requested military support. (Jewish people would have argued that it had already been under Christian occupation before that.) Eventually an enormous army drawn from many European countries was amassed, and in 1099 Jerusalem was captured and occupied. Whipping up support for the First Crusade, Pope Urban II recounted to the Council of Clermont in 1095 'a nightmare vision of defiling, polluting Muslims who tortured and eviscerated Christians in the Holy Land, raped women, and forcibly circumcised men, spreading the circumcision blood on church altars or pouring it into baptismal fonts' (Heng, 2018, p. 114). Bernard of Clairvaux (1090–1153), reviver of the Cistercian order and co-founder of the Knights Templar, whipped up enthusiasm for the Second Crusade (a dismal military failure), and even exceeded Urban's vitriol against Muslims. Muslims were not human at all. They were essentially '*malefactors*, agents of evil in the world'. Heng observes: 'On Bernard's authority, then, whoever killed a *malefactor* was not a homicide, a killer of a human, "but if I may so, a *malicide* [malicida]," a killer only of evil' (Heng, 2018, p. 115, citing Mastnak, 2002, p. 125, n. 262). Yes:

On the authority of one of the great churchmen of the century, a killer of Muslims was not really a destroyer of human beings. In elevating war into a world contest against evil, human bodies had become epiphenomenal. A killer of Muslims was only a destroyer of evil itself. (Heng, 2018, p. 115)

In a Holy War, *God* does the fighting. Genocide is inevitable and just, just as it was in Numbers 31, where even the attempt to show mercy was punishable by more rape and death. The details of the massacre of Muslims and Jews in Jerusalem in 1099 are too sickening to recall: 'an unremitting orgy of slaughter, dismemberment, torture, and flowing blood that appalls (*sic*) and nauseates modern scholars' (Heng, 2018, p. 123).

The war of the Crusades was fuelled by an ideological war in which Muslims were a single, common, despicable, vile enemy. In 1143 a Latin translation of the Qur'an was complete. Heng speaks of the 'epistemological capture' of the Qur'an later, after printing was invented. The 'real meaning' of the text becomes controlled by calumnies and falsehoods invented by Christians: 'Invidious fables promulgated about the Prophet pivot on constructing Islam as a lie, and Islam's Prophet as a cunning, deceitful, ambitious, rapacious, ruthless, and licentious liar' (Heng, 2018, p. 116). The cannibalism of the Christian forces – consuming the bodies of their enemies for food – is well attested. Muslims are further dehumanized by being animalized. In these centuries the notion of a 'race' of people is solidified. Not only are Muslims understood as a single entity, defined by their religion, Christians too began to see themselves as a race, in fact a 'blood race', in two senses: saved collectively by the blood of Christ; and identified collectively as the race whose blood is shed by Muslims. Solidarity in the face of the other becomes a racial bond.

The Crusades are believed by some historians to constitute an experiment in European colonial expansion, 'an early model of the European Colonial experience rooted in territorial occupation and political dominion, economic extraction, ideological reproduction, and evidence of a "colonial mentality" and colonial relations' (Heng, 2018, p. 124). Any non-Christian citizen of the world could now be regarded as a potential slave. With a mindset that assumed the superiority of Christians over all peoples, and the supremacy of their papal leader over all lands, the era of colonialism had already begun.

Here is a troubling question: how does the history of relations between Jews and Christians, and Muslims and Christians, affect these relations *now*? We have worked through many instances where violence has been justified both in, and on the basis of, scripture: where a male hierarchy has subordinated women and slaves; where the purity criterion has demeaned the bodies, lives, roles and careers of women; where deeply religious men have conducted an agonized war against their own bodies; where slavery is a natural fact factored deeply in Christian social understanding; where queer bodies are shown no mercy. There are too many silences in traditional accounts of the church's history. If the study of the Crusades can be left solely to the historians (whose proper task it is), that does not absolve theologians from examining the (im)moral basis of the theology which encouraged them. Is theology itself a system of a mistaken purity, striving to avoid contamination from past vile deeds, doctrines and bodies? Historians often warn against 'learning from history', preferring to confine themselves to narrower period detail and to eschew broader narratives. But if *no* lessons can be learned, much of the importance of historical study is lost.

A precondition for harmonious relations is the ability to find goodness in the other person, society or religion. The history of Christian missions would be unimaginably different if the missionaries had been prepared to find vestiges (or much more) of divine love and the presence of God's Spirit within the strange and 'exotic' communities and colonies they sought to convert. Since there is no place where God is not, acknowledging God where God already is, is already a primary aim of mission. The Spirit blows where she wills (John 3.8). Difference can be respected, understood and shared (with unpredictable results) or it can be stamped on and altered or replaced by a powerful Other until it is reduced to the Same without remainder. It is easy for me, an Anglican and a Protestant, taught to believe that my salvation (whatever that is) is obtained by God's grace *through faith alone*, to dismiss as unimportant the many 'works' that constitute the religious life of others, not just Christian others. I don't pray five times a day (God's continuous presence renders it unnecessary) but can't I admire the devotion of those who do, whose vision and experience of the Holy is different, differently 'traditioned' and expressed? I don't pay the *Zakat* or charity tax to benefit the poor, and I don't enjoy the disciplinary and possible health benefits of fasting during the month of Ramadan (finding it hard to go without beer even during Lent). The words of Jesus against judging *anyone* are apposite here, memorably preserved in the KJV:

> And why beholdest thou the mote that is in thy brother's eye, but considerest not the beam that is in thine own eye?
> Or how wilt thou say to thy brother, Let me pull out the mote out of thine eye; and, behold, a beam is in thine own eye?
> Thou hypocrite, first cast out the beam out of thine own eye; and then shalt thou see clearly to cast out the mote out of thy brother's eye. (Matt. 7.3–5 KJV)

The religion of which most Christians are likely to be critical is Islam. Having lived my whole life in parts of a country where the Muslim presence is tiny, I still find myself affirming unexamined assumptions and prejudices about 'them', fuelled by constant newsfeeds about the latest atrocities of Al-Shabab, Al-Qaeda, Boko Haram or 'IS' (Islamic State) and *their* triumphalist ambitions. It is easy and right to be appalled by these atrocities, ideologically fuelled, and the men who commit them. But it is just as easy to forget the barbarism on the Christian side. When I have recalled that, it is easier to understand why there are parts of the world where Christians are hated, and seething resentment stored up over centuries is yet to be addressed and released. Yes, I am enraged by the patriarchy assumed in many Muslim communities and countries, and the severe restrictions placed on women. But there are also women and men in Islamic countries and communities who are hungry for reform, for equality and justice, with whom making common cause is an obvious imperative, and some people in Islam who are enjoying 'reformed' versions of Islam already.

The notion of 'perpetually inferior bodies', the subject of this chapter, strongly suggests that the sense of superiority to be found among Christians as global citizens is what above all we Christians need to lose. It is found in the exceptionalism of the Roman Catholic and Orthodox Churches; in the myriad Protestant denominations and groups whose public faces have written all over them their superiority over other denominations and groups in their uniquely superior understanding of God's word; and in the unexamined superiority of the white race over all others (Chapter 16). Innate superiority comes in many guises – whiteness, European-ness, class, clericalism, androcentrism, sexism, saintliness, doctrinal correctness.

A minimal precondition for just personal, social and political relations is the ability to see ourselves as others see us. The chronic triumphalism of Christian hymnody ('Jesus shall reign where'er the sun/ Doth his successive journeys run' is a local favourite) is less praiseworthy when overheard by non-Christian groups of people. If we cannot repent of past Christian sins, we can at least acknowledge them. The arrogance of James and John, believing themselves adequate to be co-rulers with Jesus in his earthly kingdom was met with a rebuke: 'whoever wishes to become great among you must be your servant' (Mark 10.43). The need for humility as a Christian virtue, well attested in the NT, is not confined to the realm of the personal. It applies also to humility of thought, finding grace through deep listening, swapping certainties for tentativeness, while retaining confidence in our own inherited but chastened faith. Humble service is likely to be more effective than triumphant proclamation.

16

'Oriental' Bodies:
Colonized, Lynched and Traumatized

The bodies of this chapter belong to the millions of people whose lives were colonized by European powers; to the 4,500 women, men and children who were lynched in the Jim Crow years in the USA; to all their successors who struggle to come to terms with racial violence and the threat of violence in the present; and to all people who demean themselves by racist attitudes. The chapter begins with the legacy of colonialism and slavery, and with racism as experienced by black people in the USA. It then moves to the moral outrage of lynching and asks how such an inhumane and barbaric practice could ever have happened. The aim of the chapter is to expose the abusive theology that is deeply complicit in these events, and to inquire how and why its abusive character remains largely unacknowledged and undetected.

But first, a disclaimer. Paulo Freire (Freire, 1970) made clear that people from oppressor groups have a limited consciousness of oppression, however well motivated they may be. As an author who is a beneficiary of white power, education and wealth, and who has lived his whole life away from racial and colonial strife, please view this chapter with suspicion, especially if you are non-Caucasian. Why do I speak from this '(disad)vantage point' at all? Because I want to contribute, as a chastened theologian, to a world that is more just and to a church that is more worthy of the One it claims to represent. While I lack the requisite experience, I do not lack a passion for justice. Whether I speak wisdom or folly, or both at the same time, is for readers to judge.

Servile Bodies (3) – colonized bodies

While the Reformation was taking place in Europe, several European countries began exploring, colonizing and exploiting whole continents. European Christianity was exported first to Central and South America, then to Africa, Asia and North America. The missionaries took with them a strict understanding of marital and sexual morality, and a rigid gender binary. Both of these would clash with indigenous moralities. While it is dangerous to generalize, 'indigenous peoples quickly noted that Christian conquerors and colonists – sometimes including the clergy themselves – did not practice what they preached, but raped local women, entered into bigamous marriage, or engaged in numerous sexual relationships.' Spanish men in the Americas 'had essentially polygamous households', while 'almost all European men in the Caribbean had sexual relations with slaves or free mixed-race women, and half of all slave children in Brazil were baptized with an unknown father' (Wiesner-Hanks, 2000, pp. 143, 166).

The sense of pervasive entitlement to the bodies of colonized women and men, assumed and exercised by many white Europeans, belongs to that innate sense of superiority, backed by military, political, ecclesiastical and mercantile power, that Christian teaching gave them. Edward Said's influential book, *Orientalism* (1979), showed how European thought 'feminized' the East in order to 'conquer' it. The Occidental/ Oriental binary maps well on to the male/female binary with its distorted domination/subjugation axis or its civilized/uncivilized contrast. A similar ideology was generally deployed by the sciences, which took it for granted that nature, the earth, the seas, the mines were all material bodies that required to be controlled, dominated, exposed, opened up, objectified, 'conquered' (like mountain peaks and, in the twentieth century, even space), no matter what violation might have been required for their secrets to be revealed to the penetrating male gaze.

Marcella Althaus-Reid, an Argentinian liberation theologian familiar with poverty in Buenos Aires, wrote an explosive book, *Indecent Theology* (2000), in which (in her own terms) she sought to 'unveil the sexual ideology of systematic (even liberationist) theology'. Theology, she continued, 'is then seen in its true nature as being a sexual project from its epistemological foundation based on a sexed understanding of dualistic relationships and its legitimatory role' (Althaus-Reid, 2000, p. 7). Speaking on behalf of poor women in a heavily colonized country where Catholicism has largely replaced indigenous religions and deities, she was making several accusations: that a male God was made to authorize colonial conquests ('legitimatory role') by whatever force was necessary; that machismo masculinities drew their strength from the conquering behaviour of the conquistadores of the fifteenth and sixteenth centuries; that the asymmetrical male/female binary had come to structure social, political and domestic life and so on. But more than these, she accuses theology of operating, instead of confronting, these binaries. There had been a colonization *of thought* (the 'epistemological foundation'). Even liberation theology, with its emphasis on the relief of poverty and solidarity with oppressed peoples, she held, had failed to acknowledge the extent of its own involvement in emphasizing mind over body and spirit over flesh ('dualistic relationships'), emphasizing liberation as an intellectual project while neglecting real bodies with their 'indecent' desires, their material and sexual needs, and their concealed practices. Colonization had extended even to the way liberation theologians did their work.

Indigenous theologians commonly depict colonization as rape. There is more to this depiction than the actual rapacious behaviour of colonizers. As the Botswanan feminist theologian Musa Dube exclaimed, 'the African continent was being penetrated by the West, its male subjugator, and inseminated with Western seed to give birth to the Westernized African' (Dube, 2012, p. 2). 'The modern history of the Western colonization of Africa was a violent process of taking Africa by force. It was indeed a gang rape, so to speak' (Dube, 2012, p. 3). The Nigerian feminist scholar Amina Mama goes further. Imperialism, understood as 'a militarized expansion of capitalism', was responsible for installing patriarchal regimes 'at the heart of the modern state in Africa' (Mama, 2017, p. 265). Post independence these states *retained* their vulnerability to militarism. The imperial conquests 'bequeathed a systemic vulnerability to militarism, and to repeating cycles of conflict, characterized by sexual and gender-based violence' (Mama, 2017, p. 266). Contemporary law, politics and social policy bear the marks of the old colonialism. After African men were conscripted into service in both world wars, they were indoctrinated into forming

> male-dominant institutions that were to persist after independence. African men embraced nationalism as an assertion of masculine prowess, such that even today, post-independence politicians invoke colonial customary laws – such as the right to beat wives – in the name of masculine renditions of 'African culture'. (Mama, 2017, p. 273)

The history of colonialism reveals secrets so terrible that even experienced researchers still wince at their findings. Even before colonization an estimated 12–15 million African women, men and children were procured by slave traders and trafficked across the Atlantic. Entire regions of Africa were depopulated by the slavers. On a conservative estimate, over 12 per cent of these wretched people died on the way (Mama, 2017, p. 266). England, a country to profit more than most from trading in slaves, still doesn't know how to deal with this crime against African peoples; how to teach its national history honestly in its schools; how or whether to continue to display the public signs of the trade scattered throughout the land in statues and monuments to slave traders and colonizing colonels on horseback and in uniform. These signs exist in churches, town halls, museums, stately homes, public parks, 'ancient' universities. Only now are the complex questions surrounding reparation, or possible reparative activities being discussed (*Church Times*, 2023).[1]

Lynched Bodies

Perhaps one of the most troubling books ever to be written by a black theologian is James Cone's *The Cross and the Lynching Tree* (first published in 2011). His analysis of the complete failure of white theology to deal with racial violence is of particular interest here because of its vilification of black people, its matching failure to engage in self-criticism, its indifference to suffering, and its abusive character. Much can be learned from this white theology if it is given sufficient attention. The period Cone covers occurs after the emancipation of slaves in the USA in 1865, and after the introduction of the Jim Crow laws which severely restricted the rights and freedoms of former slaves. Yet more than 500 years after their deportation from Africa, millions of African Americans are still living in fear of violence. By the 1890s, Cone writes,

> lynching fever gripped the South, spreading like cholera, as white communities made blacks their primary target, and torture their focus. Burning the black victim slowly for hours was the chief method of torture. Lynching became a white media spectacle, in which prominent newspapers, like the *Atlanta Constitution*, announced to the public the place, date, and time of the expected hanging and burning of black victims. Often as many as ten to twenty thousand men, women, and children attended the event. It was a family affair, a ritual celebration of white supremacy, where women and children were often given the first opportunity to torture black victims – burning black flesh and cutting off genitals, fingers, toes, and ears as souvenirs. Postcards were made from the photographs taken of black victims with white lynchers and onlookers smiling as they struck a pose for the camera. They were sold for ten to twenty-five cents to members of the crowd, who then mailed them to relatives and friends, often with a note saying something like this: 'This is the barbeque we had last night.' (Cone, 2013, p. 9)

Human hatred appears almost limitless in these accounts of vengeful cruelty inflicted on innocent and silenced people. Yet to the extent that Christian beliefs fuelled such hatred, there can be no alternative to renouncing them in sorrow and abject repentance. But this is only just beginning to happen. Referring to the crucifixion of Jesus, Peter taunted the Jewish leaders in Jerusalem not just with having Jesus killed but with the appalling manner of his execution: 'The God of our ancestors raised up Jesus, whom you had killed by hanging him on a tree' (Acts 5.30; and see 10.39). How was it, Cone asks, that white people, whose beliefs were based on Christ being crucified to set them free from sin, failed to make any connection between Jesus being hung on a tree and their actions in hanging on a tree thousands of black people? Between 1880 and 1940, nearly 5,000 people died this way (not to mention countless Mexican and Hispanic people as well). Yet the similarities between their violent deaths and the death of Jesus – mob hysteria, humiliation, torture, striking of terror – were never noticed! So 'amazingly similar' were these methods of execution, writes Cone, 'one wonders what blocks the American Christian imagination from seeing the connexion' (Cone, 2013, p. 31).

A partial explanation for the 'disconnect' between conventional understandings of the meaning of the crucifixion of Jesus – the 'first lynchee' – and the victims of the lynching mobs may lie in the different doctrines of atonement. The Protestant denominations had their own 'transactional' theories of how God and humanity had become 'at one', of what was necessary for God to forgive 'sin'. The cross was in some sense necessary for white Christians to get right with God *in their souls*. For black Christians the cross meant something different – the extremity of God's identification with suffering, violence, injustice, torture and terror, agonizingly present *in their own bodies*. It meant radical solidarity of a loving God with them in their plight, offering hope that there was ultimately more to life than the oppression of the present. While not doubting for a moment the significance of the self-surrender of Jesus in Jerusalem in comprehending and revealing the character of God as Love (1 John 4.8, 17), there is a terrible danger in making his crucifixion the centre of a faith (in evangelical jargon, 'crucicentrism'). Once violence and suffering are centre stage, they become normalized, expected, even demanded. They betray their origin in HB narratives (Chapters 2 and 3) and have no place in contemporary faith (Chapter 20). Once suffering is associated with its inevitability, indifference to it ('hardness of heart' is a good biblical description) is also inevitable.

The American sociologist and civil rights activist W. E. B. Du Bois (1868–1963) condemned 'white religion' as an 'utter failure'. The 'plain facts', he wrote, are 'The church aided and abetted the Negro slave trade; the church was the bulwark of American slavery; and the church today is the strongest seat of racial and color prejudice' (cited in Cone, 2013, p. 103). Cone's description not merely of churches but of the white theologians of the twentieth century in the USA is detailed and devastating:

'One must suppose that in order to feel comfortable in the Christian faith, whites needed theologians to interpret the gospel in a way that would not require them to acknowledge white supremacy as America's greatest sin' (Cone, 2013, p. 159). Yes, a perverse theological scheme offering self-delusion was required to pretend that racism is consistent with God's will, like sexism and homophobia. In order *not* to confront these evils, a white male God and a soothing doctrinal orthodoxy supplied the means.

Inoculated Bodies

The bodies of this section belong to the white Christians whose consciences are 'inoculated' against registering the harm they think and practise. 'Inoculation' is the metaphor used by Robert Jones in *White Too Long*, speaking of 'the moral antibodies' that 'preemptively neutralize thornier questions about the current power of white supremacy in our institutions, culture, and psyches' (Jones, 2020, pp. 12–13). He speaks, as this book does, of 'wilful amnesia' in relation to a past Christians prefer to pass over because it contains so many elements too painful to acknowledge. Whiteness is 'the mortar holding together the fortress of white supremacy', while 'purity' (found to be morally damaging in earlier chapters above, and Chapter 20 below) is its chief ingredient. Raised in a household in an all-white town, where we ate only white bread, added white sugar and white salt unnecessarily to food, whitened tea and coffee with milk, and wore clothes that white washing powder made 'whiter than white' (like our teeth whitened still further with appropriate toothpaste), it took the present writer many years to become aware of the connection between whiteness, affluence, moral superiority and, of course, cleanliness.

Another feature of white theology is the desire for quick repentance. Jones calls this 'the white Christian shuffle'. This is his term for the

> subtle two-steps-forward-one-step-back pattern of lamenting past sins in great detail, even admitting that they have had pernicious effects, but then ultimately denying that their legacy requires reparative or costly actions in the present. It's a sophisticated rhetorical strategy that emphasizes lament and apology, expects absolution and reconciliation, but gives scant attention to questions of justice, repair, or accountability. (Jones, 2020, p. 27)

Similar shuffles abound in UK Christianity – the spiritual abuse shuffle, the racist shuffle, the homophobic shuffle, the gynophobic shuffle and so on. In Jones' view white Christians inoculated themselves against any suggestion of self-criticism

> by projecting an idealized form of white Christianity as somehow in-dependent of the failings of actual white Christians or institutions. The mythology – really, the lie – that white Christians tell ourselves, on the few occasions we face our history, is that Christianity has been a force for unambiguous good in the world. No matter what evil Christians commit or what violence Christian institutions justify, an idealized con-ception of Christianity remains unscathed. This conviction is so deep that evidence to the contrary is simply dismissed. (Jones, 2020, p. 35)

As usual, biblical proof texts were available to justify the cruel exercise of power. A favourite proof text for slave owners was the highly problem-atic parable of Jesus that illustrates the need for disciples to be watchful for the coming of the Son of Man by means of a slave owner meting out punishment to inattentive slaves, actually cutting one of them to pieces for misconduct (Luke 12.46 NIV). The cutting open of the bodies of slaves by lashing was a common punishment, but the next verse – 'The servant who knows the master's will and does not get ready or does not do what the master wants will be beaten with many blows' (Luke 12.47) – offered a persuasive reason for doing exactly what the saying recommended. A well-known autobiography of an American slave (Douglass, 1845) records how the endurance of slavery under a Christian owner was worse than it would otherwise be: 'his own lived experience had convinced him that Christianity's central contribution to chattel slavery was to make it *less*, not more, humane' (Jones, 2020, p. 38, author's emphasis). The 'theological blessing of slavery', continues Jones, 'paradoxically lobotom-ized white Christian consciences, severing what natural moral impulses there may have been limiting violence and cruelty' (Jones, 2020, p. 39).

The problem of how to begin to account for the cruel behaviour of these white followers of Jesus is almost insurmountable. They needed a the-ology that allowed them *not* to confront their manifest cruelties. Perhaps enough has already been documented in this book about the propensity of Christian doctrine to manufacture patriarchy, sexism, antisemitism and racism, and to place these at the service of European powers. These features of Christianity provide the background, but additional nuances can be added to these ideologies with the arrival of Protestantism. The determination to elevate the literal meaning of the text of scripture above other possibilities, along with its determination to elevate and equate the written words of the Bible with the living Word made flesh, undoubt-edly encouraged the owning of slaves and their cruel treatment. Another factor was the priority given to 'the personal Jesus paradigm' (Jones, 2020, pp. 43–4), the spiritual relationship of converted individuals with a God who has no body, divorced from the material conditions that the same followers of Jesus might have apprehended all around them, and to which Jesus himself had once surrendered:

> It's nothing short of astonishing that a religious tradition with this relentless emphasis on salvation and one so hyperattuned to personal sin can simultaneously maintain such blindness to social sins swirling about it, such as slavery and race-based segregation and bigotry. (Jones, 2020, p. 43)

The Protestant God who sacrificed 'His' 'Son' is both unspeakably violent and unspeakably unjust, so it was perhaps inevitable that believers swayed by the image of this violent God themselves became unspeakably violent and unspeakably unjust in following 'Him', inoculating themselves against awareness of their own sins, even as they rejoiced in divine forgiveness.

Unhealed Bodies

Tracey Michael Lewis-Giggetts has written deeply and movingly about the trauma of African Americans in the face of racial violence. It is a semi-autobiographical, theological reflection from a contemporary African American woman whose life and family have been deeply touched by it. In the pages of *Then They Came for Mine*, readers learn the sense in which most African Americans still suffer, individually and collectively, from trauma, from 'what we carry inside from our ancestors as a result of the very real systemic racism and violence we encounter regularly' (Lewis-Giggetts, 2022, p. 28). Readers learn how racial trauma manifests itself physically, how black Americans internalize how white people think of them, and encounter racism in their daily lives. This violence encompasses 'all America's institutions and systems (judicial, legal, religious, policing, religious, economic)' (Lewis-Giggetts, 2022, p. 59). But in the next few paragraphs and without deflecting attention from the pain of black Americans, I will draw from her book insights about what racism does to *white* people. Instead of the familiar idea of black people internalizing the vilifying view of white people about black people, the process will be reversed. What do we need to internalize? How are white people, and in particular Christians, seen by this godly black Christian woman? How do we manage so to diminish ourselves?

As Lewis-Giggetts describes the need for black people to be healed from racial trauma, she makes it clear that white people too need to be healed, and they need to understand their need for it. A principal charge is that we have lost our capacity for empathy. If we still had it, we could not go on as we do. Responsible, directly and indirectly, for so much pain and violence, part of us has been numbed by our insensitivity to suffering. It is a condition of the soul that is not confined to white Americans. White people can't

> deal with how both the legacy and current demonstrations of racism and white supremacy still infect them. Eschewing discomfort in favor of color blindness has had devastating effects on the ability of the church to dig up this deep-rooted sin at the source. (Lewis-Giggetts, 2022, p. 21; see also pp. 121–2)

Seen from her perspective, white Christian discipleship is imperilled because our lack of empathy mars the image of a God of love within us. We don't see how we have become infected by belief in our own supremacy and inoculated against self-criticism. Failure in love for others has led to failure in self-love, to a dissatisfaction with ourselves that we dare not name. This failure impedes the healing of black people too: 'The healing of Black and Indigenous people from racial violence and the trauma that is birthed from it nearly always requires accountability from those who either perpetrate or benefit from that violence' (Lewis-Giggetts, 2022, p. 31). There is yet more pain to be endured from supposed white allies who say or do nothing. It is the 'collective inaction of so-called woke white people within the body of Christ that burns us the most' (Lewis-Giggetts, 2022, p. 87). Our 'silence is violence', akin to the violent silence that routinely follows reports of *sexual* abuse in the churches (Chapter 20).

The need for a white theology that upholds all these evils, either excusing them or, better, not drawing attention to them – so the facing up to them can be indefinitely postponed – is aptly demonstrated in *Then They Came for Mine*, and overlaps with the themes of this book. In this theology there has to be a 'manufactured hierarchy' of value, insists Lewis-Giggetts, drawn up by powerful ecclesiastical and political leaders, *requiring* the inferiority of marginalized groups. Yet there is no way of reconciling the hierarchy with the core belief that everyone – yes, everyone – is made in the 'image of God'. Then there is the question of white evangelism – 'the very skewed, colonizing, missionary mindset of many white Christians "who disregard" the real possibility that Jesus may already be there, just not in a form they recognize'. They 'fail to see anything of value in those communities already, a blessing for them waiting in the midst of the people the white Christians are claiming to save' (Lewis-Giggetts, 2022, p. 43). Here is a charge that can be made about much of the European missionary effort, and much contemporary evangelism as well.

Another feature of white theology is a sacralized version of identity politics. This is the appeal to the type of unity Christians claim to have through their faith in Christ. Because *Christian* identity is thought to exceed in importance all other identities, especially those of race, sexuality and gender, the invalid conclusion is regularly drawn that other identities don't matter, because 'once we become believers our only identity is found in Christ' (Lewis-Giggetts, 2022, p. 49). This identity enables all other identities to be regarded as less important, or even unimportant, especially if they cause discomfort to white Christians. It provides another way of overlooking systemic inequality and its causes.

We noted in Chapter 12 that the Latin word for 'Lord' is *Dominus*, and suggested an incompatibility between the modern presentation of Jesus as 'the Servant King' and the One who conquers everyone and everything. White theology authorizes racial domination, violently when necessary. 'That need for control and, dare I say, domination is one major factor that leads to the false notions and stereotypes that are the foundations of white supremacy' (Lewis-Giggetts, 2022, p. 82). 'Scientific' or 'biological' racism – the pseudo-scientific belief that empirical evidence exists to justify white racial superiority – is the obvious example of a 'false notion'. The characterization of black women as the scheming biblical queen Jezebel (eaten by dogs as punishment for her crimes) (Douglas, 2019) is another. An element of healing for black people is to free themselves from these 'authorized' yet false stereotypes. But there is healing needed too for the white majorities who do not realize how they *hurt themselves* by their desire to control, and by subscribing to racial stereotypes that underwrite their quest for certainty.

Much of the theology in this book deserves the label 'abusive theology', like the white theology Lewis-Giggetts finds, constricting and demeaning her and her community. But the charge of lack of empathy – a simple but far-reaching criticism – might be made of the entire theological tradition:

The theology that many people are attempting to create around their lack of empathy is even more devastating. Some have bought into a bad theology that says empathy is wrong, even sinful, because holy compassion would demand that they set aside their doctrine – the very thing that needs investigation. They've convinced themselves and others that empathy is some kind of idolatry – a way to put the love and care of each other above the love of God – as opposed to the very core of God's intention for creation. (Lewis-Giggetts, 2022, pp. 126–7)

But the simple judgement here – that doctrine overrules compassion – does not stop with white American Protestantism. It has been present throughout these pages. I have said nothing about apartheid in South Africa, an appalling doctrine of white Protestant Christians reinventing the Reformer John Calvin's idea of an 'elect' chosen people. Once again the HB idea of purity was evoked and applied to whiteness. Once again the HB was plundered for proof texts. Conveniently the story of the tower of Babel was pressed into service, a principal tool 'with which to unlock God's providence in the world, namely, the punishment of those who seek unity and the ordaining of separate *volke* (people/nations) as an "order of creation"' (de Gruchy, 2006, p. 396).

Abusive theology, and its vilifying consequences for particular bodies, still seems pervasive and finds fertile soil in political conservatism and the renewed politics of nationhood. But not all white theology endorsed slavery. In particular, liberal Protestants in the USA came to view its abolition as a Christian imperative. There are lessons to be learned from the liberal Protestants 150 years ago. Principal among them is that the abolitionists could not use the Bible directly to advance their case because, as we have seen, the Bible and tradition assumed and supported it. What, then, was to be done? The answer was to appeal to principles *found* in the Bible, to argue from these and to hear the voice of God in the human conscience. But this required seeing the Bible differently, less as an inerrant document containing moral instruction for all time and more as a historically based series of writings relative to their times. In this they were indebted to European biblical criticism, and equally to the widespread acceptance of Darwinian evolution. The popular notions of progressive development among species, nations and peoples, however misleading, aided the new understanding of what was called 'progressive revelation'. Liberal theologians saw progressive revelation not only between the covers of the Bible but in nature and history, including – for them – the abolition of slavery and 'enlightened' scientific understanding.

But liberal Protestantism never became a powerful force in the American churches (see Oshatz, 2011). It developed into the Social Gospel Movement on the one hand and Free Religion on the other, best represented by Unitarianism. For many intellectuals it served 'as a spiritual halfway house between orthodoxy and secular humanism' (Oshatz, 2011, p. 145). Also:

For antislavery Protestants and their liberal heirs, the discovery of historical consciousness represented an enormous loss of theological and moral simplicity. The Bible was no longer a transparent record of the moral law, and being a good Christian required determining the meaning of Christian revelation for one's own time. (Oshatz, 2011, p. 147)

This loss of theological and moral simplicity was too great for many Christians and church leaders to take. It is always simpler to appeal to the authority of the Bible or the pope, however harmful or plain irrelevant the consequences. Religious fundamentalism abhors complexity. That is why it became a new force in the next century. But the suggestion that liberal Christians have no alternative than to rely on their private experiences, and their consciences, is not quite right. There are many *gains* to be registered as well. What a relief it is to be delivered from the urge to dominate, to pretend always to be right! What a relief it is to embrace complexity instead of fearing it! *Renewal* of faith becomes possible when we realize that certainty is unachievable. What a relief to embrace a larger and properly divine concept of God who as Spirit is always present and discoverable among all peoples and creatures! What is required (assuming it is not too late) is a renewal of empathy that extends to all people and to the earth itself. Liberal theology can help with this. It is a positive antidote to abusive theology, on the way to a more worthy representation of Jesus. Alongside liberation theologies, and aided and amplified by appropriate liturgical, sacramental and practical observances, it seeks to rethink doctrine positively and constructively.

Notes

1 The Church of England is beginning to ponder the extent of its wealth derived from the slave trade. It has set aside £100 million to establish a fund to 'address the past wrongs of slavery' from which church investments are said to have benefited (*Church Times*, 2023).

17

Spousal Bodies:
Not What They Seem?

Mindful of the exposure of doctrine that stifles compassion, poignantly described by Lewis-Giggetts in the previous chapter, this chapter is about the doctrine of marriage and its effects on married people. I have outlined and defended a revisionary approach to Christian marriage in several books. It seemed to me, and still does, that the living tradition of marriage offers the virtues of commitment and mutual empowerment; the best environment overall for the safety and well-being of children; and the lived realization of the Christian theological themes of sacrament and covenant, together with the understanding of deep love and mutuality they are capable of unfolding. Sadly, many marriages are not like this, whether or not they are conducted in church and formally blessed. Many descriptions of marriage, including some of my own, are unrealistic, ignoring the dynamics of real marriages. It is necessary to examine this gap between theology and reality.

The legacy of patriarchy, hierarchy, misogyny and sexism described in earlier chapters still flows through countless marriages, causing dissonance and unhappiness, and is yet to be acknowledged and dealt with. Arguments over homosexuality have taken the spotlight off the theology of marriage and the skewed interpersonal dynamics it often generates, while the struggle for equal marriage (inside and outside the churches) has served to solidify the centrality of marriage as the socially approved framework for living together and for sexual relations. It may even have hindered the task of making *heterosexual* marriage more equal. Gay communities the world over are not unanimous about extending marriage to embrace them. Freedom from persecution and prejudice would be a start. While same-sex marriage normalizes the presence of out gay people in society, the refusal of normalization and the living out of alternative relationships to marriage are also, for many, healthy features of gay life that are in danger of being lost. The official teaching of almost all the churches, against almost universal practice, is that intimate relations belong only within marriage. The Methodist Church in Britain is a happy exception to this (2019, sections 2.5–2.6). This chapter is about the suitability of marriage, theologically understood, as the framework within which human eros is to be understood and practised. The bodies of this chapter belong to married couples: those married lives that are both intimate and fulfilling, and those that carry the marks of physical violence and psychological, physical and emotional trauma. The positive place of physical, bodily enjoyment within personal relationships as these are understood and expected in the churches is postponed to Chapter 18. The impact of abusive theology on queer bodies follows in Chapter 19.

Regulated Bodies

We have seen that the NT does not wholeheartedly endorse marriage. There is a variety of views about marriage in the NT, a growing distaste for sexual intercourse even within marriage, and an uneasy compromise arrived at by Augustine between regarding marriage as equal in value to celibacy (Jovinian) and disparaging marriage almost completely (Jerome). Nonetheless the great majority of Christians married, and in 1215 marriage was declared a sacrament but was always second best to celibacy. All licit sexual activity was confined within it, and married Christians became accustomed to being quizzed about their sex lives, and even their thoughts, when they went to confession. Aquinas' strictures about lust became determinative for godly Christians with any spark of sexual desire in their lives.

Aquinas' dislike of full heterosexual sex between an unmarried man and an unmarried woman (simple fornication) is sound. Without the life commitment of potential parents to each other and to any children they may have (which he assumes only marriage provides), the prospects for any child born of the union are 'injured'. Neither must a man enjoy a woman's body for enjoyment's sake because this is *disrespectful*, 'by reason of due honor not being paid to her'. But the enjoyment of *any* sexual intimacy not directed towards the pregnancy of a wife is doomed (as it was for Augustine). It is mortal sin. That is because 'the sin of lust consists in seeking venereal pleasure not in accordance with right reason' (Aquinas, 1974, 154.1). Right reason provides the reproductive imperative. Only the desire for children is licit desire. Kissing and touching too are mortal sins if there is any pleasure in them (Aquinas, 1974, 154.4). The worst sexual sins are those that are contrary to nature and so contrary to its Author. Within this category or 'species' of sins, the least worst is masturbation – 'the sin of uncleanness, which consists in the mere omission of copulation with another'. Anal intercourse between men is almost the worst of sexual sins. Worse still is intercourse with an animal (because a non-human species is involved) (Aquinas, 1974, 154.12).

The penitential tradition expected married couples to refrain from sex during Advent, Lent, Easter Week and Whitsun Week: on Wednesdays, Fridays and Saturdays throughout the year; in any position other than 'missionary' (men on top); and during menstruation or pregnancy. For lay folk who took these restrictions seriously, a majority of days in a calendar year were abstinent. Even with a green light flickering in the darkness above the marital bed, clearing one's imagination from temptation by demons, being careful not to over-enjoy what one was doing or to appear naked must have surrounded love-making with so many dissonances, fears, threats and difficulties that enjoyment must itself have been difficult even for otherwise eager lovers – an intended consequences of the restrictions (see Brundage, 1987, pp. 155–61). It is tempting to imagine, and also quite possible, that few people paid any attention to these restrictions. Yet by the sixteenth century, pressure for the reformation of Christian teaching about sex lay less on removing the restrictions imposed on the laity, more on the immorality of the supposedly celibate clergy. The Protestants thought compulsory celibacy was a burden practicably impossible to bear, but also unwarranted on two grounds in particular (see Crowther, 2015). God had commanded Adam and Eve to 'be fruitful and multiply', and had created marriage as the institution or ordinance within which the multiplication of the species was to happen. Luther also attacked celibacy as one of many futile attempts of Roman Catholics (along with fasting, bodily mortification, going on pilgrimages, performing acts of charity and so on) to earn their salvation through virtuous deeds or 'good works'. Rather, Christians are made right with God ('justified') by faith, and faith alone.

A present-day Lutheran pastor illustrates how the faith/works argument, far from being confined to the pages of history, enters into modern culture wars about sex and the pastoral care of sexual 'sinners'. Minister of a Lutheran congregation in Denver that consisted mainly of casualties of evangelical teaching about the body and sex, Nadia Bolz-Weber compares Luther's proclamation of being made right with God through faith in Christ ('justification by faith'), apart from any 'good works' that may have earned merit in the sight of God, with the behaviour of evangelical churches that refused to accept people who did not display the right, approved works of compulsory conservative heterosexuality:

> Luther took a hard look at the harm in his own parishioners' spiritual lives, specifically their torment from trying to fulfil the sacramental obligations that the church determined would appease an angry God.

Seeing this, Luther dared to think that the Gospel – the story of God coming to humanity in Jesus of Nazareth, and speaking to us the words of life – could free his parishioners from the harm their own church had done them. Luther was less loyal to the teachings of the church than he was to *people* ... (Bolz-Weber, 2019, p. 5, author's emphasis)

Much scholarly ink has been spilt over whether Luther's theological reflections on the human female body were positive, negative, mixed or plain contradictory (Wiesner, 1990). He could mix appreciation – 'There is nothing better on earth than a woman's love' – with contempt: 'Women are created for no other purpose than to serve men and be their helpers ... Let them bear children to death; they are created for that' (in Wiesner, 1990, p. 123). He integrated sexual intercourse into human life with a rare candour. It was 'more necessary than sleeping and waking, eating and drinking, and emptying the bowels and bladder' (Crowther, 2015, p. 671). There was no requirement for abstinence. But if (married) sex was freed from restrictions, gender roles were more restricted, and so the position of women in church and society in the sixteenth century became worse. Why so?

There are no priests in Lutheranism. In the Catholic Church, the role of women was also restricted, but there were powerful abbesses and mystics, and nuns whose charitable works were recognized and deeply appreciated. There were no such roles among Protestants. Another feature of priestly ministry was the need for lay people to come to God through priestly ministrations. Men and women found a certain solidarity in being lay, both dependent on priests, who often looked like a virtual third sex by their very (supposed) abstinence. Luther and the Protestants swept this intermediate level between God and the human away. Was this an overall gain for women? Well, no: 'Reformation theology might have removed the priest, but it replaced him with the husband' (Barr, 2021, p. 23). Luther was adamant that the role of women was to serve men. It was a belief founded in nature and affirmed by scripture. Women belonged within families under male control. They were to serve the household as loving wives and mothers. The Protestants, then as now, prioritized scripture over tradition and reason, and all the scriptures discussed earlier (Chapter 6) are given a renewed status and impetus in reinforcing patriarchy in the home, church and state. The modern family was given new theological justification and its commanding patriarchal character was strengthened.

It is tempting to think that Luther's frank recognition of the sexual needs of women and men accomplished a greater freedom or allowed a greater erotic satisfaction for both sexes. He believed that women, like men, emitted seed, so he presumably had knowledge of, and no hang-ups about, female orgasms. He thought (as most people did in the sixteenth century) that women were randier than men and their unsurveyed presence everywhere potentially disruptive. That was another reason why God had decreed through scripture that women had to be controlled.

Puritanical Bodies

English Puritans within the Church of England (in the sixteenth and seventeenth centuries) sought to return to a 'biblical' understanding of sexuality (as many evangelical Christians do today). They thought their church had not sufficiently abandoned Roman Catholic teaching and practices. The name 'Puritan' suggests a tight new sexual regime, but recent work on the Puritans suggests they were considerably more progressive than the strait-laced caricature 'Puritan' assumes (Doriani, 1996). A key text for them was Hebrews 13.4: 'Let marriage be held in honour by all, and let the marriage bed be kept undefiled; for God will judge fornicators and adulterers.' There were to be no reservations about having and enjoying sex, provided it was only in marriage. Thomas Gataker (1574–1654) believed it was the duty of every husband to follow the advice of Proverbs 5.18–19:

Let your fountain be blessed,
    and rejoice in the wife of your youth,
    a lovely deer, a graceful doe.
May her breasts satisfy you at all times;
    may you be intoxicated always by her love.

It was a duty and delight for a man to love his wife ardently. Paul could be taken at face value when he had said: 'Let the husband render unto the wife due benevolence: and likewise also the wife unto the husband' (1 Cor. 7.3 KJV) (the verse giving rise to the idea of 'the marital debt'). Yes, the Bible urged godly husbands to have regard to the sexual needs of wives in the undefiled marriage bed. Neither was the purpose of marital sex to be confined to the desire for children. The 'linking of affections' was also an end of marriage, strengthening each partner against temptation elsewhere.

Androcentrism apart, this looks affirmative, a body-positive, sex-positive, biblical theology. But the achievement of the Puritans was limited, and one wonders whether there is any theology of the body anywhere and at any time that encourages passion to spend itself and love-making to rise to the ecstasy of safe mutual surrender. *Too much* passion turns out to be as bad as adultery, and turns a man into a beast: 'Yet must modesty be observed by the married, lest the bed which is honorable, and undefiled, Heb. 13.4, in its right use become by abuse hateful, and filthy in God's sight' (Robinson, in Doriani, 1996, p. 40). Yes, there is much abuse in marriage beds, but abuse here is merely the absence of decorum (as it was for Clement; see Chapter 10). The number of times for having marital sex were to be strictly limited (Luther had recommended twice a week). The marriage bed 'must be used as seldom and sparingly as may stand with the need of the persons married' (Whately, in Doriani, 1996, p. 41). Nearly all the Puritan writers advocated prayer as necessary foreplay, petitioning the Deity to keep them from falling into sin prior to falling on each other. To remind them of the danger of immoderate passion was the threat of divine punishment in the form of miscarriages, barrenness or deformed children. The intoxication of young love, advocated in Proverbs, turned out to be metaphorical after all, as Origen, and the Catholic tradition ever since, had insisted (Chapter 11).

Doriani coolly observes that, for all the biblicism of the Puritans, there is no condemnation of passion in the Bible. Indeed, the Bible often assumes it: 'the fundamental issue is not passion as a *basis* for marriage but the legitimacy of passion *within* marriage' (Doriani, 1996, p. 47, author's emphasis). None of the Protestant Churches and sects disagreed with the legal basis for marriage hammered out in the twelfth century, which allowed a marriage to be 'valid' without any sexual relations at all. Once marriage had become a sacrament in the twelfth century, a more precise definition of it was needed. The theologian and bishop of Paris, Peter Lombard (*c.* 1096–1160), held that the declaration of vows – consent – alone made a marriage a 'real' or 'valid' marriage, though others held that it was sexual consummation or first intercourse that de facto accomplished the marital state.

What lay behind the debate was already the outcome of a millennium of negativity about sex, which we have traced in earlier chapters, exacerbated by a conundrum of the time: *was the marriage of Mary and Joseph a real marriage?* Believed never to have been consummated, 'this was one of the reasons why it was believed to be a perfect marriage' (Thatcher, 1999, p. 109). The final position in the Catholic Church was (and still is) that consent makes the marriage valid (*ratum*) and the first (successfully completed) act of sexual intercourse renders it indissoluble. Failure to consummate (*consummatum*) became a ground not for divorce but for annulment. The influence of the allegedly sexless marriage of Mary and Joseph won the day in Western Christendom and has remained ever since. The implication, if not the practice, is that a sexless marriage is the ideal marriage. If the warmth, joy and intimacy of the 'marriage bed' can be limited, or avoided, so much the better.

Violated Bodies

Speaking of marriage *theologically* runs the danger of ignoring its practical reality. If it is God's appointed way of regulating human intimacy, churches have concentrated on protecting it instead of inquiring what goes on inside it. The title of Elizabeth Koepping's recent excoriating work – *Spousal Violence Among World Christians: Silent Scandal* – opens up a reality the churches scarcely dare admit to themselves. This eloquent, fair-minded and meticulous work makes its distressing subject a distressing but necessary read. Koepping is an anthropologist and priest in the Scottish Episcopal Church. She travelled to 14 countries in six continents, having discussions 'in houses, universities and seminaries, churches, house prayer groups, informal gatherings, women's shelters' (Koepping, 2021, p. 10), listening to women from 14 different denominations describe their harrowing experiences of Christian marriage. Her research bears a quiet, unassailable authority.

Her discussion groups used the idea of three levels of violence. 'Shaking, pushing hard, slapping with a flat hand or hitting with a thin stick ... swinging her against a wall by her hair' (Koepping, 2021, p. 14) – that's just level one. All over the world, she discovered, 'the ingrained view of male and female resembles two distinctly different beings' (Koepping, 2021, p. 21), instead of a fundamental unity of the sexes. She notes two strands of Christian thought about wife-beating, 'one being that of Chrysostom and Laurence Hispanus and the other Augustine and Huguccio of Pisa. The first pair opposed, and the latter accepted violence against wives' (Koepping, 2021, p. 41). The 'rule of moderate chastising', proposed by Gratian in 1140, became canon law, and its influence remains strong. Equally harmful for wives was the framework of the household in which the husband and father could be expected to exercise correction 'by word or blow' (Koepping, 2021, p. 42) (and the wife blamed for provocation – 'she made him hit her'). She finds the legacy of the medieval church is still active, 'not only in ideas about men and women in relation to God and each other, but in the very words used to advise and control them' (Koepping, 2021, p. 60).

The distressing testimony from victims around the world, including victims of 'Church leaders as abusing husbands', evokes the hypocrisy and spiritual wreckage brought about by such abuse. There are several reasons why there are hardly any sermons preached about domestic violence, 'as several Korean pastor-friends have said, "because so many pastors beat their own wives"' (Koepping, 2021, p. 64). Church leaders are better able to twist biblical passages in order to validate their actions. They generally do nothing when violence is reported to them (Koepping, 2021, pp. 68–71). Clergy wives are afraid to report violence for fear of reprisal, bringing shame on the church or dismissal. While most married clergy would never 'dream' of harming their wives, 'their silence is sinful' (Koepping, 2021, p. 83) – a collusion with evil, for doing nothing and failing to address the abusive theology that informs violent behaviour is part of the global problem. A well-respected Indian nun was able to speak out about violence against wives only because she belonged to a worldwide order that protected her. She had 'little regard for the bulk of diocesan priests who "enjoyed side-lining when not insulting resident nuns in church so the local people know who counts"', and discerned that seminaries and churches were unwilling to see marital violence 'as a theological rather than a social issue' (Koepping, 2021, p. 105). Many clergy don't even think about or recognize the issue. They are inadequately trained to recognize or respond. Too many leaders blame feminism 'for disrupting peaceful church life' (Koepping, 2021, p. 147). There is a need for 'ministry to the abuser'; that is, the creation of safe spaces for *men* to talk with other men about reasonable and unreasonable behaviour. And there should be recognition of 'the culture card' (Koepping, 2021, p. 150), the tendency to excuse violence as something other people do, while failing to recognize what is going on nearer home.

Spousal Violence Among World Christians is mainly about *physical* violence. Exposing psychological and emotional violence and its consequences for mental and spiritual health would require another book. There is a chilling but unstated parallelism in the book between church responses to spousal violence and their responses to the abuse of children (Chapter 20). These distressing circumstances are probably global. In the 'Christian-saturated' country of Jamaica, for example, the problem of intimate partner violence is exacerbated by Christian doctrines. Church leaders are implicated. Silence about it is maintained. The doctrine of headship supports it. Victims are discouraged from disclosing it. The Bible is thought to be 'against divorce', so a violent marriage must be preserved no matter what. Non-church organizations tackling violence see churches as part of the problem (see Perkins, 2019).

Rachel Starr's *Reimagining Theologies of Marriage in Contexts of Domestic Violence* is another distressing exposure of the problem of domestic violence. Based on research on domestic violence in Britain and South America, she came quickly to see theology as a root of the problem, and sought 'to pay attention to how women's diverse experiences of domestic violence problematize Christian teaching on marriage, and to ask how marriage might be reimagined so that bodily wellbeing was central to the good of marriage' (Starr, 2018, pp. vi–vii). Christian doctrines, she asserts, have contributed to it. Without revision, they are destructive. These ambiguous attitudes to the body and sex have been the theme of the present book.

There is more violence in intimate relationships between unmarried partners than in marriages. The danger to women from male ex-partners is greater still. I am suggesting not that marriage is a dangerous institution per se but that patriarchal attitudes are dangerous in all straight couple relationships. Not all same-sex relationships are free from violence either. We noted in Chapter 12 how, for example, Augustine's three goods of marriage were integrated into a gendered framework of ruler and ruled, where marriage could never itself be a good, even on Augustine's own terms. That framework makes mutuality impossible. Starr shows how the 'good of children' has been used to deny contraception and abortion to women, and to emphasize motherhood 'as the natural vocation of women, and the means by which they are saved' (Starr, 2018, p. 60). 'While women have been praised as mothers, notably through the figure of Mary, their identity has often been restricted to a maternal one, even when they have no biological children' (Starr, 2023, p. 19). These are patriarchal attitudes. Fidelity within marriage is clearly beneficial, but emphasis on it has led to a pervasive climate of male suspicion and coercive control. Faithfulness must be 'refashioned as friendship' (Starr, 2018, p. 50), where mutuality is possible and suspicion less likely to arise. In Chapter 3 we noted how modelling marriage on the covenant between God and God's people led to a distressing imbalance or asymmetry between the two parties. It still does. Starr finds the marriage covenant in the HB prophets to be a shaming metaphor 'which still works to reinforce women's low social status' (Starr, 2018, p. 77). While the idea of covenant, qualified by mutuality, *can* be positive for women, 'covenantal models of marriage may need to be abandoned as intrinsically violent and inescapably hierarchical' (Starr, 2018, p. 82).

Sacramental models of marriage are no less dangerous. The idea of the 'indissoluble bond' has 'resulted in a lasting denial of the legitimacy of divorce within the official Roman Catholic Tradition' (Starr, 2018, pp. 104–5). Churches have emphasized the marriage ceremony instead of seeing the daily realities of married life as the possible locus of sacramental grace (Starr, 2018, p. 117). Escape from violent marriages has been made more difficult. Pastoral advice that assumes indissolubility as the default position can even risk death, especially when laced with mealy-mouthed exhortations about forgiveness. 'Dominant sacrificial understandings of atonement function in situations of domestic violence' (Starr, 2018, p. 126), finding divine justification for suffering in the following of the crucified Christ who 'also suffered for you, leaving you an example, so that you should follow in his steps' (1 Pet. 2.21). In situations of domestic abuse 'salvation is survival'. 'Making bodily survival a good of marriage would transform theological discourse on marriage' (Starr, 2018, p. 177). The three traditional goods, theologically reimagined, may yet enable marriage to be 'spaces of peace, the meeting of bodily needs and loving desires, and the development of just and right relationships' (Starr, 2018, p. 176).

Our conclusions in Chapter 5 about sundered bodies speaks constructively to the condition of heterosexual marriage in its present global forms. Wives are not to be treated as assets disposable on a patriarchal whim. The power to divorce (according to Matthew's Jesus) is limited to a husband, on the general ground of 'fornication'. But 'divorce' in the Western Church meant 'separation' without prospect of a second or a 'further' marriage, or a 'remarriage' to another spouse. A spouse was united indissolubly to her (or his) estranged partner, however miserable, cruel and intolerable the relationship became. Since 2002 the Church of England permits 'in exceptional circumstances' the further marriage of a divorced person in church. Pope Francis has 'unambiguously confirmed that in particular cases, and after a process of careful discernment, the church now officially grants the possibility to divorced and remarried Catholics to have access to the sacraments of Reconciliation and Eucharist' (Knieps-Port le Roi, 2017, p. 3). Among Orthodox Churches it is recognized that marriages become 'spiritually dead'. When a marriage dies there is no point in pretending that it lives on, in any form, amid the wreckage of broken promises and lost hopes. Second and sometimes third marriages are possible within Orthodoxy.

The theological issue yet to be fully owned is that the theology of marriage contains detrimental, mistaken and abusive elements that cause immense harm and can't be concealed by the siren voices that God calls us to suffering, or that the church cannot change its teaching. It flies in the face of experience that a violent marriage is already in grave peril, if not already terminated psychologically by the impossibility of regaining mutual love and respect. How can what has already been dissolved, even by the craftiest of verbal manoeuvres, still be regarded as 'indissoluble' in some unspecifiable sense? It is not only cruel to suggest so. It flies in the face of good sacramental theology. A closer examination of Catholic teaching reveals that a man and a woman marry themselves (by their exchange of consent in the presence of witnesses, including more recently a priest). But *they* are the ministers of their sacrament, experiencing grace (or not) as they administer their sacrament to each other throughout their marriage. That is a sacramental theology that takes the experience of grace, and of course its absence, seriously, and invites a stark contrast with some imagined infusion, administered by the church, that remains undiminished whatever the circumstances (see Thatcher, 1999, pp. 232–41).

So is marriage, theologically understood, a suitable framework within which human eros is to be enjoyed and practised? Suppose we understand the revised *goods* of marriage as faithfulness, mutuality, friendship and children (for couples who desire them), and call them *values* – marital values. Let's now make three obvious observations about them. First, some marriages clearly come to lack these marital values. If it were otherwise, there would be no divorces and no social demand for them. Second, some non-marriages nonetheless embody them. Some people remain committed to each other for life, having never promised to do so in a marriage ceremony. Most people know of children, brought up by unmarried parents, who thrive. Third, marriage then, as an institution, is no guarantor of the provision of marital values, whatever Christians believe about it being a sacrament or ordinance. Rowan Williams has rightly decried 'the insistence on a fantasy version of heterosexual marriage as the solitary ideal, when the facts of the situation are that an enormous number of "sanctioned" unions are a framework for violence and human destructiveness on a disturbing scale' (Williams, 2002, p. 316). Sexual union, he declares, 'is not delivered from moral danger and ambiguity by satisfying a formal socioreligious criterion'. Some sex *within* marriage is immoral.

These observations invite a conclusion: being married (whether or not with church involvement) and embodying marital values are not the same. And it gives rise to a tantalizing question: wherever marital values are found, should not churches be able to commend and name them as the presence and operation of sacramental grace?

Marriage – all the churches now say – is really about love. It is rarely admitted how recent this discovery really is. We learned in Chapter 6 that loving within a marriage is something a husband is commanded to do, not a reciprocal quality expected of a wife who submits to her husband in all things. The 1662 Book of Common Prayer of the Church of England describes 'holy matrimony' as 'an honourable estate' and warns that it

is not by any to be enterprised, nor taken in hand, unadvisedly, lightly, or wantonly, to satisfy men's carnal lusts and appetites, like brute beasts that have no understanding; but reverently, discreetly, advisedly, soberly, and in the fear of God; duly considering the causes for which Matrimony was ordained. (Church of England, 'Solemnization of Matrimony')

In the most recent marriage service, the warning becomes: 'No one should enter into it lightly or selfishly but reverently and responsibly in the sight of almighty God.' The brute beasts have disappeared along with the carnal lusts, and the 'Preface' informs the congregation instead that 'The gift of marriage brings husband and wife together in the delight and tenderness of sexual union and joyful commitment to the end of their lives' (Church of England, 'Marriage'). The contrast of tone and content between the two services over time (1662 and 2000) has often been noted, with varying amounts of approval or disapproval. The cultural popularity of romantic love is probably as much of an influence as any recovery of theological insights on these changes.

An issue to be explored in the next chapter is whether the older tradition, which at least *acknowledged* 'men's carnal lusts and appetites', is more honest in its candid recognition of the murky depths of desire than the twenty-first-century version of marriage, which avoids them, boldly proclaiming the delight and tenderness of sexual union. Can there be an honest Christian theology of the body that rejoices in the body's pleasures, as well as warning about its dangers?

18

Desiring Bodies:
Making Friends with Eros

The desiring bodies of this chapter belong to everyone who experiences sexual desire. Its scope could hardly be broader!

The tradition we have been studying is suspicious, to say the least, of eros, understood here as bodily desire for another (see Kamitsuka, 2015). Even the notorious papal document *Humanae Vitae* (On Human Life), which continued to prohibit the use contraception to Roman Catholics, proclaimed 'the unitive significance and the procreative significance' of marital sex (Pope Paul VI, 1968, section 12). 'Unitive significance' is a coded acknowledgement that a happier sex life leads to happier and longer-lasting marriages. But as usual there are stern caveats. There is an 'unbreakable connection' between these twin purposes, the new basis for withholding contraceptive rights from Catholic Christians. But Catholic bishops in the USA also worry about enjoying (marital) sex too much, either on fertile or infertile days. Reassuring anxious pre-copulative married couples that they 'do no wrong in seeking out and enjoying this pleasure', they are counselled that they

> ought to know how to keep within the bounds of moderation. As in eating and drinking, they ought not to give themselves over completely to the promptings of their senses, so neither ought they to subject themselves unrestrainedly to their sensual appetite. (United States Conference of Catholic Bishops, n.d.)

The Lustful Body

The ghosts of Clement, Ambrose, Augustine, Aquinas, not to mention Luther, Calvin, the Puritans and countless other male theologians, surround the lovers' bodies as they prepare to 'give themselves over' to each other. Moderation is necessary. Restraint is counselled, even though – unlike the Puritans – pre-arousal prayer is not. Given the weight and persistence of the fear of passion in all traditions of Christianity, is it even unrealistic to assume that couples can achieve a thoroughgoing celebration of bodily passion, hinted at in the coy-sounding reference to 'the delight and tenderness of sexual union and joyful commitment' of the Anglican service?

A powerful case from an unexpected source argues 'No'. In *Queer Faith*, Melissa Sanchez argues that the sexual pessimism, constructed, maintained and policed by the Christian churches, is more *honest* in its estimate of the destructive dangers of lust, and the unwelcome self-knowledge it brings with it, than the homage paid to romantic love by liberal Protestant theologians who (it is claimed) influence modern Anglican marriage liturgies. A sexual ethic characterized by 'a humbling awareness of our own propensity to guile, aggression, and self-deceit' (Sanchez, 2019, p. 16) is preferable to the fantasy version based on love. The early Anglican Prayer Book's warning that marriage is not to be undertaken 'to satisfie mens carnal lusts and appetites, like brute beasts that have no understanding' (Sanchez, 2019, p. 119), tells us more about ourselves than modern liturgical encomiums of love that gloss over *what we prefer not to know about ourselves*: 'The modern erasure of sex from the Anglican marriage ceremony exemplifies a larger principle of family values discourse that makes conjugal sex uniquely, even magically innocent' (Sanchez, 2019, p. 121). This, exclaims Sanchez, is no more than a 'Disney version of marriage' (Sanchez, 2019, p. 121). Luther, even after his recognition of the sexual urge as 'more necessary than ... emptying the bowels and bladder', and his defence of marriage for clergy, still reckoned marriage a 'hospital for incurables' (Sanchez, 2019, p. 130). For Luther and Calvin, fornication and married sexual love continued to flow from the same foul stream.

Sanchez's attack on the Anglican 'love marriage' (not, of course, confined to Anglicans) can be rebuffed on theological grounds that have little to do with frothy cultural romanticism. But it requires Christians also to be honest about their bodies and desires. In the main – if church reports are to be our guide – they are not. In reply to Sanchez, first, for nearly two centuries we have known that we are descended from 'brute beasts'. Indeed, our worst instincts may be worse than theirs, not merely inherited but intensified. It should be well known to us by now that we – people, governments – are capable of extraordinary goodness and extraordinary evil. Genocide, war, starvation, torture, universal violence against women, racism – these are horrendous and abiding evils. The strength of lust can lead to jealousy, betrayal, murder, revenge. The Bible contains several such stories. Is there a peculiar insistent pessimism to be attached to the misuse of the sexual urge that cannot be attached to other moral evils? Or is lust exaggerated because the churches' sense of good and evil is so strongly associated with it? Or has the sexual urge become distorted through the very patriarchal understandings of gender? Add shame, disgust, impurity to desire and there is little surprise it gets distorted. These mindsets encourage domination, objectification, possession and corruption. The opposition from churches in the twentieth century to sex education in schools has shown that they preferred children should remain in ignorance about sex and embarrassed to speak about it to their being given real knowledge, unmediated through centuries of guilt. Openness about bodily desires and patriarchal contortions of them are the first steps towards an honest understanding of these desires and a growing ability to balance them with other elements of personal life.

The Frustrated Body

Bodies in this section are those impinged on by impossible Christian teaching on masturbation, contraception and divorce. There are some areas of sexual life where the churches have encouraged change. Divorce and subsequent remarriage is one such area (with only the Catholic Church holding out against it). In the 1950s and 60s the Church of England advocated decriminalization of male homosexuality. But hardly anyone seems to recognize what a transformation has taken place since the sixteenth century over contraception and masturbation. Contraception was a practice Luther and Calvin abhorred. Drawing on the Onan story (Chapter 8), Luther reckoned it 'a sin far greater than adultery or incest' (references in Provan, 1989, p. 19). Elsewhere he calls it a 'Sodomitic sin'. Never lacking in candour he describes how

> Onan goes in to her; that is, he lies with her and copulates, and when it comes to the point of insemination, spills the semen, lest the woman conceive. Surely at such a time the order of nature established by God in procreation should be followed. Accordingly, it was a most disgraceful crime to produce semen and excite the woman, and to frustrate her at that very moment. (Provan, 1989, p. 19)

Luther deserves credit for at least noticing that a man arousing a woman yet leaving her unsatisfied was also a disgraceful crime. Millions of women, whether married or not, still have cause to complain about this. He was aware that the withdrawal method of contraception per se was only part of Onan's crime. Yes, the deed was a 'pollution', but his refusal to honour his responsibilities for the child he was supposed to help to conceive made his sin doubly disgraceful. For Calvin too, Onan's crime was 'doubly monstrous', not merely a polluting act but *child murder*, for Onan sought 'to extinguish the hope of the race and to kill before he is born the hoped-for offspring'. The crime of abortion cannot be expiated, wrote Calvin, but what Onan did was in the same category because 'he tried, as far as he was able, to wipe out a part of the human race' (Provan, 1989, p. 20).

We saw in Chapter 8 that abortion was regarded as child murder. Here even non-procreative sex is shrouded by this visceral designation. It was a much earlier judgement, unreformed in the sixteenth century. Augustine had taught that 'It is more serious to sin against nature than to commit adultery.' 'To act against nature is always unlawful and beyond doubt more flagrant and shameful than to sin by a natural use in fornication or adultery' (references in Noonan, 1986, pp. 172–3). The net was cast wide. Oral and anal sex were covered by acting 'against nature'. So in all probability was 'any intercourse where the form of the sexual act prevented insemination' (Noonan, 1986, p. 173). We will shortly see how arguments from nature can be used to reach a very different conclusion.

Fear of the negative consequences of wasting seed reached a peak in the eighteenth century when masturbation became a medical pathology, understood as a primary manifestation of excessive individualism (Laqueur, 1984). Samuel-Auguste Tissot, a well-regarded Calvinist Protestant neurologist, physician, professor and Vatican adviser, published the hugely influential *L'Onanisme* in 1760. It is interesting to see how the medical profession contributed to what was in effect a masturbatory panic, attributing all kinds of effects to it such as blindness, enfeeblement and premature death. 'At one point, two-thirds of all human diseases, medical and mental, were attributed to masturbation' (Patton, 1986, p. 292), including insanity, epilepsy and 'masturbatory neurosis'. It became the 'secret sin' not only because it did not result in visible pregnancy but because, in Protestant societies, it did not require confession. By the end of the last century, attitudes to it were almost completely reversed, and the *harm* caused by anti-masturbatory teaching was acknowledged and found to include anxiety, guilt, a fear of sexual activity (sexophobia) and a loss of self-love – damaging to a person's self- and social integration (Patton, 1985; and see Patton, 1986). While Christian ethical teaching once followed the medical sciences in condemning it, the harm caused by retaining the teaching is not generally acknowledged. It is another case where bodies and their desires are needlessly vilified.

The basic Christian objection to contraception was its frustration of the only licit purpose of intercourse: procreation. The great pleasure to be found in straight sexual intercourse (given of course not merely full consent but positive mutuality) was neither acknowledged nor admitted. Indeed, given its purely procreative purpose, it is difficult to see how enjoyment could be expected or obtained.

We saw in Chapter 8 that the prevention of contraceptive practices was more about preventing people having sex or exploring their bodies *at all*. There has probably been opposition to this functional, biological constraint, at least among lay Christians, in every generation. But it has a long heritage. Gnostics, who denied the goodness of creation and taught it was wrong to procreate, sometimes, like Onan, used coitus interruptus or alternative forms of infertile sexual contact to prevent procreation, thereby associating contraception with heresy. Augustine confirmed that the Manichees practised it for similar reasons in the fourth century (Noonan, 1986), as did the much-persecuted Cathars (or Albigensians) in the twelfth and thirteenth centuries. But the memoir of John Cannon, a literate English farm labourer, between 1705 and 1719, may show a shrewd circumvention of the reproductive, functional view of bodily intimacy. He records that he had pleasurable sexual relationships with three women, including mutual masturbation, yet he avoided intercourse with them all and considered them virgins when they later married other men (Hitchcock, 1996). No one knows how widespread the practice of bodily intimacies excluding sexual intercourse with ejaculation actually was.

No Christian church approved contraception until the Lambeth Conference of Anglican Bishops in 1930, provoking an angry retort from Pope Pius XI in the same year that it remained a 'grave sin' to frustrate the 'natural power' of marriage to 'generate life' (Lambeth Conference Resolutions Archive, n.d., p. 56). The Anglicans were pioneers, nearly a century ago, in promoting a profound change in sexual ethics. The bishops allowed that there could be a 'clearly felt obligation to limit or avoid parenthood', and when this obligation held, it was up to each married couple to decide for themselves what 'method' to use. The obligations were not stated, but parental inability to provide for children, or for further children, risk to the health of the mother (perhaps exhausted by an already large family), the likelihood of a seriously deformed child being born – these all counted. Not only did the Anglicans at last hand back to married couples limited power and responsibility to decide for themselves about their sex lives. They also, in their own 'method' for pronouncing about contraception, put the well-being of parents and their children first, replacing obedience to natural law with a degree of personal and private agency, and respecting them as persons. They also offered 'Christian principles' to help couples decide for themselves what to do in their sex lives, and so changed the tone of the church's voice. The church becomes the facilitator, the friend, offering guidance to those who sought it, instead of the requirement of obedience.

Humanae Vitae shocked millions of Roman Catholics by upholding the ban on all 'artificial' forms of contraception, including condoms, diaphragms and the newly available birth-control pill. The encyclical allowed 'that married people may ... take advantage of the natural cycles immanent in the reproductive system and engage in marital intercourse only during those times that are infertile' (Pope Paul VI, 1968, 12). Critics were swift to point out that 'natural family planning' of the sort that Pope Paul VI was allowing was contraception under another name (Moore, 1992, pp. 163–5). He accepted the minority report of an advisory commission, 'probably ... sharing the concern of the minority report that the Church could not repudiate its long-standing teaching on contraception without undergoing a serious blow to its overall moral authority' (Salzman and Lawler, 2008, p. 44). But by placing doctrine above people, and the good name of the church above the pastoral needs of its members, he self-administered an even greater blow to the moral authority of the church, to be superseded only by the abuse scandal (Chapter 20), which was even then beginning to come to light.

In 1981 Pope John Paul II, in the face of much dismay and open disregard among the worldwide laity, reaffirmed the Catholic Church's ban, teaching that the 'total personal self-giving' (Pope John Paul II, 1981, section 11) of *every* act of (marital) sexual intercourse was compromised by contraception – a partial withholding of each partner from the other, a failure to share the God-given power of fecundity. We saw that even the 'unitive purpose' of marriage – when married couples at last are free to give themselves permission to fuck like crazy if they want to – must be controlled and kept 'within the bounds of moderation'. A total 'un-withholding' seems impossible.

There can be no doubt that the widespread availability of contraception has increased irresponsible sexual behaviour. Indeed, I once drew attention to *agreement* between papal wrath about its use with a strand of feminism which warned that, by reducing the possibility of pregnancy, it removed from women a major reason for saying 'No' to unwanted attentions and advances (Thatcher, 2000). The benefits of contraception are ambiguous. But the continuing refusal to allow the use of condoms in the time of HIV/AIDS must rank as another prime example of the incalculable harm done by adherence to Christian teaching. Between 33.6 million and 48.6 million people have died from AIDS-related illnesses since the start of the epidemic (UNAIDS, n.d.). How many lives might have been saved if, wherever there was Catholic influence, condoms had not been forbidden (Iozzio, 2015)? In 2016 Pope Francis, while not revoking previous teaching, emphasized instead that 'decisions involving responsible parenthood' are firmly a matter of conscience: 'The parents themselves and no one else should ultimately make this judgment in the sight of God' (Pope Francis, 2015, para. 222). The Orthodox Churches and most Protestant Churches accept contraception as a fact of married life (Zion, 1992, pp. 239–62). Francis' apparent concession, while welcome, is too little too late.

The Graced Body

Graced bodies belong to people who understand themselves as desired. How? Rowan Williams, in a famous essay 'The Body's Grace', provides a theological evaluation of the desiring human body. It is an antithesis of anything 'vile', shameful or impure. Beginning with a fictional account of a woman's unsatisfactory sexual encounter and its after-effects, he observes how in the novel the woman 'has discovered that her body can be the cause of happiness to her and to another'. She refers to this as 'her body's grace'. Williams leaps on the use of 'grace' here and provides a theological definition of it that fits the woman's aroused self-awareness. 'Grace, for the Christian believer, is a transformation that depends in large part on knowing yourself to be seen in a certain way: as significant, as wanted' (Williams, 2002, p. 311). Understanding grace is central to the very purpose of the church: 'The life of the Christian community has as its rationale – if not invariably its practical reality – the task of teaching us to so order our relations that human beings may see themselves as desired, as the occasion of joy.' This is a 'newness of perception' that causes Williams to reflect ruefully on 'why the concrete stories of human sexuality' are only 'grudgingly seen as matters of grace, or only admitted as matters of grace when fenced with conditions' (Williams, 2002, p. 312). These conditions have been widely aired in this book.

I concentrate now on a single feature of this rich, positive, highly unusual essay – the theological link between fulfilled sexual relationships and the experience of *joy*. The very existence of same-sex lovers, writes Williams, queries the instrumental, functional view of sex – 'the peopling of the world'. The functional imperative of procreation does not exhaust its meaning. There is also the possibility

of nonfunctional joy – of joy, to put it less starkly, whose material 'production' is an embodied person aware of grace. The question is the same as the one raised for some kinds of moralists by the existence of the clitoris in women: something whose function is joy. If the Creator were quite so instrumentalist in 'his' attitude to sexuality, these hints of prodigality and redundancy in the way the whole thing works might cause us to worry about whether 'he' was, after all, in full rational control of it. But if God made us for joy ... ? (Williams, 2002, pp. 318–19)

These remarks intentionally subvert almost the entire Christian tradition about the sexed body while refraining from criticizing it at all, except obliquely. Thirty-five years on (the essay was first a lecture given in 1989) we might want to draw attention to the implicit or latent violence even in apparently consensual sex; note that lots of straight sex is far from being joyful; that being desired can also be threatening; and that there is little or no pleasure in clitoral stimulation as a matter merely of learned technique. These important considerations cannot be brushed aside, and Williams himself would, I suspect, acknowledge them. Let's next examine how his suggestions might be developed.

First, 'nature' is fundamental to Catholic moral thought. The Catholic moral tradition can't stop talking about it. We have repeatedly uncovered references to nature in earlier pages: to natural law, natural theology; to unnatural practices, vices against nature, unnatural intercourse, unnatural positions and so on. Even wet dreams are ultimately natural – 'motions of the body implanted by nature'. The idea of nature as a book (the Book of Nature along with the Book of Scripture), through which the purposes of God might be read, was common from the fourth century onwards.

Second, the appeal to nature only makes sense (at least among believers in God of any faith) if God is the Author of nature. 'Nature' of course is a problematic category for believers. It evokes wonder among astrophysicists, cosmologists, biologists and poets. It is also wasteful, cruel and inexplicable in its vastness. The myth of a cosmic Fall is used by Christians in an attempt to account both for human wickedness and natural disasters. But nature remains God's creation, ordered and purposed, however its manifest deficiencies are explained: 'God saw everything that he had made, and indeed, it was very good' (Gen. 1.31); 'All things came into being through him, and without him not one thing came into being' (John 1.3). God has made everything for a purpose, even if that purpose is known only to God.

The primary example of the works of nature is thought to be found in the reproductive organs of species, and the human species in particular. The very recent theological name for this is 'complementarity' (for a comprehensive critique, see Thatcher, 2020). The eager, erect penis fits the moist, awaiting vagina. How convenient! This is how God enables people to 'be fruitful and multiply' (Gen. 1.28). But unfortunately such assumptions turn out to be alarmingly naive. Being lesbian or gay is also a part of nature. Neither are some people straightforwardly heterosexual (or cisgender) (as if this needed to be pointed out). And neither are our reproductive organs merely reproductive.

Third, the clitoris is indubitably a part of nature. Half of all people have one, nestling between their legs, waiting to come out to play when appropriately cued. How did that happen? How did such a thing get there? Could it be there simply for pleasure *tout court*? Or, as Williams says, 'for joy'? And the penis too – is it really just for peeing and occasional baby-making, or is it not also for pleasure, whether alone or in company?

There is hardly a book or an article about sex in Christian theology that does not, usually piously and incontrovertibly, assert that men and women are made in the image of God. That famous text (Gen. 1.27) was used in the NT not to parrot an early version of complementarity but to go on to point to *Christ* as the image of God, just as he was referred to as the 'second Adam'. But let's remain with the standard use of the text: women and men equally are made in the divine image. So far, so good. We can forget Augustine's warning that if women want to see themselves in the image of God they must look not in a mirror but at their husbands (Chapter 12). God is imaged as much by women as by men. Well then, the divine image is just as much 'clitorocentric' as it is phallocentric. Women are endowed with an enviable organ, capable of exceeding any pleasure achieved by the mono-orgasmic male. What purpose did God have, endowing them with such potential pleasure? Remaining firmly with the now standard interpretation of Genesis 1.27, we may safely say both sexes and the relation between them are equally reflections of Godself. Therefore, as far as our imagination allows, it is as appropriate to say God has a clitoris as it is to say that God has a penis. Of course, God has no body at all in patriarchal theology. 'He "is" without body, parts, or passions.'

Fourth, given the known pleasure-giving potential of the human sex organs, why has there been such a colossal clitoral cover-up in Christianity? Any answer to that question would be a long one, so let's attempt some brief medical and theological considerations (which are very closely intertwined). The vagina has often been regarded as an inverted penis – women's genitalia being inside, and men's genitalia outside their bodies. The male body is the default body. On such a view, not only is the womb a poor match for the scrotum, but there is no place for the clitoris at all in the comparison since it is not present in the male body. However, in the seventeenth century the term 'lady penis' began to be used of the clitoris, so some connection is made between the two organs. Rufus of Ephesus (*c.* 110 CE) also mentioned that women masturbate by rubbing a zone of the anatomy that he called the *kleitoris* (Charlier et al., 2020). The anatomy of the clitoris was described in 1559 by Renaldus Columbus of Padua, who claimed that previous anatomists had overlooked the very existence of 'so pretty a thing' (Hall, 2001). The European term 'clitoris' was first coined by Reinier de Graaf in the seventeenth century, and this designation has remained. When it became known in the nineteenth century that female orgasm was unnecessary for a woman to conceive, emphasis on it waned in medical textbooks. It received a further setback when Freud distinguished between a clitoral and an imaginary 'vaginal orgasm', regarding the former as a sign of immaturity. The famous textbook *Gray's Anatomy* failed to mention the clitoris in its 1948 edition (yet another cover-up). But in 1995, the full extent of this tiny organ was revealed. It was not tiny. Advances in both anatomical dissection and magnetic resonance imaging (MRI) have helped to characterize its intricacy. Instead, it is now found to have:

> an otherworldly shape, with the nerve-rich glans merely the external protrusion of an organ that extended beneath the pubic bone and wrapped around the vaginal opening, with bulbs that become engorged when aroused. It looked like an orchid. It was beautiful. (Wahlquist, 2020)

One can imagine dour proponents of a reproductive ethic discouraging women's orgasms, since they were superfluous to the reproductive task. Better to discourage pleasure by mixing it up with phobias and pathologies. In patriarchal theology the clitoris remained covered up, unacknowledged, unspoken, unexplored. I'm grateful to Prof. Helen King for providing the references in this section, and also for pointing out that clitoridectomy was practised in nineteenth-century England, *and that the practice was endorsed by the Church of England*. In the 1860s Isaac Baker Brown founded the London Surgical Home for the Reception of Gentlewomen and Females of Respectability suffering from Curable Surgical Diseases, including epilepsy and hysteria. The cure was clitoridectomy, performed by him. After the publication of his 1866 book, *On the Curability of Certain Forms of Insanity, Epilepsy, Catalepsy, and Hysteria in Females*, Brown was expelled from the London Obstetrical Society, and the London Surgical Home was closed (see Sheehan, 1981). The *Church Times* endorsed the practice: 'The clergy will be doing a service, especially to their poorer parishioners, by bringing [the operation] under the notice of medical men.' The Archbishop of York was a patron of the Home, and the Archbishop of Canterbury was among the Vice-Presidents. There can be no doubt: FGM ('female genital mutilation') was practised in England, and the Church of England endorsed the practice.

The medical ambivalence towards the clitoris cannot be dissociated from the heavily androcentric theology explored in the present volume. The influence of religious belief on medical practice and everyday life is usually underestimated, and in Victorian Britain it remained considerable. One can almost sense the misogyny present in the movement of the surgeon's knife, exercising male power, excising the 'lady-penis', improving the imperfect female body (to make it more docile), and making a church-approved contribution to women's sexual and overall 'health'.

The Joyful Body

The joyful bodies of this section belong to women and men who have freed themselves from patriarchal attitudes towards themselves. A sexual ethic emphasizing procreation as the main purpose of sex can still overlook women's pleasure entirely, since (we now know) a female orgasm is unnecessary for pregnancy to occur. It is safe to say the lack of orgasm in many millions of women is a cause of serious and preventable unhappiness. How would a natural theology look if it took *all* the provisions of nature seriously and included the organ whose purpose is joy? If our 'parts of shame' (*pudenda*) were instead parts of joy ('*laetanda*' perhaps!)? Where 'full rational control' was *not* the last word in sexual expression? If there was more than a 'hint of prodigality' (Williams' phrases) in the joy of sex because it reflected the divine nature of the loving God, *and therefore could be expected among the creatures where the image of God is embodied*? Suppose we were to borrow Freud's term 'penis envy' (the supposed state whereby a young woman, when she realizes she does not possess a penis, envies everyone who has one), and speak instead of the real homologue of the penis – the clitoris – instead? '*Clitoral* envy' would be easily understandable. With 8,000 nerve ends – twice as many as the phallus – who would not want one? Sure, if penis envy has any remaining psychological currency left, it lies in the desire of women to share social power with men in exchange for the domination of men over women. But clitoral envy would have social outcomes too. It might lead to the desire for non-domination, to place the other beyond the urgent imperatives of the thrusting male self.

But there is no need for recourse to Freudian theory. Let's consciously unlearn Origen and his wholly mystical approach to the Song of Songs (Chapter 11 above). No longer are the senses to be plundered for metaphors that purport to tell us something about some other extra-sensory world. The longing of the lovers for each other in the Song *is* how the passionate God is already present to them (Stuart and Thatcher, 1997, p. 206). That entire 'mystical' way of thinking about God – seizing on body parts (and sounds and smells) – in order to soar above them in flights of fancy could become instead a celebration of 'the body's grace', the rediscovery of the divine flame within human passion. There will always be a place for mystical experience in theology and spirituality, but why at the body's expense?

There are many theological considerations to ignite the body's grace and banish its *dis*grace from Christian souls whose relation to their bodies may be troubled. The problem is theological – the package of beliefs that starts and ends with shame (Chapter 2). It will be taken up again in Chapter 22.

19

Queer Bodies:
Harmed Yet Hopeful?

Graced and joyful bodies were contrasted in the last chapter with lustful and frustrated bodies. The bodies of this chapter belong to LGBTIQ people who have been harmed by Christian teaching and practice, whose lives are unlikely to be graced and joyful. Rather, they have been made to endure humiliation, shunning, self-loathing, low self-esteem, exclusion, guilt and failure. In many cases they have never broken free from the oppressive teaching imposed on them. Even those on their way to recovery speak of post-traumatic stress. Such people sometimes identify as queer.

Queer theology is currently popular. 'Queer'

> originated as a word simply meaning 'strange', but over time became increasingly associated with issues of sexuality and gender. By the early twentieth century, the word had become a derogatory term for LGBT+ (lesbian, gay, bisexual, transgender, and other sexual and gender minorities) people, but also one used by some people as a form of self-identification. (Slater and Cornwall, 2022)

Queer bodies in this chapter belong to people who *are* regarded derogatorily by mainstream churches and their teachings, and to those same people as they have come to understand themselves, with or without the 'help' of Christian teaching.

Shepherded Bodies

'Shepherded' bodies are those placed under a particular physical and spiritual discipline that presents itself as 'pastoral' support. When Cardinal Ratzinger (before he became Pope Benedict XVI) wrote his 'Letter to the Bishops of the Catholic Church on the Pastoral Care of Homosexual Persons' (Ratzinger, 1986), it seemed as if he was exercising a caring *pastoral* ministry to gay people, speaking of them with respect as 'persons', not as inverts or sodomites, or other products of hate speech. While there was little about pastoral care in the Letter, there was a lot about homosexuality being intrinsically disordered, about the teaching of the church being authoritative and unrevisable, and about the impossibility of gay people forming a 'complementary union'. Bishops were warned that:

> No authentic pastoral programme will include organizations in which homosexual persons associate with each other without clearly stating that homosexual activity is immoral. A truly pastoral approach will appreciate the need for homosexual persons to avoid the near occasions of sin. (Ratzinger, 1986, para. 15)

Particularly noxious is the insistence that God wills a life of suffering for gay people:

> What, then, are homosexual persons to do who seek to follow the Lord? Fundamentally, they are called to enact the will of God in their life by joining whatever sufferings and difficulties they experience in virtue of their condition to the sacrifice of the Lord's Cross. (Ratzinger, 1986, para. 12)

The idea of joining one's personal suffering to the redemptive suffering of Jesus was once used as pastoral advice to wives coping with the labour pains of birthing and then nursing unwanted children. Conservative lesbian and gay people using the label 'same-sex attracted' (or SSA) sometimes like to think of themselves as willing sufferers for Christ's sake, as martyrs, enduring physical and spiritual trauma because it is God's (inscrutable) will that they should do so. But the appearance of pastoral care, offered to lesbian and gay people specifically, has grown substantially in the Roman Catholic Church. Courage International is an official organization – an Apostolate – devoted to it. Based on the spiritual writings of Francis de Sales (1567–1622) and developed by Fr John Harvey, Courage International has five aims: first, 'To live chaste lives in accordance with the Roman Catholic Church's teaching on homosexuality (Chastity)'; second, 'To dedicate our entire lives to Christ through service to others.' Third comes, 'To foster a spirit of fellowship' (to combat loneliness). Fourth, the value of 'chaste friendships' is recognized, followed by the need to be 'good examples to others' (Courage International, 2023). While there is a 12-step programme, borrowed from Alcoholics Anonymous, which is 'an integral part of courage discipline', visitors to the website are assured that 'the heart of the apostolate is always a personal relationship with Christ as a member of His Mystical Body – as He heals us and gives us the strength to grow in the virtue of chastity'.

The programme may help some gay Catholic Christians if they accept the teaching and the authority on which the programme is based and embrace the support it offers. There are testimonies to its efficacy on its slick and expensive website, and it would be churlish not to believe them. But there remains a mountain of difficulty with the pastoral ministry of Courage International. First, we might notice that each of the five aims is binding on *all* Christians, not just lesbian and gay people. There is nothing new about any of them. All Christians are called to live chaste lives, to devote their lives (as far as they can) to the service of others, foster a spirit of fellowship and friendship, and share their faith-filled outlook more widely. What *is* new is the *intensification* of these aims in the case of lesbian and gay Christians in the expectation (no more) that more fervent practice will address and overcome same-sex desire. For very many that is not going to happen, and for them the cognitive, emotional, psychological and spiritual dissonance between their experience and the church's expectations will be made worse.

Courage International assumes Catholic teaching about homosexuality cannot be changed, whatever the sciences and gay Christians say. It explicitly assumes the 'neodogma' of the 'complementarity of married love', which gays, because of their condition, can never achieve. Yet more troubling is the widespread assumption that chastity is the equivalent of celibacy. That is an absurd conflation. Despite its association with celibacy and virginity (and that other negation of sexual activity – continence), it is not the same. Chastity is broader – the virtue of sexual restraint, not necessarily sexual abstinence – since the Catechism of the Catholic Church rightly states that chastity is a state of life required of married people as well. 'People should cultivate [chastity] in the way that is suited to their state of life' (para. 2349). But there are other 'states of life' apart from marriage. Having sex and living chastely are not opposites. Chastity tells us whether, when and with whom to enjoy pleasurable physical intimacy. It is much too important to be lumped together with continence (which the Catechism also does).

One wonders *where the priority of love lies* throughout this whole pastoral enterprise. Its founder is an ultra-loyal Catholic. It is explained that his 'gift of love to others first bound him to the universal Church, to the Pope and the Bishops in communion with him. Fr. Harvey never worked outside of an abiding obedience to Christ and to His Vicar on earth.' It is not love for gay people, it seems, that primarily inspired him but love for the church, its hierarchy, its unbending teaching and its requirement for transparent obedience. In the safest pair of hands, then, this carefully qualified love is directed towards gay Catholics who, it is made clear, need to be *healed*. This is what loving gays means. The adaptation of the Alcoholics Anonymous programme reveals the assumption that a gay person and an addict need similar treatment, to enable them to manage or recover from a damaged state of being. Such a mismatch has serious consequences.

The programme replicates the negativity about same-sex desire and the bodies who experience it that has been sketched in earlier chapters. For many it leads to what Jarel Robinson-Brown has called 'the spiritualization of suffering' (Robinson-Brown, 2021, p. 16), the perverse assumption that mental anguish and torment, brought on by abusive theology, is somehow pleasing to God. Who wants to worship such a God? My next criticism of this attempt to heal gays is the hardest one to make because it extends analysis into the 'heart' of what looks to be a beautiful arrangement between the healed gay person and Jesus, 'the Chaste One, in order to live chastely in Him'. For:

> Prayer of the heart is the way to union of heart with the Sacred Heart of Jesus. It is this union of one's heart with the Sacred Heart of Jesus which also brings healing and strength to the family members and friends of persons with SSA [same-sex attraction].

These pious words, presumed to describe the process of religious healing, may just be pious words, nothing more. They may be profound, they may not. They may point to an ineffable experience but if they do, the experience is beyond both description and examination. They may be a con trick with beautiful words and deleterious consequences.

This mystical uniting of the heart with the heart of Jesus is the precursor to the efficacious 12 steps that wean the errant queer person from their erroneous and sinful ways. Indeed, the second aim, 'To dedicate our entire lives to Christ through service to others', may itself be little more than posturing with holy words. The aim may also be read, not too unkindly (I hope), as entering a life of unhealthy self-examination and self-absorption (albeit based on the sacraments, spiritual direction and reading, prayer and meditation, confession and so on, and not on 'service to others'). At least eros for the forbidden other is dealt with not by denial. It's now OK to be gay and Catholic. 'Shepherded' gays are permitted to be 'out' to each other, to their families and their church. But that God-given aching for intimacy with a cherished other is not allowed expression. Chaste friendships are encouraged, though one wonders how chaste these are and where the required boundaries are drawn.

'Converted' Bodies

Fortunately not all gay Catholics take the route of the Courage Apostolate in working out their salvation. New Ways Ministry and Rainbow Catholics offer alternative perspectives. The 'converted' bodies of this section have suffered attempts to convert them from gay to straight, by conversion therapy. A mainly Protestant and evangelical organization founded in 1976, Exodus International held out the hope that the reorientation of same-sex attraction was possible. In 2006 it had over 400 local ministries in 19 countries. But in 2012 the then president, Alan Chambers, declared that conversion therapy did not work and was actually harmful. He and several other prominent members apologized for the pain and havoc they had caused to the lives of sincere innocent Christians. The organization closed, and the harm it caused to believing Christians who opened themselves to its ministry can never be measured. On a smaller scale, another evangelical 'ex-gay ministry', Courage UK, also closed in the same year after 25 years of activity (Marks, n.d., 'Post Courage'), and for a similar reason. Jeremy Marks, its director, explains:

> Over time, though, I noticed that the people coming to us for help and hope were becoming depressed and even suicidal. It became clear that our teaching – that people must remain celibate, unless they *really* felt they were ready for heterosexual marriage – was harming people.
>
> Another few years after that, I realized that the people who were doing well were the ones who had accepted their sexuality and found partners. They thrived with love in their lives. I had to recognize we had been wrong the entire time, even if we acted with the best intentions. Openly LGBT people were flourishing in the way I thought we would have, if we'd managed to change. (Marks, n.d., 'Jeremy's Story', author's emphasis).

Courage International wants gays to be healed. Union with the heart of Jesus releases the required therapy. It wants gay people 'to turn away from' a sinfully active sex life; that is, to be 'converted'. Whether this is conversion therapy depends on how wide the definition of that term is allowed to become. The *OED* defines it as:

> Therapy or treatment intended or claimed to change or suppress a person's sexuality or gender identity, esp. to make a gay or bisexual person heterosexual, or to make a transgender person identify with their birth sex; the practice of attempting to change or suppress a person's sexuality or gender identity in this way.

The topic is increasingly prominent in all the media. Several films, like *Pray Away* (2021) and *Boy Erased* (2018), detail and dramatize the havoc inscribed on the lives of innocent victims by Christians following Christian teaching. When I wrote this chapter (January 2023), the British government had promised legislation to ban the practice, but had delayed its implementation because of media pressure about the inclusion of trans people within the proposed Bill.

It is certain that this lamentable practice continues in many evangelical and fundamentalist churches throughout the world. Reports of similar abuse come from all the major world faiths. The Ban Conversion Therapy website (n.d.) posts testimonies of sufferers. Here are two of them, sufficiently graphic to illustrate the harm it causes. George was told: 'God would never make me gay. Instead, it was the work of demons, and was likely a result of an early life experience.' The conversion therapy arranged for him 'involved the laying on of hands and intensive prayer, the casting out of demons, being forced to describe my homosexual experiences and to repent publicly'. The prayers, he recalls, were lengthy and loud, 'two adults shouting and pushing down on my head, forcing me to my knees'. He too did not realize that what he was undergoing was conversion therapy. He writes:

> The lasting impact of conversion therapy is undeniable. It has taken a lot of years for me to work out who I am, and to embrace that and accept it. It was only last year, aged 38, that I finally accepted that I am gay. In order to accept the person I have always been, I have now broken a good man's heart, turned over my children's world, set off a bomb in my life and been through a huge mental health crash. I am devastated by the pain that's been caused.

Justin was raised in 'a born-again evangelical household'. For six years, he writes:

> I would be down the front of the church every Sunday, with people laying their hands on me, speaking in tongues ... Going through an exorcism is an incredibly emotionally traumatising experience. There is a definite expectation of a reaction to 'prove' that it's working and that the Holy Spirit has 'exorcised the demon within'. Afterwards, you are left alone, lying there shaking, crying, screaming and thinking, 'Did it work?', 'Is that me?', 'Am I normal now?', only to realise very quickly that it didn't. You're then left thinking, 'What's wrong with me?'

Similar stories to these are legion, and attested around the world. In other cases the gap between conservative teaching about sexuality and the experience of non-heterosexual Christians is so great it has led to suicide (Mann, 2015). There is 'spiritual dissonance', a variant of 'cognitive dissonance'. The latter is the experience of the gap between beliefs and generally accepted knowledge; the former is the gap between personal faith, or personal identity, and the religious system that condemns it. Clearly, spiritual dissonance can be too great a burden to carry. The Evangelical Alliance, a UK organization claiming to be made up of hundreds of organizations, thousands of churches and tens of thousands of individuals, continues (at the time of writing) to support the practice of conversion therapy. Behind the veneer of contrition for the harm their tradition has already caused to hapless casualties, the Alliance still shows an alarming lack of awareness of the abusive character of conversion therapy and the abusive theology that supports it. I suspect the argument it uses is used worldwide. First the contrition: 'There are many practices that are a shameful aspect of our history, and Christians should express profound regret for any part they have played in perpetuating the stigma, discrimination and harm towards people because of their sexuality' (Webster, 2021). Well, that was easily said. There is no mention of the abiding, abusive theology that brought these calamities about. Next, apparently innocuously, they insist that the proposed legislation to ban conversion therapy is likely to compromise religious freedom. Such freedom is sacrosanct. Aiming for the high moral ground, they assert:

> However, where an individual chooses to seek pastoral and prayer support, we believe that the best approach is to allow them the support they want to respond to their sexual orientation and desires in a way they choose. For Christians, this means that they are able to live in accordance with their beliefs.

But this 'support' may include all the abuses just described and endured, since a vulnerable individual may choose, or be persuaded to choose, 'to seek pastoral and prayer support', while remaining unaware of the intense religious pressures surrounding them, unaware that conversion therapy is being attempted, and unaware also of the prolonged psychological and spiritual dissonance that is likely to follow. This is a woeful failure to recognize real lasting harm caused by deeply held religious beliefs and practices.

The ignorance of the Evangelical Alliance about the harm it causes may also be displayed in the image on their website (in January 2023) that illustrates its position on the inviolability of religious freedom. Showing a young woman, back to camera, with hands of two other young women laid on her shoulders while a third is in attendance, all of them praying, is intended to depict a peaceful, gentle, consensual prayer scene with no coercion, no dominant males present (for once), and the one prayed for receiving the help she has freely requested. But the picture may be open to a more sinister interpretation. Is it designed to indicate that conversion therapy is harmless, freely chosen, freely given, prayerfully sought, gently administered? Are all those contrary testimonies really about something else? Thankfully not all British evangelicals think this way.[1]

Troubled and Troublesome Bodies

Conversion therapy is used in harmful attempts to make lesbian and gay people straight. But it is also used on people who are gender dysphoric and considering gender transitioning; and on intersex and bisexual people. Lesbian and gay people who are cis-gender are troubled by the expected social norm of compulsory heterosexuality. But the bodies of intersex and trans people are troubled by social norms in a more direct way. Intersex people trouble the social expectation that all human bodies belong, or ought to belong, to one or the other of two rigidly defined sexes. They are of course troubled by these expectations, especially if they are Christians worshipping in complementarian churches where sex differences continue to matter. Trans women and men are troubled by the misunderstanding and misinformation that circulates around them. They too trouble social assumptions about fixed sexed and gendered identities (see Thatcher, 2020, for extended theological discussion of the theological issues pressing in on intersex and trans people; and Cornwall, 2015a, for definitions, and the differences between each (Cornwall, 2015b)).

When the UK Government consulted in 2018 about the reform of the Gender Recognition Act of 2004, 'a torrent of anti-trans rhetoric' was unleashed (Beardsley, 2023, p. 27). Some feminists are troubled by whether trans women are 'real' women. Some journalists prey on women's genuine concern to protect their own safe spaces by inflaming the fear that trans women may be predatory men in disguise, lurking in public toilets about to pounce, or in women's refuges. Others point to unrest between the LGB and T constituencies. The LGB Alliance is a lesbian-led secular organization that objects to LGBT groups 'where it is "transphobic" to reject partners of the opposite sex who "identify" as lesbians' (LGB Alliance, 2020). In these circumstances, when campaigning groups clash, clear understanding of and empathy for trans people is needed more than ever, especially in churches.

What do Christian trans people want? They want to be listened to, and not regarded through polarized lenses (O'Brien, 2016, p. 50). They want non-transgender majorities to understand the traumatic conditions under which they generally live their lives. Some transsexual people want medical intervention in order to bring their bodies into line with their social expression, but there is disagreement on classifying gender dysphoria as a medical condition (Woolley, 2016, p. 43). Others testify that 'the journey they undertake is primarily a social, spiritual and psychological one, and while the physical changes are important milestones they are only one aspect of a complex journey' (Dowd and Beardsley, 2018, p. 115). Christian trans people are weary of their misrepresentation in, or of being ignored by, church documents. Roman Catholic trans people suffer the full force of Vatican polemic against them. They are said to be duped by 'gender ideology', and found guilty of the sin of hubris in attempting to choose the sex other than that which God intended for them. I have roundly dismissed this allegation elsewhere (Thatcher, 2020, pp. 72–6).

There have always been intersex people, or 'Bodies in Between' (Green, 2013). And they often caused 'social disruption', because if they did not manifest a predominant sex by the time they reached puberty, they 'had the potential to disrupt the practices of prayer, burial rights, and any number of circumstances' (Green, 2013), including ordination, the right to own property, and the legitimacy of individual marriages. Intersex people, if their condition is known, trouble most churches, and in turn are troubled by them, because they do not conform to the male–female binary in which so much conservative theology is invested. Sara Gillingham writes as someone born with variations in sex characteristics (VSC). She explains this means: 'I do not fit into the typical understanding of what it is to be male or female' (Gillingham, 2019). She endured irreversible corrective surgery when she was one year old, causing her continued stress, and her true condition was concealed from her until her forties. She was invited to join the Living in Love and Faith (LLF) project. I suspect her experience is typical of many intersex Christians. She writes:

I have faced discrimination in church, and from Christians outside church; I have been called 'possessed' and 'an abomination'; I have had rumours spread about my gender and embodiment; and have been worn down by the constant drip of being called 'disordered'. The Church has, largely unwittingly, 'othered' people from birth if they do not fit normative assumptions about what it is to be made in God's image …

The difficulty for the bishops [in LLF] is that I am still judged by some to be disordered, someone created as a result of the Fall, someone in need of being corrected or in need of surgeries which, research shows, have such detrimental outcomes for countless people's mental and physical health – including mine.

She later felt compelled to resign from the project, like Beardsley who also resigned, 'citing "dishonesty and hostility" from both conservative and liberal Christians' (*Church Times*, 2019).

The 'B' in LGBTIQ is frequently overlooked (Robinson, 2015). Bisexual people are hardly mentioned in LLF. They complain of being misunderstood and confused by lesbian and gay people, but some bisexual Christians situate themselves deliberately on the boundary between gay and straight, and lesbian and gay, finding in that very space that they make their own contribution to the overcoming of sexual binaries and hierarchies. 'My bisexuality,' writes one, 'far from being a sin, disease, or case of confusion, might be God's way of working gracefully in me against exclusivism and categorization, on behalf of God's joyful and inclusive kingdom' (Udis-Kessler, 2000).

There is a growing number of groups of people whose bodies have become subjects of theology at the present time, outside the designation LGBTIQ. 'A severe drawback in our obsession with bodies as sites of sexual misdemeanor', writes Robinson-Brown,

> is that it has rendered us immune to all that our flesh can teach us – we have neglected the basic human sacrament of bodily interaction as we have become imprisoned by a rupture in communion, a fear of the flesh. (Robinson-Brown, 2021, p. 29)

Queer theologies, like this book, address this 'fleshly immunity', and so do other recent theologies. Foremost among these is disability theology (surveyed by Creamer, 2015; and see Eiesland, 1994; Brock, 2021; Jacobs and Richardson, 2022), which begins, and finds wisdom in, the experiences of many types of disability. Trauma theologies (a still newer category) begin with the many experiences of trauma experienced by traumatized people (see O'Donnell and Cross, 2020, 2022). Even the miscarrying body becomes the creative basis for rethinking traditional doctrines as theology is reimagined out of 'messy origins' (O'Donnell, 2022).

'Christian churches', writes Shelly Rambo, 'must reckon with their histories of harm against women' (Rambo, 2020, p. xvi), and also with the harm done to men and to children. They 'have not simply failed to witness trauma inflicted by others; they are sites of trauma's perpetration' (Rambo, 2020, p. xvii). The people whose bodies are troubling to the churches and who are troubled and damaged by their teaching, and yet who remain active within them, are the heroes and heroines of this book. Here is powerful testimony to the virtues of faith, hope and love, even during and after the traumas involved in belonging. But we have yet to examine the church itself as 'a site of trauma's perpetration'– a 'vile body' – the subject of the next and even more troubling chapter.

Notes

1 Jayne Ozanne is a tireless campaigner in the UK for the full acceptance of LGBTQ+ people inside and beyond the church. She identifies as an out lesbian and 'affirming' evangelical, and has a strong following among British Christians, especially through the ViaMedia.News weekly blog. She is the director of the Ozanne Foundation, and the Founder of the UK's Ban Conversion Therapy Coalition. Through the Foundation a successful initiative was taken to establish the Global Interfaith Commission on LGBT+ Lives.

20

The Church:
A Vile Body?

The vile body in this chapter belongs to the church: yes, to the church who throughout its history has abused children, and women (and men too), continues to abuse them and often denies that it has done so. That is why, with the greatest regret, the church may be characterized in this way. In Chapter 1 we noted six areas shaped or influenced by bad theology: the absence of women's leadership in most of the worldwide church; increasing violence against women; spiritual abuse; racism; homophobia; and sexual abuse, together with its concealment. The intervening chapters uncovered some of the roots of this theology. Inasmuch as this vilification continues, then the church must see itself as responsible for it – a reviling, or vile, body. In this chapter there is a reflection on the outcomes of the Living in Love and Faith (LLF) process, and some indication given of the extent of the abuse crisis in the worldwide church, and the Roman Catholic Church in particular. A further examination of the abusive theology underlying it is postponed until Chapter 21.

A Repentant Body (The Church of England)?

During the writing of this book the LLF process has come to an end. The bishops of the Church of England (Bishops of the Church of England, 2023) issued a summary response document. They are 'deeply sorry' for 'the ways the Church of England has treated LGBTQI+ people', and 'for this we repent'. They say they have been studying the scriptures and 'reflecting on the Church's tradition'. They are 'united in our condemnation of homophobia'. They re-commit themselves to the six 'Pastoral Principles', summarized in the document as 'the need to address ignorance, to cast out fear, to acknowledge prejudice, to speak appropriately into oppressive silence, to admit hypocrisy and to pay attention to power'. They set themselves a programme for 'future work', but this does not appear to include the church's urgent self-examination in response to the IICSA's reports. There are to be new 'Prayers of Love and Faith', which 'will offer clergy a variety of flexible ways to affirm and celebrate same-sex couples in church, and will include prayers of dedication, thanksgiving and for God's blessing'. Drafts of these prayers are published already (General Synod, 2023), and will be available before this book appears. Even before the drafts emerged, the Archbishop of Canterbury declared in advance he would not use them.

These prayers must not be understood to confer any marital status on same-sex couples who wish to marry or who are already civilly married. No, there is only one 'Holy Matrimony, which remains the lifelong union of one man and one woman, as set forth in its canons and authorized liturgies'. There weren't sufficient votes in the House of Bishops to recommend any change to the church's doctrine of marriage. Same-sex marriages are not real marriages, although the bishops say they 'want to find ways of affirming same-sex couples'. The continuing practice of conversion therapy is still exercising their minds because 'Guidance for good practice in praying with others' is to be produced. However, 'while the material would need to reference questions of coercion, this would not be its main focus'. Of course not. This book closes before these developments have been completed.

In 2017 the Archbishop of Canterbury admitted the 'need' for 'a radical new Christian inclusion in the Church' (Archbishop of Canterbury, 2017). Six years later the bishops say, 'We *continue to seek to be* a church that embodies "the radical new Christian inclusion"' (Bishops of the Church of England, 2023, emphasis added) – a tacit admission that the whole project fell short of its own aims. The blessings are a gain, and for some the most that could have been achieved from the LLF process. Others are bitterly disappointed. The white Christian shuffle of Chapter 16 has become the straight Christian shuffle. There has been a small shuffle forward. Some have drawn attention to the parallels between the behaviour of the bishops in issuing this document and the behaviour of abusers. Why so?

Given the church has not rid itself of abusive theology, the suggestion is not surprising. The church admits it has been 'profoundly wrong', yet with no thought of abandoning the theology of sexuality that vilifies LGBTIQ people and is responsible for the 'homophobic response in our churches'. The bishops have been studying the scriptures. Which ones? Certainly not the ones we have examined in this book, which are morally objectionable, and which *obscure* claims about God's unbounded love that the church wants to proclaim. They are silent about these, just as the church has also been silent about the abuse going on in its midst. Do the bishops not see the connection between homophobia and epistemic injustice deeply rooted in a particular type of theology? Have they even heard of it? Let's view this apology from the point of view of the people to whom it is given. Soft apologies generally make matters worse for victims and intensify their suspicions. There have been countless apologies for racism in the church. The church has had to apologize for the number of apologies it has made while making little improvement. Now it is apologizing, yet again, to the same people.

'For this we repent.' Is this not abusive behaviour, typified by the untrustworthy apologies survivors of domestic abuse receive from their abusers? Are LGBTIQ people to be expected to *accept* the apology, again as victims are often pressured to do? What is saying sorry worth if it is not accompanied by a radical change of behaviour (which the doctrine of repentance exists to promote), and an admission that the theology responsible for homophobia was, and remains, abusive? Earlier generations required penances sometimes lasting for years in the attempt to ensure that repentance was genuine, and real sorrow for wrongdoing encouraged. Is homophobia really to be condemned? What penances might the church itself prescribe for itself, to give meaning to its repentance? Over how many years? The Lambeth Conference of 1998 condemned the 'irrational fear of homosexuals' while 'rejecting homosexual practice' (whatever that was) as 'incompatible with Scripture'. How will the latest condemnation be any more effective? As long as the vilifying theology is in place, LGBTIQ people will be vilified.

We saw in the previous chapter a great need for wariness when pastoral guidance is issued. Does there not need to be a frank examination whether *any* of these pastoral principles, illustrated by expensively produced videos languishing on YouTube, has been transparently applied and upheld? '*The need to address ignorance.*' What confidence can there be that ignorance has been addressed, when history was written out of the formal discussions as the project progressed (King, 2020)? That is certainly *paying attention to* power – using it to avoid difficult conversations about scripture, about history (and in particular about marriage). The bishops say they have consulted the church's tradition, yet the themes of the present volume have not been acknowledged or discussed. Indeed, one might suspect they have been kept hidden for fear that, in discovering them, doctrine and practice would need to change.

'*Cast out fear*'? LGBTIQ people will be able to speak a lot about that. I wonder whether the arguments in the Church of England about sexuality over the last half century, culminating in LLF, have been conducted *in a climate of fear*; fear of offending conservative minorities, fear of their threats of withdrawal, schism and withholding of funds; fear of disunity (!); fear of offending African churches in countries where gay people live in fear *of their lives*; fear of re-examining the bad theology that taints women, upholds whiteness, keeps LGBTIQ people in the closet; fear of coming out; fear of being wrong.

'*Acknowledging prejudice*'? Well, that was always going to be difficult when there is disagreement about what counts as justified belief. As we saw in Chapter 1, *epistemic* violence is embedded in systems of knowledge that hurt people. If we inherit such a system we need help in recognizing the violence in it. Appealing to the system merely keeps the violence hidden, just as the ecclesiastical system of bureaucracy kept abuse hidden. In England, though not in Scotland and Wales, theology continues not merely to authorize but to insist upon inflicting pain on lesbian and gay Christians, as well as on the women priests who are called to work alongside the men who still have the audacity to think that ministry belongs solely to them. The 'vile affections' (Chapter 6) and sodomitic bodies (Chapter 13) may not be described in such colourful terms, but the discrimination giving rise to them remains.

'*Speak appropriately into oppressive silence*'? Saying what? 'We are sorry'?

Admitting hypocrisy? How did the bishops themselves think their statement had avoided it?

Vulnerable Bodies

When the scale of child abuse committed by members of the Roman Catholic Church became known in the 1990s, the question put was how such an aberration was possible. Now we have an answer. It was not an aberration:

> the conditions informing the clerical sense of entitlement, and the code of silence that sustains it, are embedded in the very fabric of church doctrine from at least the fourth century, increasing over time. Indeed, the degree of secrecy surrounding clerical vice has sharply risen over the course of the twentieth century. (Elliott, 2020, p. 236)

This devastating and unpalatable conclusion is supported by a wealth of evidence in Dyan Elliott's ground-breaking book *The Corrupter of Boys: Sodomy, Scandal, and the Medieval Clergy*. A church council in the fourth century (Elvira, 309 CE) had already threatened with permanent excommunication 'those who sexually abuse boys' (Canon 72) (Laeuchli, 1972, p. 47). The eighth-century *Penitential of Bede* notes the offence of priestly sodomy with children, and prescribes penances whose severity increases in accordance with the rank of the priest (for a list of instances, see Doyle, 2003). Peter Damian's shocked denunciation of widespread sodomy among the clergy (Chapter 13) sounded an alarm. The reforms of the eleventh century included a further attempt to enforce compulsory celibacy. Priests were banned from living with their wives, disparagingly called concubines. They could always be sold to the Turks as slaves. But the imposed celibacy may not have lessened the sexual activity of the clergy. It may have merely deflected it. While sex with women was more difficult to hide, and formally prohibited, disclosure of sex between men, or between men and boys, was less likely. There was something called 'the unmentionable sin' (a neologism in the eleventh century), but since it was unmentionable, no action could be taken against it. It gave the church licence to avoid dealing with it. By turning clerical concubinage into the *real* scandal, attention was diverted away from the other sexual scandal – men's rape of other men and of boys.

IICSA reported that people who were abused sometimes failed to report the abuse because they could not bring themselves to use the required vocabulary or because they didn't want anyone to think they were gay. 'Unmentionability' has not gone away. Elliott suggests that many clerics turned to boys in order to fill the emotional and physical void left behind by the departure of wives and children. Children or young men in monasteries and schools were particularly vulnerable to grooming and exploitation. Behind the walls of church institutions the unmentionable sin was protected from the public gaze and public prosecution. The Gospels contain many warnings against causing someone to 'stumble'; that is, to hinder or damage a person's moral or spiritual development. The Greek word for 'stumble' is 'scandal', and Matthew's Gospel preserves a particular saying of Jesus:

> If any of you put a stumbling-block before one of these little ones who believe in me, it would be better for you if a great millstone were fastened around your neck and you were drowned in the depth of the sea. Woe to the world because of stumbling-blocks! Occasions for stumbling are bound to come, but woe to the one by whom the stumbling-block comes! (Matt. 18.6–7)

Yet by a pernicious irony the church, in order to preserve its good (!) name, and so avoid 'scandal', often tacitly *approved* of the scandal of sex with children. Provided it was concealed (and a highly elaborate system of evasion, denial, prevarication and procrastination existed for this purpose), it was still regarded as an evil, but a *lesser* evil than the greater evil of priests having sex with each other or with women, and the greatest evil of all – bringing the good name of the church into disrepute. That quiet toleration of it still exists. Only sustained outrage and clamour from *outside* the church has made a difference. As Jesus also said: 'For nothing is hidden that will not be disclosed, nor is anything secret that will not become known and come to light' (Luke 8.17).

Priests were required to be officially blameless, without sin. Only they could distribute the sacramental elements to their congregations at the Mass. Only they could pardon the sins of their flock (and of course their own sins) and ensure they escaped eternal punishment. But this blamelessness seemed not to extend to relations with women, even after the reforms of the eleventh century. Many parishes in England *preferred* priests with concubines, in order to protect their wives and daughters from predatory advances (Elliott, 2020, p. 232). But the laity *were* scandalized by priests having sex with minors, and as sex with women became more difficult, sex with boys became more likely. And so the need for concealment became more pressing. Elliott concludes:

> The clergy's sexual abuse of minors preexisted modern understandings of sexual orientation by centuries. It is a sad by-product of compulsory celibacy, a discipline that enables predatory behavior and rewards its concealment – all in the service of avoiding scandal. (Elliott, 2020, p. 238)

After the Reformation, the Catholic Church hierarchy was anxious to maintain a religious 'exceptionalism', proclaiming their superiority over the new Protestant Churches. Any public recognition of clerical sexual misbehaviour would compromise its efforts at ecclesial superiority, so had to be denied, or concealed, with increasing rigour and determination.

Pope Francis, in *As a Loving Mother*, wrote:

> The Church loves all her children like a loving mother, but cares for all and protects with a special affection those who are smallest and defenseless. This is the duty that Christ himself entrusted to the entire Christian community as a whole. Aware of this, the Church is especially vigilant in protecting children and vulnerable adults. (Pope Francis, 2016)

Unfortunately his church has not lived up to his aspirational, maternal description of its work with children, which flies in the face of the facts. The point of the letter was to inform bishops and priests that failure to take action in the case of *any* allegations of abuse could result in removal from office. This failure of course was part of the worldwide scandal, running directly contrary to the title of the letter. Nonetheless it was a positive papal intervention.

Abused Bodies – a worldwide scandal

No one will ever know the extent of the clerical abuse of minors by Catholic priests. Statistics were until recently not kept. Concealment operated at every turn.[1] Attention to the scandal worldwide began in the USA in the 1980s (Keenan, 2012, pp. 17–23), although the Mount Cashel Orphanage scandal in Newfoundland broke in 1971 and dragged on for two decades (Cahill and Wilkinson, 2017, p. 60). A milestone in the USA was reached in 1992 when an investigation by the newspaper *The Boston Globe* led to the prosecution of five Roman Catholic priests. The 2015 film *Spotlight* was based on this investigation. Subsequent investigations revealed a pattern of abuse and concealment in many dioceses in the USA, aggravated by the behaviour of bishops transferring accused priests to different dioceses, where they continued their pattern of offending. The independent organization BishopAccountability.org has kept a massive and still growing database of cases of abuse. It reports that more than 1,360 US priests and religious ordained and vowed before 1950 are known to be accused of abusing children. It 'has identified 95 Catholic bishops worldwide accused publicly of sexual crimes against children and 43 Catholic bishops worldwide who have been accused publicly of sexual wrongdoing against adults only'. The US bishops themselves have made public that there are 6,721 bishops, priests and seminarians accused of abuse, a figure likely to be a fraction of the number of crimes committed. The church has paid out nearly $4 billion dollars in lawsuits over clerical sexual abuse (including the abuse of men and women) going back to the 1980s. It is estimated there are around 100,000 victims in the USA alone (*Newsweek*, 2022).

Chapter 1 described the behaviour of the Anglican and Roman Catholic Churches in England and Wales regarding the abuse of children up to the present day. Sexual abuse and denial are probably a feature of all churches. An independent commission similar to IICSA (Chapter 1) reported in France in 2021. It said that 216,000 people over the age of 18 had been subjected to violence or sexual assault during their minority by clerics or other Catholic religious authorities in France, from 1950 to 2020. This number of victims climbs to 330,000 if lay people working in institutions of the church are added (Teller Report, 2021). In Italy, the country where the highest number of Catholic priests resides, it is reckoned there are hundreds of thousands of cases which have never come to light. There the Vatican has enjoyed a pact with the Italian state allowing it to handle cases of abuse against its priests, denying accusers justice in the secular Italian courts. Almost 5,000 victims were identified in a 2023 report in Portugal, where church officials themselves admitted the actual number was 'much higher than the Church was able to calculate' (Luxmoore, 2023, p. 12).

A similar pact between church and state existed in Ireland, where for decades cruelty against children in church institutions, including the so-called Magdalen Laundries and 'industrial schools', was allowed to remain undisturbed and unchallenged. The Ryan Report (2009) showed beyond doubt that children in institutions suffered terrible physical, emotional and sexual abuse. Thousands of allegations of abuse went unheeded, while abusers would be transferred, only to reoffend. The Irish state failed completely to enforce any of its guidelines around children's education, health or welfare. The anonymization of all accused in the Report inhibited justice being done and accused individuals being identified.

In 2014, at Tuam, Galway, in the west of Ireland, a mass grave containing the bodies of 795 children was found at a former Mother and Baby Home run by the Bon Secours Sisters of the Roman Catholic Church (Weber and Glimois, 2022; BBC News, 2021; Corless, 2020). The unspeakable enormity of this discovery has so far eclipsed any determination of the Irish authorities to investigate it. The home operated between 1925 and 1961. The homes were a system of internment and mandatory labour for pregnant, unmarried women. Tens of thousands of children were forcibly separated from their mothers. The distress of mothers was ignored. Harsh treatment was thought to provide a deterrent against 'fornication'. Children born 'out of wedlock' were stigmatized. Many children died of preventable diseases (in particular, gastroenteritis, caused by lack of breast milk), and over 35,000 surviving children from such homes were sold to Irish and American families. Ireland, newly independent from Great Britain, and led by the Catholic Church, saw itself as *pure* – a state expected of Irish citizens almost all of whom were Catholics. What could be more impure than sex outside marriage? No sanctions were imposed on the fathers of these children. The full shocking story of these homes is yet to be told. When it emerges, the theological dimension cannot be neglected. The near total patriarchal control; the abuse of power; the contempt for women and children; the secrecy; the lack of accountability; the compliance and obedience of nuns who ran the homes; the injustice ... Yes, the church is a vile body. Even now it will not acknowledge the full extent of its crimes.

In 2017, an Australian royal commission similar to IICSA in England and Wales (Chapter 1) reported on institutional responses to child sexual abuse. In the same year an exhaustive report, *Child Sexual Abuse in the Catholic Church*, estimated that:

the prevalence (i.e. rate of offending) of child sexual abuse by priest perpetrators in Australia is likely to hover in the 5.5–8.5% range, using unweighted figures and a little higher using the weighted figures. The Australian evidence is clear that the prevalence amongst religious brothers who are teaching or caring for vulnerable children in residential care varies from 15–40%. (Cahill and Wilkins, 2017, p. 195)

From January 1980 until February 2015, church authorities paid out more than $276 million in response to claims of child sexual abuse (RCT Abuse Law Team, 2017). The number of women worldwide abused by clergy is likely to be much higher than that of children (Clough, 2022). The number of victims cannot be counted. It has probably gone on since before the days of Samuel (d. 1012 BCE, according to a standard chronology), whose sons 'lay with the women who served at the entrance to the tent of meeting' (1 Sam. 2.22). The seriousness of the abuse crisis in Australia led to a series of reports. The 2017 report, *Child Sexual Abuse in the Catholic Church* (Cahill and Wilkinson, 2017), an independent and influential review of all previous reports, confirms what we know from similar reports in the USA and Europe. It is equally critical of seminary training, noting the misogyny and homophobia that was 'baked into' the curriculum and *habitus* (the values, dispositions and expectations of particular social groups, and the means of their enforcement, which are acquired through the activities and experiences of everyday life) of Catholic seminaries. The 'celibacy problem encouraged a tendency to stereotype a little over half the species as a perilous mass threat. This wariness and fear of women spilled too easily into contempt, and the cramping of emotional development' (Cahill and Wilkinson, 2017, p. 139, citing Kenneally, 2017, p. 4). But as we have noted already, contempt is a phenomenon locked into systemic racism, anti-Semitism and sexism, and was already locked into ministerial training:

> The organisational culture of the seminaries and houses of formation was undeniably devoid of the adult feminine and a maturely understood sexuality, and it was a deeply homophobic environment suffused with a fear of homosexual activity: The feminine was represented either as unreachable as in the case of the Virgin Mother, as insipid and deferential to the power of the male, or as seductively evil in the figure of the temptress Eve. (Cahill and Wilkinson, 2017, p. 139)

Pope Francis appears to understand this need for a radical change in the 'organisational culture' of the entire church. He writes:

Looking back to the past, no effort to beg pardon and to seek to repair the harm done will ever be sufficient. Looking ahead to the future, no effort must be spared to create a culture able to prevent such situations from happening, but also to prevent the possibility of their being covered up and perpetuated.

He calls for prayer, penance and fasting

that can make us hunger and thirst for justice and impel us to walk in the truth, supporting all the judicial measures that may be necessary. A fasting that shakes us up and leads us to be committed in truth and charity with all men and women of good will, and with society in general, to combatting all forms of the abuse of power, sexual abuse and the abuse of conscience. (Pope Francis, 2018)

Francis' sincerity is unquestionable. He is aware of the ghastly record bequeathed to him, and the contrition required throughout the church. But perhaps even he scarcely comprehends the scale of the required task. Three times in half a sentence he mentions abuse – of power, of sex and of conscience – but there is no word of the *abusive theology* that authorizes and legitimizes these evils. High on the list is compulsory celibacy itself, followed by the warped understanding of sexuality, the insistence on hierarchical authority with its requirement of obedience; the sense of superiority of the ordained 'third sex' as it sees itself as superior to everyone else, ontologically different, and particularly different from women and children.

It is a safe bet that no church is free from sexual abuse committed by and covered up by its leaders. John Howard Yoder, the distinguished Mennonite pacifist theologian (1927–97), abused women students throughout his ministry, and even spun a version of sexual politics and relationships justifying his actions (Cramer et al., 2014; Pitts, 2015). He has now become a case study in constant denial, manipulation and prevarication by church authorities. Jean Vanier (1928–2019) in 1964 founded L'Arche, an international federation of communities spread over 37 countries for people with developmental disabilities and those who assist them. Yet he was found to have had manipulative and emotionally abusive relationships with six women, including nuns, usually in the context of giving 'spiritual guidance' (BBC News, 2020). These writers are still among the most revered among Christians. A damning report about the serious sexual wrongdoing of the Anglican bishop Peter Ball (Gibb, 2017), who abused many boys and men over a period of 20 years, found his priority 'was to protect and promote himself and he maligned the abused. The church colluded with that rather than seeking to help those it had harmed, or assuring itself of the safety of others.' The book *Bleeding for Jesus* (Graystone, 2021) tells the true story of how John Smyth QC, a well-known Anglican barrister, used his role in the church to abuse more than 100 men and boys in three countries. He liked to recite Luke 12.47 – 'That slave who knew what his master wanted, but did not prepare himself or do what was wanted, will receive a severe beating'– while administering his 'fatherly discipline' (Harvey and Woodhead, 2022, p. 14). Scores of respected church leaders turned a blind eye to his history of abuse over many years.

In 2022 an independent report in the USA concluded:

> For almost two decades, survivors of abuse and other concerned Southern Baptists have been contacting the Southern Baptist Convention (SBC) Executive Committee (EC) to report child molesters and other abusers who were in the pulpit or employed as church staff. They made phone calls, mailed letters, sent emails, appeared at SBC and EC meetings, held rallies, and contacted the press … only to be met, time and time again, with resistance, stonewalling, and even outright hostility from some within the EC. (Guidepost Solutions, 2022, p. 3)

The SBC is the largest Protestant denomination in the USA. Reading this report may induce nausea among readers as they learn about the lies, secrecy, inactivity, contempt for survivors and for evidence, fear of prosecution and liability, and outright hypocrisy of their all-male leaders. It became known that the Executive had a list of 700 Baptist leaders accused or found guilty of sexual abuse of children. By the end of 2022, 380 leaders and volunteers have so far faced prosecution. The accused include a former president and vice-president. Sometimes the denials took a theological form. The reports of abuse were said to be fabrications, inspired by the devil to discredit the good name of the Southern Baptists and discredit their efforts at world evangelism.

Behind this abuse is a warped, conservative theology. Southern Baptists and Catholics have much in common despite their obvious differences. Women definitively cannot be ordained, not even as deacons. Misogyny is wrapped in scripture. Southern Baptists and Roman Catholics find common cause in opposition to abortion and homosexuality in the USA. Their leaders, like the Curia, are obsessed with secrecy. They cannot cope with uncertainty. They insist on unchallengeable authority, found in their own androcentric interpretations of the Bible instead of in the authority of the pope and the Congregation for the Doctrine of the Faith.

Notes

1 For a summary of recent statistics and developments in Belgium, Germany, The Netherlands, Poland, Spain and Italy, see Cahill and Wilkinson, 2017, pp. 86–96.

21

Abused Bodies:
Abusive Theology

Abused Bodies – abusive theology

There has been copious analysis of the abuse crisis in the Catholic Church, both internal and external, and from multidisciplinary perspectives. Few of these have been *theological*. It is now widely understood that theology has been underrated in the sociological and psychological analyses of the abusing church (Cahill and Wilkinson, 2017, p. 213). They have underestimated the abusive nature of the beliefs and doctrines that conservative churches affirm and proclaim. Perhaps they can't imagine anyone believing some of the abusive theology found in these churches. We noted earlier the close association between a patriarchal order or set of institutions; misogyny as the enforcement of patriarchy; and sexism as the rationalization and justification of misogyny. Misogyny is the founding dualism of the patriarchal order. It establishes women as other and inferior, and then establishes further large groups of people – Jews, blacks, slaves, homosexuals, 'others' – who are discriminated against for not being 'the same'. The sexism that justifies misogyny *is* abusive theology. Feminist philosophy has a word for this: 'mansplaining'. The *OED* defines it: 'Of a man: to explain (something) needlessly, overbearingly, or condescendingly, esp. (typically when addressing a woman) in a manner thought to reveal a patronizing or chauvinistic attitude.' All theology down to the latter half of the twentieth century is written by men. How could this not be defective? No inheritor of Christian traditions can blame men for being men and writing like men, and they are not blamed here. What lies at fault is that the mansplaining goes on with little if any recognition of the harm it causes or the vastness of the new knowledge and heightened social awareness that exposes its inadequacy.

We find the patriarchal order everywhere. It was a system of control that once pronounced every world citizen under the domination of Christ's vicar on earth (Chapter 15) and sought to control the lives of all its members, not just their sex lives but even their thoughts. Compulsory celibacy lies behind the Catholic abuse crisis, but it is not the whole truth about it. Celibacy was still being lauded in 1967 as 'a brilliant jewel', which 'retains its value undiminished even in our time when the outlook of men and the state of the world have undergone such profound changes' (Pope Paul VI, 1967). In seeking to understand the abuse crisis, I found the meticulous, comprehensive and deeply compassionate work of Marie Keenan (2012) most helpful. She interviewed nine priests who were found guilty of abusing children in Ireland, and one of her findings complexifies what might be meant by 'evil' and 'good'. While in no doubt about the appalling nature of their crimes, she did not find them to be 'evil' paedophiles. Depicting the priests as 'monsters' may be an effective cultural coping strategy, distancing 'us' from 'them', but there is a sharper point to be made here. Rather, the offending priests were all ordinary men trying to do good, men whose ministry as priests, to say nothing of their responsibilities as social beings, went badly wrong. Asking why led to answers involving the totality of the institution they tried to serve – their formation, the theology they inherited, the culture of fear and silence surrounding priests, their isolation and abject defeat in the well-meaning attempt to live an impossible life. As we have found in confronting racism, sexism and homophobia earlier in this book, malaise cannot be located in individuals alone. It has a structural, systemic, institutional dimension.

Polluted and Humiliated Bodies

All the offending priests in Keenan's study had a deep sense of God's calling to the priesthood and were determined to devote their lives to the service of God and the church. But more, much more, is required of priests, particularly the demand of *purity*. The sexual ignorance of the offending priests at the time of their training is striking. There was no language for talking about their adolescent desires; only vague talk about 'bad actions' and 'bad thoughts' that were regarded as mortal sins. The men:

> learned that purity, like celibacy, was a 'gift' from God, and they tried the recommended lessons of praying to the Blessed Virgin for the gift of purity and saying three Hail Mary prayers in the morning to cure all bad thoughts and desires. The problem was that they had to ask and pray for the 'gift', but when they didn't receive it, the failure was internalized. 'They' had failed to receive the gift because of their unworthiness. Further spirals of prayer and personal failure, shame, and guilt became the norm. (Keenan, 2012, pp. 135–6)

But this notion of purity is disastrous for the health of the person whether or not she or he is a priest. We have seen that purity, and the near antonym that derives from it – pollution – is directly descended from the ritual anxiety and disgust in the HB about ejaculating and menstruating bodies, extended into early Christian thought. It is directly linked to misogyny and (in Christianity) to discomfort with almost *any* sexual experience. Ancient Israelite and early Jewish purity laws, we saw, excluded most people from being counted among the holy, just as they were designed to do. They are not binding on Christians, as Paul clearly taught. Otherwise, circumcision would be binding on male converts too. But Christians intensified their own plight by *internalizing* impurity, where there are no means of washing it away or prescribing remedies.

Jesus, we saw, was more interested in purity of the heart, which lay in not wanting to commit murder, adultery and so on. There is a wealth of difference between a man wanting to have sex with another man's wife and having (and enjoying) erotic thoughts. We saw how the document *The Teaching of the Twelve Apostles* warned against importing HB teaching into Christian practices, not least the practice of remaining at home during the time of their menses (Chapter 13). The Holy Spirit is not fazed by menstruating and ejaculating bodies, nor by the harmless fantasies entertained countless times a day by healthy men (and women), whether priests or not. Purity culture needs to go, along with obsessive attempts to control sexual impulses. Instead, what is needed is emphasis on integrity, honesty, empathy, good character and good practice, which have the best chance of resulting in healthy and pleasurable sexual expression.

Another failing in conventional Catholic sexual morality is its act-centred approach to personal conduct, instead of a relational one that includes society and context. The entire penitential tradition was and remains centred on particular individual sins and appropriate penances for them. It helped to bring about 'a moral perspective which focused on individual acts, on regarding the moral life as a matter of avoiding sin, and on turning moral reflection into an analysis of sin in its many forms' (Gula, 1989, p. 26). Here we have arrived at a barely believable characteristic of the mentality of sex offenders. All of Keenan's offenders regarded their offending as sins against God, not against the victim. They had broken rules for which *divine* forgiveness and restitution through penance was essential and the need for *human* forgiveness was never entertained. No, says Keenan, this type of thinking was *not* distorted. It was authentic Catholic thinking:

From their study of Catholic sexual ethics they understood sexual sin as direct offense against God but not as a direct offense against a person, who happened to be on the receiving end of the sex 'act', and who was a minor. It was on God that they focused their concerns, not on the child they were abusing. This can at one level be seen as in harmony with Catholic moral teaching. A purity ethic rather than a relational ethic predominates. (Keenan, 2012, p. 167)

There was little thought for the victims or the consequences for them in the short or long term. The men themselves came to see how wrong these attitudes were, but the unacknowledged harm caused to their victims is replicated in the churches' treatment of abuse survivors when the abuse is eventually reported, and the churches called to account. Churches have no problem about recognizing child abuse as a grave sin against God, but they have been pitifully slow to recognize it as a sin against the victims, and as a *crime*. Abusive theology tolerates abuse.

The lack of thought for victims, the failure of empathy for them, is a striking feature of abusive behaviour that goes all the way back *to the victimhood of Jesus, and the failure to recognize the sexualized violence he suffered in his last hours.* David Tombs (2022) and others (Reaves, Tombs and Figueroa, 2021) have drawn attention to this. The Gospel of Matthew records that Jesus was stripped naked (27.28). His nakedness was part of the violent public humiliation he suffered at the hands of Roman soldiers. That the soldiers cast lots for his clothes (Matt. 27.35; Mark 15.24) confirms what we already know but fail to acknowledge: 'the historical certainty that Jesus was crucified naked, in line with Roman practice'. This is a certainty 'literally covered up by centuries of Christian art' (Dawson, 2021). What else may have happened to him on the way to the cross? Are even the Gospels silent about that?

The victimhood of Jesus is emphatically not a matter of conjecture. The mockery, humiliation and appalling violence he suffered is recounted in all four Gospels. The disturbing parallel lies between the covering up of the genitals of Jesus on the cross in Christian art and theology, and the covering up of the violence endured by victims of sexual abuse, female and male. The reassuring erasure of Christ's nakedness by a convenient loincloth in countless depictions of the crucifixion erases the stripping and exposure of his violated, pierced body. The cloth is there for *our* sakes. We the viewers are spared, shielded from, the shocking truth of the violation of the Christ. The denial of his nakedness is very telling – as if sexual abuse of the Messiah is too defiling to contemplate. Yet the church also drapes a cloth over the shocking violence it has committed – too shocking to contemplate. Victims see the obfuscation of their complaints as further abuse, as revictimization, as denial (Figueroa Alvear and Tombs, 2019). If the churches had responded with survivor-centred and trauma-informed ways of addressing the crises as they came to light, outcomes for victims and offenders would have been very different.

Submissive and Repressed Bodies

How did abusers regard children? Keenan makes a suggestion that takes some unpacking. Some priests when they related to children regarded them as friends and co-equals! How so? Because the priests had become so accustomed to obedience to doctrine and to being bossed about by their superiors, so numbed by constant submissiveness, that they felt deprived of agency. They could relate easily to children and youths as friends and equals just because of their *lack* of power, not because of their power over the children as authority figures:

> at the level of the sexual and the emotional, their narratives paradoxically indicate that they saw children and young people as potential 'friends' and 'equals'. Thus, it was the men's interpretation of 'equality', their blindness to power in the sexual and emotional sphere (i.e., their sexual and emotional immaturity) and their lack of understanding of childhood vulnerability and sexuality that was part of their problem. (Keenan, 2012, p. 138)

Their 'submissiveness in the seminary diminished their sense of personal authority and autonomy as well as their moral judgement' (Cahill and Wilkins, 2017, p. 225). There was another reason why the abusers Keenan interviewed chose boys (apart from their easier availability). At least the boys weren't women! Yes, intimacy with boys was a sin, but it wasn't adultery! You can only commit adultery with a woman! At least intimacy with boys and youths need not be a threat to celibacy (Keenan, 2012, p. 12).

Keenan's subjects all said they experienced acute difficulties over trying not to pleasure themselves by masturbating. It is apparently, and very believably, a major item for confession, 'the great sexual terror in the struggle for sexual purity' (Cahill and Wilkins, 2017, p. 228): 'Within the seminary environment, masturbation was known as "self-abuse", and this was highly problematic for all of the men because it contravened their understanding of purity and chastity. Six of them were in their 30s before they first masturbated' (Keenan, 2012, p. 136). But the very notion of self-abuse is counterproductive because it links the *real* abuse of victims with the harmless and victimless pleasure of private orgasm, mischaracterized as an abuse of the priest's own body. Any kind of sexual pleasure, and even the thought of it, is to be banished. The damage done to victims of abuse is linked via the notion of self-abuse to the need for harmless release. The former is vile abuse; the latter is no abuse at all. But this repression of desire and release is, like the system of act-based morality, based on Catholic teaching that has outlived its usefulness. Sr Margaret Farley defended the practice in her brave and pioneering work *Just Love*, pointing out that the discovery of 'self-pleasuring' could contribute positively to the well-being of women and men, their self-understanding, self-knowledge, and to their relationships (Farley, 2006, p. 236). The Vatican condemned the book for confusing the faithful, and ordered Catholics not to read it (*New York Times*, 2012). Its response indicates how threatening to patriarchy *any* revisionary perspective in sexual ethics is perceived to be.

Sacrificial Bodies?

Some of the men spoke to Keenan of how much 'they subjected their sexual and emotional life to a process of intellectualization, a process that they also perfected during their time in the seminary' (Keenan, 2012, p. 139). This may be a fault of almost all theological institutions associated with churches. The 'man of reason' (Lloyd, 1984) inhabits them, confusing and replacing the growth of moral, spiritual and emotional wisdom with intellectual dominance and accomplishment. That was true of my own (more gentle and less rigorous) ordination training, decades before any mention of sexuality was allowed to disturb the curriculum. But at least I was allowed to have (and had) a fiancée then (even though she was not allowed in college after 10.30 p.m. – my immediate expulsion ('sending down') would follow detection), and one or two friends, also in ordination training, with whom secrets could be honestly shared. This intellectualism was barely diminished many years later. I was invited to a closed conference of ministers and ordinands in a theological college, which was called, in private and out of term, to discuss the ministers' own sexuality and for some their homosexuality. That sounded like real progress. However, my preparation for the event was interrupted by a firm request: 'Please confine your contributions to the history and theology of marriage.' And so it was. Students directed polite academic questions to the expert who was parachuted in (me), and he (me) obeyed the script unquestioningly, sounding off about divorce in the NT or Luther's dislike of betrothal, or some such, conniving with the intention to discuss sexuality personally and existentially, while all the time avoiding it.

In Catholic and Orthodox Christianities the Virgin Mother is ubiquitous, and in Protestantism she is regularly ignored or trivialized. I think the earlier analysis of her rise to become the God-bearer (Chapter 7), together with her veneration accompanying the church's fear of sexual sin, comes into play here. She is not given special veneration in the NT. Her later adoration is associated with the increasing revulsion for having sex and the need to remove the mother of the Lord from any suggestion of having had it.

But it is possible that this goddess-like figure of female purity is little or no help to seminarians struggling with their sexuality. In their devotion to her she belongs with their devotions to God. So while her presence feminizes and softens the stern and demanding male deity, she leaves in place his stern and demanding masculinity, percolating through the church hierarchy requiring obedience from his feminine church. She occupies the *place* where the hierarchy wants her to be: unreachable and untouchable, while *acting* as the hierarchy want her to be, passive and obedient, relieving priestly frustration. She is the poor answer to the need of straight priests for real, feminine company. She listens to their prayers and understands their needs, yet she does nothing to help them. She cannot, for she is a displacement. A displacement (in psychology) is 'the substitution of one idea or impulse for another, as in dreams, obsessions, etc.; the unconscious transfer of intense feelings or emotions to something of greater or less consequence' (*OED*). The deeper revisionary problem goes beyond Mary because it goes beyond the male God with his male hierarchy operating like God over his female church. The solution lies in the recovery of the feminine in God's own being, rendering feminine compensation for manly obedience to the male God unnecessary.

Clergy in training for the Catholic priesthood have little understanding of the near impossibility of remaining faithful to their sacred vow of celibacy, and little understanding of the sexuality of the human person that will conspire against their best efforts. The church too does not prepare men for the difficulties they will encounter, nor does it support them in their struggles, nor give them opportunity, apart from confession, to be honest with themselves. The first flush of enthusiasm that accompanies the call to the priesthood is also an exposure not simply to the promptings of the Holy Spirit but to unrealistic and even deluded expectations of what may be achievable even with the Spirit's help. That is why commentators speak of 'clerical sacrifice' or 'the sacrificial psychology of the clergy ideal'.

There are several strands to the exploration of clerical sacrifice. First, there is the undoubted willingness of clergy and religious to take vows of poverty, chastity and obedience, sometimes at great personal cost to themselves. The crucified Christ is undoubtedly part of their inspiration.

He is 'the Son of God, who loved me and gave himself for me' (Gal. 2.20). 'Rejoice in so far as you are sharing Christ's sufferings, so that you may also be glad and shout for joy when his glory is revealed' (1 Pet. 4.13). What could be more Christ-like than willingly suffering for Christ's sake? Second, there is the willingness of the hierarchy of the Catholic Church to sacrifice their priests to a life of obedience and unrelieved loneliness, in short to a life that is impossible to live. There is little or no post-ordination support for such clergy, whose relationship to their superiors is likely to be fraught. A bishop cannot be simultaneously a pastor and a disciplinarian (as Anglicans have also learned). The life of priests is known to be like this; that is why Keenan accuses the church of institutional hypocrisy. It knowingly prepares men for an impossible life while ignoring the cruelty that comes with it. Keenan asks:

> How can ... the Catholic Church ensure that its candidates for priesthood and religious brotherhood receive the right psychological constitution and attitude that will help them make good moral choices and avoid cruelty and suffering? When will such formation programs include a theology of power in which authority in the Catholic Church is reconfigured to include not just an understanding of the obligations when 'under' authority but also an understanding of the responsibilities of those 'in' authority? (Keenan, 2012, p. 263)

Third, there is the distinction, nearly always blurred, between necessary and unnecessary sacrifice. Necessary sacrifice in the Christian life, clerical or lay, may include openness to persecution, hardship, ridicule and discrimination in the service of Christ. Jesus told his disciples: 'If any want to become my followers, let them deny themselves and take up their cross and follow me' (Matt. 16.24). There is ample evidence of this in the worldwide church. Dietrich Bonhoeffer said: 'When Christ calls a man, he bids him come and die' (Bonhoeffer, 1959, p. 99). He too paid the ultimate price. Many Christians will endure hardship in their love of neighbour. But there is also a willingness among laity and clergy alike to take upon themselves, and to advocate for others, a burden of sacrifice, of self-denial, of mental or psychological suffering that may be wholly unnecessary. Lesbian and gay students have regularly shared with me their misapprehension about the compulsory celibacy their conservative churches want to impose on them. Does God really require this? At this point the distinction between necessary and unnecessary sacrifice becomes useful. I ask them to think about the saying of Jesus:

Come to me, all you that are weary and are carrying heavy burdens, and I will give you rest. Take my yoke upon you, and learn from me; for I am gentle and humble in heart, and you will find rest for your souls. For my yoke is easy, and my burden is light. (Matt. 11.28–30)

The inference is clear. Reconsider the abusive theology that considers celibacy an obligation for anyone outside compulsory heterosexuality. It may indeed be a calling. But it may be a step towards a desperate and unfulfilled life.

Bodies Abused by Theology

The abusive theology unearthed in earlier chapters distorts not only clerical sacrifice but almost any theology of sacrifice. The violence of God in the Bible is frightening, but it never seems to be repudiated by Christians of almost any persuasion. Its dark shadow (if nothing more) remains permanently rooted in the heart of Christian theology. Jesus is known as the 'Son of God' sent by the Father to suffer and die on the cross for the sins of the world. The metaphorical character of the designation 'Son' is obvious. God is no literal human father. Also obvious is that the metaphorical character of the designation is frequently overlooked. When this happens, a father knowingly sends his son to die a cruel death, which in some theories should be ours but which by faith we can escape. In a leap of divine injustice, the punishing god cruelly abuses his son for our sins, instead of punishing us, and we should be grateful, sacrificing ourselves to God in our response to this great Paschal event of divine mercy. These theories are morally lamentable (they operate under the label 'penal substitution') because they make God the Father the divine child abuser. Divine violence is justified, even against children, and divine *in*justice is justified too.

A standard Christian theology of the body has also been abusive. It assumes a catastrophic human Fall in which all womankind is perceived as the primordial temptress, and where the primordial sin is disobedience. Whereas soul and body may have been perceived as a single entity ('hylomorphism', as Aquinas taught, following Aristotle), the distinction between them was often experienced as an existential chasm. On one side the body is unruly, needing vigilance and firm control in ever more extreme forms. On the other side lies the soul, ill-equipped to deal with the desires of its unruly body, surrounded by demons or evil thoughts that no amount of prayer and acts of bodily mortification will ever overcome. Worse, the 'will', abstracted as something separate from the body, is characterized by weakness, unable to control the body's desires and the soul's wandering thoughts.

The problem is that negative elements still predominate. Any theology is abusive if it does not allow the human person to engage in appropriate self-care. LGBTIQ people know this full well. That is why they mainly avoid churches. The cognitive dissonance between beliefs and reality becomes so great it becomes unbearable. The second 'great commandment' of Jesus was, 'You shall love your neighbour as yourself' (Matt. 22.39), adding, 'On these two commandments hang all the law and the prophets.' Self-love, then, is a precondition of the love of neighbours, as this commandment requires. Any theology that encourages self-hatred, shame, guilt and so on, is abusive because it saps the ability to self-affirm and diminishes the requirements to love God and neighbour. It locates sin in the body's desires instead of in the wider structures that shape and inform sinful individuals. Thankfully there are other ways of thinking about the body (Chapter 22) that are more positive.

22

Glorious Bodies:
Loving in the Afterlife, Loving After All

This last chapter returns to the verse with which we began – Paul awaiting his post-mortem encounter with Jesus Christ: 'Who shall change our
vile body, that it may be fashioned like unto his glorious body' (Phil.
3.21 KJV). There are more positive estimates of the body in Paul. It is
'a temple of the Holy Spirit' (1 Cor. 6.20; see Rom. 12.1). If these had
been emphasized, Christian thought about the body might have had a
different trajectory. We will keep our bodies after we have died. It is hard
even to imagine the possibility of bodily life after death, especially if it
requires the reconstitution of billions of decomposed or cremated human
bodies. Assuming suspension of incredulity for a moment, we can at
least continue to *imagine* what life after death might be like, what shape
our forthcoming glorious bodies might take. And our imagining (if it is
informed by Christian faith) will be framed by two prerequisites. It will
be based on the conviction that Jesus Christ arose from death, that death
is not the end. And the 'glorious body' will be a *body*; that is, like our
bodies now it will be *somatic*, recognizably a body, though transformed
in some way ('a spiritual body', as Paul also said – 1 Cor. 15.44), just as
the Gospels record the resurrected Christ as still recognizably Jesus, yet
also different.

Glorious Bodies – an anatomy

The emerging churches affirmed the resurrection of the body, or – perhaps
to emphasize still further the corporeality of heaven – the resurrection of
the *flesh*. But there was a further prerequisite to this belief – our genitalia
would remain behind in the grave. In heaven we wouldn't need them.
As the coyly titled book *Resurrecting Parts* asserts and records, early
Christians advocated 'a particular kind of body and flesh that has been
safely extricated from sexual desires and acts' (Petrey, 2016, p. 4). It is
important that these early theologians, like us, were using their imagination in order to speculate what a perfected existence – eternal life in and

with God – might be like. But suppose in *our* imaginings we found no use for the assumption that our 'parts' of shame were parts of *shame*? Suppose we *retained* them in the next life, perhaps without their reproductive function, but with their pleasure-giving function retained or even enhanced?

Remaining with the imagination (as eschatology must) it is exciting to envisage what might happen if, as Christians suppose, God, in the outpouring and outworking of divine love, finally banishes all that opposes it, and the beings made in the divine image are able to love one another as God loves them? This is what having a glorious body might amount to – that blessed state of affairs in which everything once thought vile that belonged to the body and its actions belongs no more. All that would be definitively missing from this vision would be the detritus from *broken* relationships this side of heaven – abuse, violence, exploitation, domination, pleasure-seeking as opposed to pleasure-giving, self-loathing, envy, jealousy, betrayal and so on. Many varieties of expressions of love might be possible in eternity – from celibate loving to polyamory. Perhaps sexual ethics *now* could be rejuvenated by allowing eschatology to shape the relationships that we anticipate in the *eschaton* where the bliss of eternal love becomes a reality. Several theologians urge this route upon us, at least as a complementary pathway through the minefield that is sexual ethics. Perhaps it is a route for all of Christian ethics to follow.

This imaginative kind of surmising has been aptly named 'sexchatology' (Cornwall, 2013, pp. 153–64). Two book-length studies have developed the vision of sexual love, restored and beatified in God's eschatological future, aptly titled *Sex on Earth as it is in Heaven* (Jung, 2017) and *Under the Bed of Heaven* (McCarty, 2021). The church badly needs the spiritual nourishment and the imaginative vision that an alternative vision of eschatology can provide. Instead of golden streets, choirs of angels and ranks of the redeemed (with hymn sheets and no genitals) praising God, think instead of embodied personal existence held together by the power of divine love. What delights and ecstasies might await in glory?

No More Vile Bodies

This section is a thought experiment for people of faith who have not given up on the virtue of hope, and who still cling to the belief that love is stronger than death. It is grounded in faith, hope and love, and so is an activity never merely theoretical and abstract but with one eye on what may be God's future for all God has made, and the other eye on where and how transformation needs to happen now. When God is glorified there will be no more patriarchy, racism, no more sex and gender hierarchies, no more slavery and no more abuses of power that make these evils possible. We might begin our experiment by imagining how wrong we Christians were in much that we did and continue to do in our earthly existence, starting not with sexual relationships but with our relations with the Jewish people of God. We might see (if we remember then what was in the Bible) what Paul was getting at when he argued that the church was more like a wild olive shoot grafted on to a mature olive tree, sharing its 'rich root' (Rom. 11.17) than a sapling with roots in its own soil. We remain lodged and supported by that mature tree. If we have our scriptures in the next life, will we be able to see what terrible mistakes we made with them in this life (Chapter 15), using them to persecute, subjugate, exploit and kill? Perhaps there will be space to repent there of all our harms against Jewish people, and eventually to receive forgiveness not merely from God but from the Jewish people themselves.

We will wonder why it took almost 2,000 years to get rid of slavery, ignoring the material consequences of slavery for millions of people, wondering why our scriptures (and theologians) endorsed it (Chapter 12) and why we were so criminally slow in failing to read them differently and redemptively. We might see, if we lived in a rich country, how many of us benefited from the miserable existence of others, and continued to do so as exploitation assumed different, legal and illegal, forms. We will be able to ponder, if we are able to share in God's omniscience, why Christians were detested in many parts of the world and how complicit our ancestors were in giving good cause for resentment. Where God is light the colour black will no longer be associated with darkness, sin, cursedness and inferiority, because *God's* light enables the rich colours of created light to illuminate everything else in all its colourful diversity, including in the human case everyone black, brown, white or varying shades of each. 'God is light and in him there is no darkness at all' (1 John 1.5). Darkness will no longer be available as a synonym for all that is feared or hated because there will be no more fear, only the light of God illuminating the glorious bodies that God created in the divine image and now fully restores. Perhaps we will appreciate afresh the appropriateness of rainbows as a sign of God's covenant with the former earth (Gen. 9.8–17).

Misogyny and sexism may be the founding sins of 'fallen' humanity. In the old narrative, Eve, the temptress, brings about the fall of the human race (Gen. 3). Only after the fall does Cain murder his brother Abel (Gen. 4). Continuing with the experiment, we will come to see how absurdly mistaken we were in blaming womankind for the condition of humanity, adding to the classical views of women's all-round inferiority and subjugation in relation to men, authorizing the gender hierarchy and the necessary force to require it. If we were to continue the thought experiment begun here and extend it to the stories told by earlier chapters, what contrasts might emerge?

Men would no longer view the bodies of women with disgust (nor women internalize such views). We will all be able to see that disgust, like impurity, should have played no part in our thinking about bodies. Naked or clothed, bodies will be without shame. If we do not create in heaven, our bodies may no longer emit the fluids associated with impurity in a former life. Purity exists elsewhere – 'Blessed are the pure *in heart*, for they will see God' (Matt. 5.8). There will be no gender hierarchy to generate inferiority and contempt. Since our bodies are now glorious ('glorified') they cannot be 're-viled'. There will be no more violence against women because men will see the self-serving ideology that kept women in their (subordinate) place for the evil thing it was, and will understand that from primordial sexism all other dominations followed. The male body will no longer be held up as the 'default body', with lesser (female) bodies seen as 'faulty'.

Eros will no longer be seen as an internal enemy to be tamed because we will be purged of the possessiveness that drives it. In our still-sexed bodies desire will be integrated with spirit, with each other and with God. We will be able to respond positively to other people whose bodies allure us. We will be able to experience for ourselves what 'no longer male and female' (Gal. 3.28) means. A rigid distinction between male and female will be seen to belong to the old order that has passed away.

Virginity will no longer be prized because men will not be regarding women who have had sex as defiled property unworthy of purchase. But those men and women who chose to be or to become celibate in this present life will be free to remain celibate in the life to come (or not), adding to the diversity of experiences of love already there. We will no longer have use for old nineteenth-century medical distinctions between homosexual or heterosexual people because we will no longer have an imaginary need to stigmatize as 'other' people who loved but who loved differently. Who knows what possibilities might arise? Perhaps we will all be bi, or at least bi-curious. At least we know that if there is a heaven at all, it will be a place of safety for everyone, unlike the churches in this present life. For us to be the people we once were, we will need to recognize each other and so maintain much of our identity. People who struggled with their gender identity, who transitioned or who didn't but wished they had, they will be content with the glorious bodies they have come to be and inhabit. Will there be queer people in heaven? Queer people on earth defy categories. In heaven categories won't matter, so perhaps everyone or no one will be queer. If the categories don't matter, perhaps even that category-that-is-not-a-category – queer – will be redundant.

There will be no women priests in heaven because there will be no priests there. They too will be redundant. Priests minister in earthly churches but there will be no churches in heaven: 'I saw no temple in the city, for its temple is the Lord God the Almighty and the Lamb' (Rev. 21.22). Churches belonged to a former world where reconciliation with God had only just begun. But once reconciliation is achieved, we will realize how temporal and earthly churches actually were. We will see that the 'treasure' we had then we kept in 'clay jars' (2 Cor. 4.7, or 'earthen vessels', KJV), and that we worried more about keeping the jars clean and holy than about the treasure that was in them.

We won't be mystifying sex, allegorizing it as Origen and countless other priests and theologians did. We won't need to look past our bodies and bodies that attract us in order to find God. There will be no more self-loathing brought about by wearing the 'yoke' that was made for oxen (Matt. 11.29–30), not for God's loving children to wear. Perhaps we who taught and preached will marvel at our cavalier and unworthy readings of the scriptures that allowed us to defend and prefer racial purity, race and gender hierarchies and heteronormativity. How could we have thought we were right when we had caused so much suffering?

'Inglorious Bodies'– still with us

Returning to this present life, how much more remains to be done! In the world there is an epidemic of violence against women (Storkey, 2015; Thatcher, 2020). Women cannot feel safe at night, alone, in public spaces (despite the presence of surveillance cameras recording their every step) (Chapter 1). There is an outpouring of disdain and contempt on social media directed against women who are successful, by angry young men who need urgent help in dealing with their resentment at the crumbling of patriarchy and their inability to see women as equal to them in deserving and achieving respect. Yet in my own church, women are required to tolerate 'two integrities', according to which some male priests and bishops do not recognize female priests and bishops, and can choose (and do) not to be ordained by them, or by any other males who have been ordained by women. There are 'male headship churches' who can opt for alternative (male) episcopal oversight, the great majority of which do not (because they dare not?) own up to their discrimination against women publicly (WATCH, 2020). These churches think they can safely preach the gospel while simultaneously sending a different message: that women are second-class church members, polluting, defiling and tainting the pure line of apostolic (male) descent (Catholic); or that women are for ever in subjection to men because the Bible says so (evangelical Protestant). The matter is wrongly theorized and understood as a clash of warring tribes and theological positions within the church. The matter is about the toleration of abusive theology in a church that has already lost its nation's trust. Its records on race, on abuse, on LGBTIQ people can all be understood and explained by abusive theology, by the old story of regarding particular bodies as inferior, impure, 'vile'.

Racism remains a scourge in the world, yet the enormity of the theological edifice that justified it has been largely denied or forgotten. Diarmaid MacCulloch characterizes as 'poison' the 'centuries-old heritage of antisemitism festering in the memories of countless ordinary twentieth-century Christians on the eve of the Nazi takeover'; a poison that also led 'Christian Lithuanians, Poles and many others gleefully to perpetrate bestial cruelties on helpless Jews who had done them no harm' (MacCulloch, 2014, p. 208). Racism has stubbornly remained in the churches, while in the USA the persistence of white racism in the form of 'Christian nationalism' threatens the very fabric of that troubled society. The legacy of grossly distorted interpretations of scripture is deep and long lasting, confirming their egregious character. But racism depends on the belief (nothing more) that one group is superior to another. It shares its sense of superiority with patriarchy, and while it exists throughout the world (probably in every country), the uneasy haunting thought is that Christians are deeply implicated in its manufacture and are usually unprepared to face our complicity in its manufacture and maintenance. Abusive theology may speak in more hushed tones here, but its legacy still needs to be owned, even as it re-emerges in secular contexts – social media, football, fashion and in countless other aggressions and micro-aggressions.

Bodies in a 'Post-Abusive Theology'

In their reflections on a post-abusive theology, Harvey and Woodhead (2022) speak of Un*knowing God* (their title; see also Chapter 1). We have seen that abusive theology, like the vile bodies it creates, is with us still. Who knows how much theology has to be 'un-known'; how much of what we thought we 'knew' about God has to be discarded, for an affirming, post-abusive theology to emerge? Theological considerations are ultimately rational ones, but if they do not bring well-being to us in our psychological, emotional, relational and spiritual states of being, what use are they? In these final paragraphs I visit the classical themes of Christian theology showing how they may be read more positively.

God. When we speak of God we do not know what we are talking about. That is because, if there be God, God is the ultimate mystery, beyond the grasp of human thought. Since God is not a creature, God is beyond any creaturely distinctions, especially the distinction between male and female.

Christ. The earliest disciples of Jesus of Nazareth, all Jews in occupied Palestine, believed he was the promised Messiah. He was known as 'the Son of God'. The Fourth Gospel made the daring connection between the God of the Jews and Jesus by means of the idea of 'the Word' (in Greek, *logos*) (John 1.1–18). He is who and what this God 'speaks'. Whatever the word 'God' might have meant, its meaning now for the fledgling church has to be discerned through Jesus, God's own self-disclosure.

But this Word was unique in imaging the divine. All things were said to have come into being through this Word. The very cosmos itself acquires its self-understanding through it. This Word is called 'life' and 'light', 'the true light, which enlightens everyone'. The Word is no Jewish or Christian possession because he/she/it operates beyond the bounds of any and every religious or ethnic community, 'the light of all people'. True, the Word was not known, but was and remains the immanent power of all life, creating and sustaining it, the moral and spiritual light that shone in darkness, 'and the darkness did not overcome it'. The Word (and the Hebrew Wisdom on which the Word is partly based) is not confined to Judaeo-Christian traditions.

Incarnation. Incarnation means en*flesh*ment: 'And the Word became flesh and lived among us' (John 1.14). Human flesh (not just male human flesh) is what God becomes. Indeed, why restrict 'flesh' to humans at all (the Greek word for 'flesh' – *sarx* – doesn't)? The material world is the world of flesh. The gross damage inflicted on the natural world by humans may belong to the human disregard for flesh. There could be no higher evaluation of the fleshly world for Christians than that Godself, the very divine Word, becomes it. Flesh itself becomes the revelation of God's being. Bodies are not vile. One of them is the means through which the divine is disclosed. God is the eternal One, known supremely in flesh.

Atonement. This is believed to be the process whereby God and whatever is not God become 'at one' with God and with each other. Early Christians, being Jews, were steeped in the thought of the HB and well acquainted with the Day of Atonement, Yom Kippur (Lev. 23.27–28). On that day the high priest performed elaborate rituals to 'atone' for the sins of the people. The rituals included the blood of a specially sacrificed bull, and a goat, while a second goat (the 'scapegoat') was driven out, bearing with it the sins of the people for another year. This ancient practice inevitably led to Jesus being seen as the sacrifice for sin, by shedding *his* blood, or being seen as the scapegoat – 'the Lamb of God who takes away the sin of the world!' (John 1.29).

But there were already limits to this kind of imagery, even within the Jewish faith. Beyond it, who could make sense of this violent God who needed a blood bath in order for 'his' people to be saved from their sins? The idea has led to the expectation and valorization of violence and suffering, the normalization of violence at the heart of Christian faith, and the creation of a god that no thoughtful moral person can believe in any longer. The idea of atonement with God does not require sacrifice in order to 'work'. Christian doctrine affirms the union of two natures, the divine and the human, in the one Christ. Jesus achieves 'at-one-ment' between the created world and God in his own being just by being here. He 'lived among us, and we have seen his glory' (John 1.14). Here is a 'glorious body', not above history but immersed in it. Skipping around the complexities and bellicose arguments surrounding the Person of Christ in the first centuries of church history, a simple point to be retained is that all flesh is united with God by Jesus who, being God, represents the unity of God and flesh by being who he is.

The cross. An early hymn (Phil. 2.5–11) depicts a 'pre-existent' Jesus, the divine Son, who 'emptied himself' (Phil. 2.7) by descending from heaven, leaving his 'glory' behind. Jesus was always a troublemaker to the religious establishment – scribes, Pharisees, priests – as much as he troubled the occupying Romans as a dangerous insurrectionist. But the biographies of Jesus that the Gospel writers provide show that Jesus was unflinching in his mission, undeterred by opposition from the different factions of Judaism, prepared (yet understandably hesitant – Matt. 26.42) even to endure crucifixion for the sake of his mission to reveal the divine love of the One he called 'Father'.

One of the earliest (and most neglected) books in the NT is the Letter to the Hebrews, a remarkable book that draws on the sacrificial system of the HB to create the 'once for all' sacrifice of Christ on the cross. The argument is complicated, deeply set in the theological thought and ritual practice of the day. But a clear theme emerges: the sacrifice of Christ is emphatically *not* something to be imitated but something that brings all talk about and practice of sacrifice to an end. 'We have been sanctified through the offering of the body of Jesus Christ once for all' (Heb. 10.10), the author exclaims. Christ has offered 'for all time a single sacrifice for sins' (10.12). 'For by a single offering he has perfected for all time those who are sanctified' (10.14). Yes, the people of God can expect persecution and suffering and must endure it bravely. But they don't need to think about continual atonement, continual worrying about sin, continual imitation of Christ's sacrifice. Christ 'our great high priest' (4.14) renders the entire sacrificial system unnecessary (which is why Nonconformists call their ministers 'ministers').

Trinity. In Chapter 18 we noted how, in Rowan Williams' essay, the life task of the Christian church is 'teaching us to so order our relations that human beings may see themselves as desired, as the occasion of joy'. The most sophisticated word picture for the Christian God is the doctrine of the Trinity. Williams found there the root of all desire, its endless circulation between the Persons of the one God overflowing into the making of the world as an act of (divine) love. To think of God as the interaction of three 'Persons' is already to stretch the threads of analogy between human and divine persons. However, I am eager to persist with it. In God the Persons are co-equal. There are no hierarchies in God. The Persons are not sexed, or (to say the same thing) are 'beyond gender'. That is because they are divine, uncreated. The Persons exist only in relation to each other. They do not exist in isolation. The Trinity subverts the idea that God is a single divine individual, the divine Monarch, with an inscrutable masculine will, and posits instead a model of mystery, interpenetration and participation. With appropriate care, theologians striving for racial and sexual justice may find unexpected inspiration here.

Spirit. The Spirit is by far the most neglected Person of the Trinity. Locating her presence throughout creation (like the Word), instead of confining her to the activities of church, enables us to find the Spirit wherever her 'fruits' are found. Those fruits are 'love, joy, peace, patience, kindness, generosity, faithfulness, gentleness, and self-control. There is no law against such things' (Gal. 5.22–23). Christians have no monopoly on these fruits (recognizing them beyond the churches gives a whole new meaning to mission).

Eucharist. There are many meanings of 'body' in the NT in addition to the 'vile body' with which we began. The church calls itself the very 'body of Christ'. In the Eucharist the body of Christ assumes another form – bread and wine. The Eucharist repeats the words of Christ, 'This is my body', every time it is celebrated. But 'This is my body' is what we 'say' to our partners when we make love with them. There are many unexplored parallels to be made between the experience of receiving the body of one's beloved in the intimacy of love-making and receiving the body of Christ in the Eucharist. Both of these are life-sustaining, life-enhancing, life-creating activities. They engage all our senses, especially the less prominent ones of touch, taste and smell. The abandonment of the self in the giving over of oneself to another, one of the many rich possibilities of love-making, is exceeded only by God's self-abandonment on a cross, the complete giving over of Godself in self-surrender. There is ample unexplored scope here for a eucharistic theology of the body and sexuality.

Bible. The Bible is the textual foundation of Christian faith. Without it we would know nothing about the faith or about its origin among the Jewish people. But while the Bible is a foundation it is most definitely not also the building that has been erected on top of it. We have examined many biblical passages (drawn from both the HB and the NT) that elicit from readers moral and spiritual revulsion, and there is no point in pretending otherwise. Perhaps one day Protestant and Reformed Churches will come to see it was a damaging mistake to confuse the Word made flesh with the words of scriptures; to confuse the Word of God – God in person – with an ancient library of books, however holy. Whenever the Bible is called 'the Word of God' or 'God's Word', the personal is confused with the propositional; the eternal with the temporal; flesh with text. It is the idolatrous elevation of the Bible to divine status that is the ultimate source of abusive theology. The Jesus of John's Gospel warns against idolizing scripture: 'You search the scriptures because you think that in them you have eternal life; and it is they that testify on my behalf' (5.39). Paul too was exasperated by the scriptural literalists of his day, rounding on them for confusing textual law with the Holy Spirit. He is a minister, he retorted, 'of a new covenant, not of letter but of spirit; for the letter kills, but the Spirit gives life' (2 Cor. 3.6). How ironic that a multitude of believers taught to call the Bible the 'Word of God' miss altogether what the Bible 'says' about who and what the Word of God is, and ignore the very warnings it makes about idolizing it. Once that mistake is made it is inevitable that the ancient cultures to which the Bible belongs get transposed into the present.

Tradition. The Catholic mistake, if it is a mistake, lies less with scripture, more with tradition. Scripture and tradition are given equal weight in the Catholic Church – 'For both of them, flowing from the same divine wellspring, in a certain way merge into a unity and tend toward the same end' (Pope Paul VI, 1965, para. 9). But while tradition (at least when it is understood as official church teaching) is taken more seriously than is generally found in Anglicanism, there is still little sense, even after the Second Vatican Council that once promised so much, that tradition itself develops, and that much of it – however adequate it may once have been – is wholly inadequate for the present and future church. It is patriarchal, and sexism is its long-running justification. From patriarchy comes hierarchy, and from hierarchy come the vile activities that have been referenced in this book – slavery, misogyny, racism, colonialism, homophobia, androcentrism, abuse and so on. Repeating tradition, instead of endlessly refining it, repeats the evils associated with it.

The kingdom or 'reign of God'. The abandonment of biblicism and of tradition as something fixed will not lead to the collapse of faith. Indeed, it points to the recovery of it, drawing on classical themes and doctrines and amplifying them. Paul looked forward to obtaining a 'glorious body' in the afterlife. The reign of God that Jesus proclaimed was grounded in (but not confined to) the present life. He healed people who were sick in body and mind, fed the hungry, championed the marginalized and the poor, castigated the rich, exposed the hypocrisy of the religious leaders of his day, and proclaimed that all this was a 'breaking-in' of God's kingdom. The cross is the culmination of a self-enacted parable of divine love, of openness and forgiveness even of the soldiers who nailed him to it. Chapter 9 reminded us of another vision of Paul, of a time when 'There is no longer Jew or Greek, there is no longer slave or free, there is no longer male and female; for all of you are one in Christ Jesus' (Gal. 3.28). However much Paul knew about Jesus, and whatever he may have meant, and whatever later interpretations were laid on what he wrote, the vision yet remains of a future where race, class and gender no longer matter, and which is also always 'breaking-in'. Yes, there may always be people who won't want to be 'in Christ Jesus' in this world or the next. God will have God's own way of including them.

Bibliography

Acts of Paul and Thecla, n.d., trans. Jeremiah Jones (1693–1724), New York: Fordham University Source Books, https://sourcebooks.fordham.edu/basis/thecla.asp (accessed 13.6.23).

Aelred of Rievaulx, 1977, *Spiritual Friendship*, trans. M. E. Laker, Kalamazoo, MI: Cistercian Publications.

Allen, Charlotte, 2018, 'Peter Damian's Counsel', *First Things* 287, November, pp. 9–12.

Allison, James, 2006, *Undergoing God: Dispatches from the Scene of a Break-In*, London: Continuum.

Althaus-Reid, Marcella, 2000, *Indecent Theology: Theological Perversions in Sex, Gender and Politics*, London and New York: Routledge.

Andreades, Sam A., 2015, *enGendered: God's Gift of Gender Difference in Relationship*, Wooster, OH: Weaver Book Company.

Anglican Communion, Resolution 1.10(d), https://www.anglicancommunion.org/resources/document-library/lambeth-conference/1998/section-i-called-to-full-humanity/section-i10-human-sexuality.aspx (accessed 13.6.23).

Anon., 1893, Introduction, Jerome, *Against Jovinianus (Book 1)*, https://www.newadvent.org/fathers/30091.htm (accessed 13.6.23).

Aquinas, 1974 (print edition 1920), *Summa Theologiae*, https://www.newadvent.org/summa/3154.htm#article5 (accessed 13.6.23).

Archbishop of Canterbury, 2017, 'Statement from the Archbishop of Canterbury following today's General Synod', 15 February, https://www.thinkinganglicans.org.uk/7470-2/ (accessed 13.6.23).

Archbishops of Canterbury and York, 2021, 'The Archbishops' Statement in response to the Anti-Racism Taskforce Report', https://www.archbishopofcanterbury.org/news/news-and-statements/archbishops-statement-response-anti-racism-taskforce-report (accessed 26.6.23).

Aristotle, 2014, *On the Generation of Animals*, trans. Theodorus Gaza, CreateSpace Independent Publishing Platform.

Armstrong, Karen, 1986, *The Gospel According to Woman: Christianity's Creation of the Sex War in the West*, London and Sydney: Pan Books.

Athanasius, 1892, *Life of Antony*, trans. H. Ellershaw, in Philip Schaff and Henry Wace (eds), *Nicene and Post-Nicene Fathers*, Second Series, Vol. 4, Buffalo, NY: Christian Literature Publishing Co., https://www.newadvent.org/fathers/2811.htm (accessed 26.6.23).

Augustine, 1984, *City of God*, Harmondsworth: Penguin Classics.

Augustine, n.d., *On the Good of Marriage*, section 1, https://www.newadvent.org/fathers/1309.htm (accessed 26.6.23).

Babylonian Talmud (Tractate *Yebamoth*, folio 34b), https://www.halakhah.com/yebamoth/yebamoth_34.html#PARTb (accessed 26.6.23).

Ban Conversion Therapy, https://www.banconversiontherapy.com/about (accessed 26.6.23).

Barnabas, Letter of, n.d., trans. J. R. Lightfoot, in *Early Christian Writings*, http://www.earlychristianwritings.com/text/barnabas-lightfoot.html (accessed 26.6.23).

Barr, Beth Allison, 2021, 'Woman's Work through Time', *Church Times*, 25 June, p. 23.

Barton, John, 2020, 'The Old Testament', in Timothy Larsen (ed.), *The Oxford Handbook of Christmas*, Oxford: Oxford University Press, pp. 67–76.

BBC News, 2020, 'L'Arche founder Jean Vanier sexually abused women – internal report', 22 February.

BBC News, 2021, 'Irish mother and baby homes: Timeline of controversy', 13 January, https://www.bbc.co.uk/news/world-europe-54693159 (accessed 26.6.23).

Beardsley, Christina (Tina) SMMS, 2023, 'Trans People and *LLF*', *Modern Believing* 64.1, pp. 26–35.

Beattie, Tina, 2010, 'The Catholic Church's Scandal: Modern Crisis, Ancient Roots', *Open Democracy*, unpaginated, https://www.opendemocracy.net/en/catholic-churchs-abuse-scandal-modern-crisis-ancient-roots/ (accessed 26.6.23).

Bennett, Jana Marguerite, 2017, *Singleness and the Church: A New Theology of the Single Life*, Oxford: Oxford University Press.

Benson, Ophelia and Jeremy Stangroom, 2009, *Does God Hate Women?* London & New York: Continuum.

Bishops of the Church of England, 2023, *Living in Love and Faith: A Response*, 20 January, https://www.churchofengland.org/media/29238 (accessed 26.6.23).

Blyth, Caroline, Emily Colgan and Katie Edwards (eds), 2018, *Rape Culture, Gender Violence, and Religion: Biblical Perspectives*, Cham, Switzerland: Palgrave Macmillan.

Bolz-Weber, Nadia, 2019, *Shame-Less: A Sexual Reformation*, Norwich: Canterbury Press.

Bonhoeffer, Dietrich, 1959, *The Cost of Discipleship*, revised and unabridged, New York: Macmillan.

Boswell, John, 1995, *The Marriage of Likeness: Same-Sex Unions in Pre-Modern Europe*, London: HarperCollins.

Boyarin, Daniel, 2007, 'Against Rabbinic Sexuality: Textual Reasoning and the Jewish Theology of Sex', in Gerard Loughlin (ed.), *Queer Theology: Rethinking the Western Body*, Malden, MA and Oxford: Blackwell, pp. 131–46.

Brakke, David, 1995, 'The Problematization of Nocturnal Emissions in Early Christian Syria, Egypt, and Gaul', *Journal of Early Christian Studies* 3.4, pp. 419–60.

Brenner, Athalya and Carole R. Fontaine (eds), 2000, *The Song of Songs: A Feminist Companion to the Bible (Second Series)*, Sheffield: Sheffield Academic Press.

Brock, Brian, 2021, *Disability: Living into the Diversity of Christ's Body* (Pastoring for Life: Theological Wisdom for Ministering Well), London: SCM Press.

Brown, Peter, 1990, *The Body and Society: Men, Women and Sexual Renunciation in Early Christianity*, London and Boston, MA: Faber & Faber.

Browning-Mullis, 2020, 'Why We Use "Enslaved"', 4 May, https://www.telfair.org/article/why-we-use-enslaved/#:~:text=For%20example%2C%20we%20use%20phrases,by%20the%20actions%20of%20another (accessed 26.6.23).

Brownson, James V., 2013, *Bible, Gender, Sexuality: Reframing the Church's Debate on Same-Sex Relationships*, Grand Rapids, MI: Eerdmans.

Brundage, James A., 1987, *Law, Sex, and Christian Society in Medieval Europe*, Chicago, IL: University of Chicago Press.

Burridge, Richard A., 2007, *Imitating Jesus: An Inclusive Approach to New Testament Ethics*, Grand Rapids, MI: Eerdmans.

Bynum, Caroline Walker, 1988, *Holy Feast and Holy Fast: The Religious Significance of Food to Medieval Women*, Oakland, CA: University of California Press.

Bynum, Caroline Walker, 1992, *Fragmentation and Redemption: Essays on Gender and the Human Body in Medieval Religion*, New York: Zone Books.

Cadden, Joan, 1995, *The Meaning of Sex Difference in the Middle Ages*, Cambridge: Cambridge University Press.

Cahill, Desmond and Peter Wilkinson, 2017, *Child Sexual Abuse in the Catholic Church: An Interpretive Review of the Literature and Public Inquiry Reports*, Melbourne: Centre for Global Research, School of Global, Urban and Social Studies, RMIT University.

Callan, Maeve, 2012, 'Of Vanishing Fetuses and Maidens Made-Again: Abortion, Restored Virginity, and Similar Scenarios in Medieval Irish Hagiography and Penitentials', *Journal of the History of Sexuality* 21.2, pp. 282–96.

Castelli, Elizabeth, 1993, '"I Will Make Mary Male": Pieties of the Body and Gender Transformation of Christian Women in Late Antiquity', in Julia Epstein and Kristina Straub (eds), *The Cultural Politics of Gender Ambiguity*, London: Routledge, pp. 21–41.

Catechism of the Catholic Church, 1994, https://www.vatican.va/archive/ENG 0015/__P85.HTM

Charlier, Philippe, Saudamini Deo and Antonio Perciaccante, 2020, 'A Brief History of the Clitoris', *Archives of Sexual Behavior* 49.1, pp. 47–8, https://link. springer.com/article/10.1007/s10508-020-01638-6#citeas (accessed 26.6.23).

Church, F. Forrester, 1975, 'Sex and Salvation in Tertullian', *Harvard Theological Review* 68.2, pp. 83–101.

Church of England, 2017, *Responding Well to Domestic Abuse: Policy and Practice Guidance*, London: Church House Publishing, https://www.churchofengland. org/sites/default/files/2017-11/responding-well-to-domestic-abuse-formatted-master-copy-030317.pdf (accessed 26.6.23).

Church of England, 2020, 'About Living in Love and Faith', https://www.church ofengland.org/resources/living-love-and-faith/about-living-love-and-faith (accessed 26.6.23).

Church of England, 2021, *From Lament to Action: The Report of the Archbishops' Anti-Racism Taskforce*, London: Church House Publishing, https://www.church ofengland.org/sites/default/files/2021-04/FromLamentToAction-report.pdf (accessed 26.6.23).

Church of England, *Common Worship*, n.d., 'An Order for Night Prayer (Compline) in Traditional Language', http://justus.anglican.org/~ss/commonworship/ word/nighttrad.html (accessed 27.6.23).

Church of England, n.d., 'Marriage', https://www.churchofengland.org/prayer-and-worship/worship-texts-and-resources/common-worship/marriage#mm093 (accessed 27.6.23).

Church of England, n.d., 'The Form of the Solemnization of Matrimony', https:// www.churchofengland.org/prayer-and-worship/worship-texts-and-resources/ book-common-prayer/form-solemnization-matrimony (accessed 27.6.23).

Church Times, 2019, 'UK News in brief', 31 May, https://www.churchtimes.co.uk/articles/2019/31-may/news/uk/uk-news-in-brief (accessed 27.6.23).

Church Times, 2023, 'Church Commissioners to set aside £100 million to compensate for slave-trade links', 10 January.

Clement of Alexandria, 1991, *Stromateis, Books 1–3*, The Fathers of the Church, Vol. 85, trans. John Ferguson, Book 3, Washington, DC: Catholic University of America Press, https://www.jstor.org/stable/j.ctt284w4w?turn_away=true (accessed 27.6.23).

Clines, David J. A., 2020, 'The Ubiquitous Language of Violence in the Hebrew Bible', in J. van Ruiten and K. van Bekkum (eds), *Violence in the Hebrew Bible: Between Text and Reception*, Leiden: Brill, pp. 23–41.

Clough, Miryam, 2022, *Vocation and Violence: The Church and #MeToo*, London and New York: Routledge.

Cohn-Sherbok, Dan (ed.), 2015, *Holocaust Theology: A Reader*, Exeter: Exeter University Press.

Collins, Adela Yarbro, 2007, 'Renewed Proclamation', in Harold W. Attridge (ed.), *Mark: A Commentary*, 1517 Media, pp. 293–395 https://doi.org/10.2307/j.ctvb 6v7zz.26 (accessed 27.6.23).

Commission of Investigation Report into the Catholic Archdiocese of Dublin (The Murphy Report), 2009, www.bishop-accountability.org/reports/2009_11_26_ Murphy_Report (accessed 27.6.23).

Concannon, Cavan W., 2017, 'Debating Dionysios: Sexual Politics and Second-Century Christianity', in Cavan W. Concannon, *Assembling Early Christianity, Trade, Networks, and the Letters of Dionysios of Corinth*, Cambridge: Cambridge University Press, pp. 122–54.

Concannon, Cavan W., 2017, *Assembling Early Christianity: Trade, Networks, and the Letters of Dionysios of Corinth*, Cambridge: Cambridge University Press.

Cone, James H., 2013 (2011 hardback), *The Cross and the Lynching Tree*, Maryknoll, NY: Orbis Books.

Congregation for the Doctrine of the Faith, 1986, *Letter to the Bishops of the Catholic Church on the Pastoral Care of Homosexual Persons*, https://www.vatican. va/roman_curia/congregations/cfaith/documents/rc_con_cfaith_doc_19861001_ homosexual-persons_en.html (accessed 27.6.23).

Congregation for the Doctrine of the Faith, 2021, 'Responsum to a dubium regarding the blessing of the unions of persons of the same sex, 15.03.2021', March, https://press.vatican.va/content/salastampa/en/bollettino/pubblico/2021/ 03/15/210315b.html (accessed 27.6.23).

Conway, Colleen M., 2008, *Behold the Man: Jesus and Greco-Roman Masculinity*, Oxford: Oxford University Press.

Cooper, Donna, 2012, 'Was Tertullian a misogynist? A Re-examination of this Charge based on a Rhetorical Analysis of Tertullian's Work' (PhD thesis), University of Exeter, https://encore.exeter.ac.uk/iii/encore/record/C__Rb2604483 (accessed 27.6.23).

Cooper, Kate, 2013, 'The Bride of Christ, the "Male Woman", and the Female Reader in Late Antiquity', in Judith Bennett and Ruth Karras (eds), *The Oxford Handbook of Women and Gender in Medieval Europe*, Oxford: Oxford University Press, pp. 529–41.

Corless, Catherine, 2020, 'Lecture 91: The Tuam Mother and Baby Home', *YouTube*, 19 November, https://www.youtube.com/watch?v=JnCmj4sKDmo (accessed 27.6.23).

Cornwall, Susannah, 2013, *Theology and Sexuality*, London: SCM Press.

Cornwall, Susannah, 2015a, 'Troubling Bodies?', in Susannah Cornwall (ed.), *Intersex, Theology, and the Bible: Troubling Bodies in Church, Text, and Society*, New York: Palgrave Macmillan, pp. 1–26.

Cornwall, Susannah, 2015b, 'Intersex and Transgender People', in Adrian Thatcher (ed.), *The Oxford Handbook of Theology, Sexuality, and Gender*, Oxford: Oxford University Press, 2015, pp. 657–75.

Courage International, 2023, https://couragerc.org/about/ (accessed 27.6.23).

Cramer, David, Jenny Howell, Paul Martens and Jonathan Tran, 2014, 'Theology and Misconduct: The Case of John Howard Yoder', *Christian Century*, 4 August.

Creamer, Deborah Beth, 2015, 'Disabled People', in Adrian Thatcher (ed.), *The Oxford Handbook of Theology, Sexuality, and Gender*, Oxford: Oxford University Press, pp. 676–87.

Crean, AnneMarie, 2019, *Irish Examiner*, 19 May, https://www.irishexaminer.com/lifestyle/arid-30925312.html (accessed 20.10.22).

Crompton, Louis, 1985, *Byron and Greek Love: Homophobia in Nineteenth-Century England*, Berkeley, CA: University of California Press.

Crowther, Kathleen, 2015, 'Sexual Difference', in Ulinka Rublack (ed.), *The Oxford Handbook of the Protestant Reformation*, Oxford: Oxford University Press, pp. 667–87.

Crummell, Alexander, 1862, 'The Negro Race Not under a Curse: An Examination of Genesis IX.25', in *The Future of Africa, being Addresses, Sermons, etc., etc., Delivered in the Republic of Liberia*, New York. Cited in David M. Goldenberg, 2003, *The Curse of Ham: Race and Slavery in Early Judaism, Christianity, and Islam*, Princeton, NJ: Princeton University Press.

Dabhoiwala, Faramerz, 2013, *The Origins of Sex: A History of the First Sexual Revolution*, London: Penguin Books.

Dawson, Rosie, 2021, 'Was Jesus sexually abused?', *Church Times*, 1 April.

de Franza, Megan, 2015, *Sex Difference in Christian Theology: Male, Female, and Intersex in the Image of God*, Grand Rapids, MI: Eerdmans.

de Gruchy, Steve, 2006, 'Religion and Racism: Struggles around Segregation, "Jim Crow", and Apartheid', in Hugh McLeod (ed.), *The Cambridge History of Christianity: Volume 9, World Christianities c.1914–c.2000*, Cambridge: Cambridge University Press, pp. 385–400.

de Wet, Chris L., 2015, *Preaching Bondage: John Chrysostom and the Discourse of Slavery in Early Christianity*, San Francisco, CA: University of California Press.

de Wet, Chris, 2017, 'Revisiting the *Subintroductae*: Slavery, Asceticism, and "Syneisaktism" in the Exegesis of John Chrysostom', *Biblical Interpretation* 25.1, pp. 58–80.

de Wet, C. L., 2019, '"The Barbarians Themselves are Offended by our Vices:" Slavery, Sexual Vice and Shame in Salvian of Marseilles' *De gubernatione Dei*', *HTS Teologiese Studies/Theological Studies* 75.3, pp. 1–8.

de Wet, Chris L., 2021, 'Nemesius of Emesa on Desire, Pleasure, and Sex: A Case of the Medical Making of an Early Christian Sexual Culture', *Religion and Theology* 28.3–4, pp. 206–32.

Deane, Jennifer Kolpacoff, 2011, *A History of Medieval Heresy and Inquisition*, Lanham, MD: Rowman & Littlefield.

DeConick, April D., 2011, *Holy Misogyny: Why the Sex and Gender Conflicts in the Early Church Still Matter*, London: Continuum.

Devisse, Jean, 1979, *The Image of the Black in Western Art: From the Early Christian Era to the "Age of Discovery"*, trans. William G. Ryan, Vol. 2, Part 1: 'From the Demonic Threat to the Incarnation of Sainthood', New York: William Morrow.

Didache, n.d., New Advent, https://www.newadvent.org/fathers/0714.htm (accessed 27.6.23).

Disney, Lindsey and Larry Poston, 2010, 'The Breath of Life: Christian Perspectives on Conception and Ensoulment', *Anglican Theological Review* 92.2, pp. 271–95.

Doriani, Daniel, 1996, 'The Puritans, Sex, and Pleasure', in Adrian Thatcher and Elizabeth Stuart (eds), *Christian Perspectives on Sexuality and Gender*, Leominster: Gracewing, pp. 33–52.

Douglas, Kelly Brown, 2019, 'Stereotypes, False Images, Terrorism: The White Assault upon Black Sexuality', in Donald L. Boisvert and Carly Daniel-Hughes (eds), *The Bloomsbury Reader in Religion, Sexuality, and Gender*, London: T&T Clark, pp. 16–27.

Douglass, Frederick, 1845, *Narrative of the Life of Frederick Douglass, an American Slave, Written by Himself*, Boston, MA: Anti-Slavery Office (electronic edn, Chapel Hill: University of North Carolina, 1999), https://docsouth.unc.edu/neh/douglass/douglass.html (accessed 27.6.23).

Dowd, Chris and Christina Beardsley (eds), 2018, *Transfaith: A Transgender Pastoral Resource*, London: Darton, Longman & Todd.

Doyle, Thomas P., 2003, 'Roman Catholic Clericalism, Religious Duress, and Clergy Sexual Abuse', *Pastoral Psychology* 51.3, January, pp. 189–231.

Dube, Musa W. (2012), 'Introduction: The Scramble for Africa as the Biblical Scramble for Africa: Postcolonial Perspectives', in Musa W. Dube, Andrew M. Mbuvi and Dora Mbuwayesango (eds), *Postcolonial Perspectives in African Biblical Interpretations*, Atlanta: Society of Biblical Literature, pp. 1–28, p. 2.

duBois, Page, 2008, *Slaves and Other Objects*, Chicago: University of Chicago Press.

Dunning, Benjamin H., 2019, 'Same-Sex Relations', in Benjamin H. Dunning (ed.), *The Oxford Handbook of New Testament, Gender, and Sexuality*, Oxford: Oxford University Press, pp. 574–91.

Ehrman, Bart D., 2005, *Misquoting Jesus: The Story Behind Who Changed the Bible and Why*, New York: HarperCollins.

Eiesland, Nancy, 1994, *The Disabled God: Toward a Liberatory Theology of Disability*, Nashville, TN: Abingdon Press.

Elliott, Dyan, 1999, *Fallen Bodies: Pollution, Sexuality, and Demonology in the Middle Ages*, Philadelphia, PA: University of Pennsylvania Press.

Elliott, Dyan, 2020, *The Corrupter of Boys: Sodomy, Scandal, and the Medieval Clergy*, Philadelphia, PA: University of Pennsylvania Press.

Farley, Margaret, 2006, *Just Love: A Framework for Sexual Ethics*, New York: Continuum.

Feinstein, Eve Levavi, 2014, *Sexual Pollution in the Hebrew Bible*, Oxford: Oxford University Press.

Feldman, David M., 1968, *Birth Control in Jewish Law*, New York: New York University Press.

Figueroa Alvear, R. and D. Tombs, 2019, 'Recognising Jesus as a Victim of Sexual Abuse: Responses from Sodalicio Survivors in Peru' ('When Did We See You Naked?' No. 3), Centre for Theology and Public Issues, University of Otago.

Freire, Paulo, 1970, *Pedagogy of the Oppressed*, New York: Continuum.

Galer, Sophia Smith, 2022, 'The sex myth that's centuries old', 20 April, https://www.bbc.com/future/article/20220419-how-the-hymen-myth-destroys-lives (accessed 27.6.23).

General Synod [of the Church of England], 2023 (GS2289), 'Living in Love and Faith – A Response from the Bishops of the Church of England', https://www.churchofengland.org/sites/default/files/2023-01/GS%202289%20Living%20in%20Love%20and%20Faith.pdf (accessed 27.6.23).

Gibb, Dame Moira, 2017, *An Abuse of Faith: The Independent Peter Ball Review*, 22 June, https://www.churchofengland.org/safeguarding/overview/news-and-views/independent-report-churchs-handling-peter-ball-case (accessed 8.7.23).

Gibson, Edgar C. S. (trans. and Notes), 1894, *The Conferences of John Cassian*, https://www.ccel.org/ccel/cassian/conferences.i.html (accessed 8.7.23).

Gillingham, Sara, 2019. 'My Intersex Story', *Church Times*, 22 February, https://www.churchtimes.co.uk/articles/2019/22-february/features/features/my-intersex-story (accessed 27.6.23).

Glancy, Jennifer A., 2003, *Slavery in Early Christianity*, Oxford: Oxford University Press.

Global Interfaith Commission on LGBT+ Lives, 2020, 16 December, https://globalinterfaith.lgbt/ (accessed 27.6.23).

Gnostic Society, n.d., *Gospel of Thomas*, trans. T. O. Lambdin, The Gnostic Society Library: The Nag Hammadi Library, http://www.gnosis.org/naghamm/gthlamb.html#:~:text=%20%20%201%20%281%29%20And%20he%20said%2C,is%20in%20your%20sight%2C%20and%20that...%20More%20 (accessed 27.6.23).

Gombis, Timothy G., 2005, 'A Radically New Humanity: The Function of the Haustafel in Ephesians', *Journal of the Evangelical Theological Society* 48.2, pp. 317–30.

Gould, Stephen Jay, 1981, *Natural History*, https://www.zoology.ubc.ca/~bio336/Bio336/Readings/GouldHyena1981.pdf (accessed 27.6.23).

Graystone, Andrew, 2021, *Bleeding for Jesus: John Smyth and the Cult of Iwerne Camps*, London: Darton, Longman & Todd.

Green, Monica, 2013, 'Caring for Gendered Bodies', in Judith Bennett and Ruth Karras (eds) *The Oxford Handbook of Women and Gender in Medieval Europe*, Oxford: Oxford University Press, pp. 345–61.

Grimm, Veronica, 1996, *From Feasting to Fasting: The Evolution of a Sin*, London: Routledge.

Gudorf, Christine, 2003, 'Contraception and Abortion in Roman Catholicism', in Daniel C. Maguire (ed.), *Sacred Rights: The Case for Contraception and Abortion in World Religions*, Oxford: Oxford University Press, pp. 55–74.

Guidepost Solutions, 2022, *Report of the Independent Investigation*, 15 May, https://www.sataskforce.net/updates/guidepost-solutions-report-of-the-independent-investigation (accessed 27.10.22).

Gula, Richard M., 1989, *Reason Informed by Faith: Foundations of Catholic Morality*, New York: Paulist Press.

Hall, Lesley A., 2001, 'Clitoris', in Colin Blakemore and Sheila Jennett (eds), *The Oxford Companion to the Body*, Oxford: Oxford University Press.

Harvey, Nicholas Peter and Linda Woodhead, 2022, *Unknowing God: Toward a Post-Abusive Theology*, Eugene, OR: Cascade Books.

Heng, Geraldine, 2018, *The Invention of Race in the European Ages*, Cambridge: Cambridge University Press.

Hillerbrand, Hans J., 2017, 'About the Jews and Their Lies, 1543', in Hans J. Hillerbrand, Kirsi I. Stjerna and Timothy J. Wengert, *The Annotated Luther, Vol. 5, Christian Life in the World*, Minneapolis, MN: Fortress Press.

Hitchcock, Tim, 1996, 'Redefining Sex in Eighteenth-Century England', *History Workshop Journal* 41.1, pp. 73–90.

Homer, G., 1929, *Didascalia Apostolorum: The Syriac Version Translated*, Oxford: Oxford University Press, https://womenpriests.org/tradition/didasc-the-didascalia-apostolorum/#abandon (accessed 27.6.23).

Hopkins, Keith, 2017 [1965], 'Contraception in the Roman Empire', in Christopher Kelly (ed.), *Sociological Studies in Roman History*, Cambridge: Cambridge University Press, pp. 1–54.

House of Bishops [of the Church of England], 2020, *Living in Love and Faith: Christian Teaching and Learning about Identity, Sexuality, Relationships and Marriage*, London: Church House Publishing.

IICSA (Independent Inquiry into Child Sexual Abuse), 2020a, *The Roman Catholic Church: Investigation Report*, November, https://www.iicsa.org.uk/key-documents/23357/view/catholic-church-investigation-report-10-november-2020.pdf (accessed 27.6.23).

IICSA (Independent Inquiry into Child Sexual Abuse), 2020b, *The Anglican Church: Investigation Report*, October, https://www.iicsa.org.uk/publications/investigation/anglican-church/executive-summary (accessed 27.6.23).

IICSA, n.d., https://www.iicsa.org.uk/about-us (accessed 27.6.23).

Ilan, Tal, 2019, 'Jewish Women's Life and Practice in the World of the New Testament', in Benjamin H. Dunning (ed.), *The Oxford Handbook of New Testament, Gender, and Sexuality*, Oxford: Oxford University Press, pp. 222–37.

Iozzio, Mary Jo, 2015, 'HIV/AIDS', in Adrian Thatcher (ed.), *The Oxford Handbook of Theology, Sexuality, and Gender*, Oxford: Oxford University Press, pp. 538–53.

Jacobs, Naomi Lawson and Emily Richardson, 2022, *At the Gates: Disability, Justice and the Churches*, London: Darton, Longman & Todd.

James, M. R., 1924, *The Apocalypse of Peter*, in *The Apocryphal New Testament – Translation and Notes*, Oxford: Clarendon Press, http://www.earlychristianwritings.com/text/apocalypsepeter-mrjames.html (accessed 27.6.23).

Jantzen, Grace, 1995, *Power, Gender and Christian Mysticism*, Cambridge: Cambridge University Press.

Jennings, Theodore W., 2003, *The Man Jesus Loved: Homoerotic Narratives from the New Testament*, Cleveland, OH: Pilgrim Press.

Jennings, Theodore W. Jr, 2005, *Jacob's Wound: Homoerotic Narrative in the Literature of Ancient Israel*, New York: Continuum.

Jennings, Theodore W. Jr, 2015, 'Same-Sex Relations in the Biblical World', in Adrian Thatcher (ed.), *The Oxford Handbook of Theology, Sexuality, and Gender*, Oxford: Oxford University Press, pp. 206–21.

Jerome, 1964, *Homily 18: On Psalm 86 (87)*, in *The Homilies of Saint Jerome, Volume 1 (1–59 on the Psalms)*, trans. M. L. Ewald, Washington, DC: Catholic University of America Press.

Jerome, n.d., *Against Jovinianus, Book 1*, https://www.newadvent.org/fathers/30091.htm (accessed 27.6.23).

Jerome, n.d., *Letter to Eustochium (Letter 22)*, https://www.newadvent.org/fathers/3001022.htm (accessed 27.6.23).

Jerome, n.d., *The Perpetual Virginity of Blessed Mary*, https://www.newadvent.org/fathers/3007.htm (accessed 27.6.23).

John Paul II, 1994, *Ordinatio sacerdotalis* ('On Reserving Priestly Ordination to Men Alone'), para. 1, http://www.vatican.va/content/john-paul-ii/en/apost_let ters/1994/documents/hf_jp-ii_apl_19940522_ordinatio-sacerdotalis.html (accessed 27.6.23).

Johnson CSJ, Elizabeth A., 'Mary, Mary, Quite Contrary', *U.S. Catholic*, December, pp. 12–17.

Jones, Robert P., 2020, *White Too Long: The Legacy of White Supremacy in American Christianity*, New York: Simon & Schuster.

Jones, Scott C., 2003, 'Wisdom's Pedagogy: A Comparison of Proverbs vii and 4Q184', *Vetus Testamentum* 53.1, pp. 65–80.

Jung, Patricia Beattie, 2017, *Sex on Earth as it is in Heaven: A Christian Eschatology of Desire*, Albany, NY: SUNY Press.

Justin, n.d., *The First Apology*, https://www.newadvent.org/fathers/0126.htm (accessed 27.6.23).

Kamitsuka, Margaret D., 2019, *Abortion and the Christian Tradition: A Pro-Choice Theological Ethic*, Louisville, KY: Westminster John Knox Press.

Kamitsuka, Margaret, D., 2015, 'Sexual Pleasure', in Adrian Thatcher (ed.), *The Oxford Handbook of Theology, Sexuality, and Gender*, Oxford: Oxford University Press, pp. 505–22.

Kaplan, Lindsay, 2019, *Figuring Racism in Medieval Christianity*, Chicago, IL: University of Chicago Press.

Kazen, Thomas, 2002, *Jesus and Purity Halakhah: Was Jesus Indifferent to Impurity?* Stockholm: Almqvist & Wiksell International.

Keenan, Marie, 2012, *Child Sexual Abuse and the Catholic Church: Gender, Power, and Organizational Culture*, Oxford: Oxford University Press.

Keneally, T., 2017, 'Crimes of the Father', *The Tablet* 271.9204, 10 June.

King, Helen, 2013, 'Female Fluids in the Hippocratic Corpus: How Solid was the Humoral Body?', in Peregrine Horden and Elisabeth Hsu (eds), *The Body in Balance*, New York: Berghahn, pp. 25–49.

King, Helen, 2017, 'The Vulva goes on Pilgrimage', 18 April, https://mistaking-histories.wordpress.com/2017/04/18/the-vulva-goes-on-pilgrimage/ (accessed 27.6.23).

King, Helen, 2020, 'Living in Love and Faith: Doing History', 12 November, https://modernchurch.org.uk/prof-helen-king-living-in-love-and-faith-doing-his tory (accessed 8.7.23).

King, Helen, 2023, 'Born-Again Virginity', 27 February, https://viamedia.news/2023/02/27/born-again-virginity/ (accessed 27.6.23).

Knieps-Port le Roi, Thomas, 2017, 'Introduction', in Thomas Knieps-Port le Roi (ed.), *A Point of No Return? Amoris Laetitia on Marriage, Divorce and Remarriage*, Berlin: LIT Verlag, pp. 1–8.

Knust, Jennifer Wright, 2006, *Abandoned to Lust: Sexual Slander and Ancient Christianity*, New York: Columbia University Press.

Knust, Jennifer W., 2019, 'Marriage, Adultery, and Divorce', in Benjamin H. Dunning (ed.), *The Oxford Handbook of New Testament, Gender, and Sexuality*, Oxford: Oxford University Press, pp. 521–38.

Koepping, Elizabeth, 2021, *Spousal Violence Among World Christians: Silent Scandal*, London: Bloomsbury Academic.

Kraemer, Ross S., 2019, 'Thecla', in Benjamin H. Dunning (ed.), *The Oxford Handbook of New Testament, Gender, and Sexuality*, Oxford: Oxford University Press, pp. 485–502.

Kramer, Heinrich and James Sprenger, 1948, *Malleus Maleficarum*, n.p.: Kessinger Publishing.

Kuefler, Mathew, 2001, *The Manly Eunuch: Masculinity, Gender Ambiguity, and Christian Ideology in Late Antiquity*, Chicago, IL: University of Chicago Press.

Laeuchli, S., 1972, *Power and Sexuality: The Emergence of Canon Law at the Synod of Elvira*, Philadelphia, PA: Temple University Press.

Lambeth Conference Resolutions Archive from 1930, n.d., Resolution 15, https://www.anglicancommunion.org/media/127734/1930.pdf?year=1930 (accessed 27.6.23).

Laqueur, Thomas W., 1984, *Solitary Sex: A Cultural History of Masturbation*, New York: Zone Books.

League of Saint Peter Damian, https://www.stpeterdamian.com/ (accessed 19.5.22).

Levack, Brian P., 2013, 'Introduction', *The Oxford Handbook of Witchcraft in Early Modern Europe and Colonial America*, Oxford: Oxford University Press, pp. 1–11.

Lewis-Giggetts, Tracey Michael, 2022, *Then They Came for Mine: Healing from the Trauma of Racial Violence*, Louisville, KY: Westminster John Knox Press.

LGB Alliance, 2020, 'Written Evidence submitted by LGB Alliance', November, https://lgballiance.org.uk/ (accessed 27.6.23).

Liberman, Anatoly, 2014, 'Beggars, Buggers, and Bigots, Part 2', https://blog.oup.com/2014/03/beggar-beguine-word-origin-etymology/ (accessed 27.6.23).

Lillis, Julia Kelto, 2016, 'Paradox *in Partu*: Verifying Virginity in the *Protevangelium of James*', *Journal of Early Christian Studies* 24.1, pp. 1–28.

Lillis, Julia Kelto, 2020, 'No Hymen Required: Reconstructing Origen's View on Mary's Virginity', *Church History* 89.2, pp. 249–67.

Lings, Renato, 2013, *Love Lost in Translation: Homosexuality and the Bible*, Victoria: Trafford Publishing.

Lings, K. Renato, 2021, *Holy Censorship or Mistranslation? Love, Gender and Sexuality in the Bible*, Pradesh, India: HarperCollins.

Lipsett, B. Diane, 2019, 'Celibacy and Virginity', in Benjamin H. Dunning (ed.), *The Oxford Handbook of New Testament, Gender, and Sexuality*, Oxford: Oxford University Press, pp. 557–72.

Lloyd, Genevieve, 1984, *The Man of Reason: Male and Female in Western Philosophy*, London: Methuen.

Loader, William, 2010, *Sexuality in the New Testament: Understanding the Key Texts*, London: SPCK.

Loader, William, 2015, 'Marriage and Sexual Relations in the Biblical World', in Adrian Thatcher (ed.), *The Oxford Handbook of Theology, Sexuality, and Gender*, Oxford: Oxford University Press, pp. 189–205.

Long, Sam, Lewis Steller and River X. Suh, 2020, 'Gender-Inclusive Biology', https://www.genderinclusivebiology.com (accessed 27.6.23).

Lowen, Mark, 2022, 'Assignment: Italy's hidden sins'(BBC World Service podcast), https://www.bbc.co.uk/sounds/play/w3ct1gyp?xtor=ES-212-%5B50369_world

servicenewsletter170222%5D-20220218-%5Bbbcrworldservice_assignment_italy_image%5D (accessed 19.10.22).

Luxmoore, Jonathan, 2023, 'RC leaders in Portugal pledge action on abuse', *Church Times*, 17 February.

MacCulloch, Diarmaid, 2014, *Silence: A Christian History*, New York: Penguin Random House.

MacCulloch, Diarmaid, 2020, 'Living in Love and Faith' (blog), https://modern church.org.uk/prof-diarmaid-macculloch-living-in-love-and-faith (accessed 27.6.23).

Maier, Harry O., 2018, *New Testament Christianity in the Roman World*, Oxford: Oxford University Press.

Malina, Bruce J., 2001, *The New Testament World*, 3rd edn, Louisville, KY: Westminster John Knox Press.

Mama, Amina, 2017, 'Colonialism', in Fionnuala Ní Aoláin et al. (eds), *The Oxford Handbook of Gender and Conflict*, Oxford: Oxford University Press, pp. 265–75, p. 265.

Mann, Rachel, 2015, 'However could God love someone like me?', *Church Times*, 16 January.

Manne, Kate, 2018, *Down Girl: The Logic of Misogyny*, New York: Oxford University Press.

Marjanen, Antti, 2007, 'Gnosticism', in Susan Ashbrook Harvey and David G. Hunter (eds), *The Oxford Handbook of Early Christian Studies*, Oxford: Oxford University Press, pp. 204–17.

Marks, Jeremy, n.d., 'Post Courage', https://postcourage.net/ (accessed 27.6.23).

Marks, Jeremy, n.d., 'Jeremy's Story', https://www.banconversiontherapy.com/jeremys-story (accessed 27.6.23).

Martin, Dale B., 2006, *Sex and the Single Savior: Gender and Sexuality in Biblical Interpretation*, Louisville, KY: Westminster John Knox Press.

Mary, Margaret, 1954, 'Slavery in the Writings of St. Augustine', *The Classical Journal* 49.8, May, pp. 363–9.

Mastnak, Tomaz, 2002, *Crusading Peace: Christendom, the Muslim World, and Western Political Order*, Oakland, CA: University of California Press.

Maunder, Chris, 2019, 'Mary and the Gospel Narratives', in Chris Maunder (ed.), *The Oxford Handbook of Mary*, Oxford: Oxford University Press, pp. 21–39.

Mauriceau, François, 1683, *The Diseases of Women with Child, and in Child-Bed*, 2nd edn, trans. and enlarged by Hugh Chamberlen, London: John Darby.

Maxwell, John Francis, 1975, *Slavery and the Catholic Church: The History of Catholic Teaching Concerning the Moral Legitimacy of the Institution of Slavery*, Chichester and London: Barry Rose Publishers.

McCarthy, Niall, 2019, 'The Death Toll of Europe's Witch Trials', *Statista*, 29 October, https://www.statista.com/chart/19801/people-tried-and-executed-in-witch-trials-in-europe/ (accessed 27.6.23).

McCarty, Richard W., 2021, *Under the Bed of Heaven: Christian Eschatology and Sexual Ethics*, Albany, NY: SUNY Press.

McDonald, Chine, 2022, 'Choice to side with the slaves', *Church Times*, 7 January, https://www.churchtimes.co.uk/articles/2022/7-january/features/features/choice-to-side-with-the-slaves (accessed 27.6.23).

McGuire, Anne, 2019, 'Nag Hammadi and Related Literature', in Benjamin H. Dunning (ed.), *The Oxford Handbook of New Testament, Gender, and Sexuality*, Oxford: Oxford University Press, pp. 371–86.

Medina, José, 2021, 'Feminism and Epistemic Injustice', in Kim Q. Hall and Ásta (eds), *The Oxford Handbook of Feminist Philosophy*, Oxford: Oxford University Press, pp. 409–17.

Methodist Church in Britain, 2019, *God in Love Unites Us*, https://www.methodist.org.uk/about-us/the-methodist-church/marriage-and-relationships/archive-marriage-and-relationships-2019/the-2019-marriage-and-relationships-report/ (accessed 27.6.23).

Methodius, *Banquet of the Ten Virgins (Discourse 1)*, https://www.newadvent.org/fathers/062301.htm (accessed 27.6.23).

Meyer, Marvin (trans.), n.d., *The Gospel of Philip*, in The Nag Hammadi Library of The Gnostic Society, http://gnosis.org/naghamm/GPhilip-Meyer.html (accessed 27.6.23).

Miller, J. E., 1995, 'The Practices of Romans 1:26: Homosexual or Heterosexual?', *Novum Testamentum* 37.1, pp. 1–11.

Mistry, Zubin, 2013, 'The Sexual Shame of the Chaste: "Abortion Miracles" in Early Medieval Saints' Lives', *Gender and History* 25.3, pp. 607–20.

Moore, Gareth, 1992, *The Body in Context: Sex and Catholicism*, London: Continuum.

Moore OP, Gareth, 1995, *A Question of Truth: Christianity and Homosexuality*, London: Continuum.

Moughtin-Mumby, Sharon, 2008, *Sexual and Marital Metaphors in Hosea, Jeremiah, Isaiah, and Ezekiel*, Oxford: Oxford University Press.

National Safeguarding Steering Group, 2022, *Past Cases Review*, 2, October, https://www.churchofengland.org/safeguarding/past-cases-review-2?mc_cid=cddb27f416&mc_eid=a6fd5d5397 (accessed 27.6.23).

New Ways Ministry, https://www.newwaysministry.org/about/.

New York Times, 2012, 'Vatican Scolds Nun for Book on Sexuality', 5 June, https://www.nytimes.com/2012/06/05/us/sister-margaret-farley-denounced-by-vatican.html.

Newsweek, 2022, 'The Catholic Church has Paid Nearly $4 Billion over Sexual Abuse Claims, Group Says', 19 October.

Niditch, Susan, 2021, 'Blood and Hair: Body Management and Practice', in Francesca Stavrakopoulou (ed.), *Life and Death: Social Perspectives on Biblical Bodies*, London: Bloomsbury, pp. 27–42.

Nixey, Catherine, 2017, *The Darkening Age: The Christian Destruction of the Classical World*, London: Pan Books.

Noonan, John, 1986, *Contraception*, Cambridge, MA: Harvard University Press.

O'Brien, Michelle, 2016, 'Intersex, Medicine, Diversity, Identity and Spirituality', in Christina Beardsley and Michelle O'Brien (eds), *This is my Body: Hearing the Theology of Transgender Christians*, London: Darton, Longman & Todd, pp. 45–55.

O'Donnell, Karen and Katie Cross (eds), 2020, *Feminist Trauma Theologies: Body, Scripture and Church in Critical Perspective*, London: SCM Press.

O'Donnell, Karen, 2022, *The Dark Womb: Re-Conceiving Theology through Reproductive Loss*, London: SCM Press.

O'Donnell, Karen and Katie Cross (eds), 2022, *Bearing Witness: Intersectional Perspectives on Trauma Theology*, London: SCM Press.

Oakley, Lisa and Justin Humphreys, 2019, *Escaping the Maze of Spiritual Abuse: Creating Healthy Christian Cultures*, London: SPCK.

Olsen, Glenn W., 2011, *Of Sodomites, Effeminates, Hermaphrodites, and Andro-gynes: Sodomy in the Age of Peter Damian*, Toronto: Pontifical Institute of Mediaeval Studies.

Olyan, Saul, 1996, '"And with a male you shall not lie the lying down of a woman": On the meaning and significance of Leviticus 18:22 and 20:13', *Journal of the History of Sexuality* 5.2, pp. 179–206.

Origen, 1957, *The Song of Songs, Commentary and Homilies*, trans. R. P. Lawson, New York: Newman Press.

Oshatz, Molly, 2011, *Slavery and Sin: The Fight against Slavery and the Rise of Liberal Protestantism*, Oxford: Oxford University Press.

Outler, Albert C. (trans.), 1955, *Augustine: Enchiridion: On Faith, Hope, and Love*, Philadelphia, PA: Westminster Press, http://www.tertullian.org/fathers/augustine_enchiridion_02_trans.htm#C23.

Oxford English Dictionary, https://www.oed.com/ (accessed 27.6.23).

Patton, Michael S., 1985, 'Masturbation from Judaism to Victorianism', *Journal of Religion and Health* 24.2, pp. 133–46.

Patton, Michael S., 1986, 'Twentieth-Century Attitudes Toward Masturbation, *Journal of Religion and Health* 25.4, pp. 291–303.

Perisanidi, Maroula, 2018, 'Zonaras's Treatise on Nocturnal Emissions: Introduction and Translation', *Nottingham Medieval Studies* 62, pp. 33–59.

Perkins, Anna Kasafi, 2019, 'Christian Norms and Intimate Male Partner Violence: Lessons from a Jamaica Women's Health Survey', in Antipas L. Harris and Michael D. Palmer (eds), *The Holy Spirit and Social Justice: Interdisciplinary Global Perspectives: History, Race and Culture*, Lanham, MD: Seymour Press, pp. 240–63.

Petrey, Taylor, 2016, *Resurrecting Parts: Early Christians on Desire, Reproduction, and Sexual Difference*, London and New York: Routledge.

Pitts, Jamie, 2015, 'Anabaptist Re-Vision: On John Howard Yoder's Misrecognized Sexual Politics', *Mennonite Quarterly Review* 89.1, January, pp. 153–70.

Pope Francis, 2016, 'As a Loving Mother', Apostolic Letter 'Motu Proprio', https://www.vatican.va/content/francesco/en/apost_letters/documents/papa-francesco_lettera-ap_20160604_come-una-madre-amorevole.html (accessed 27.6.23).

Pope Francis, 2015, *Amoris Laetitia*, https://www.vatican.va/content/dam/francesco/pdf/apost_exhortations/documents/papa-francesco_esortazione-ap_20160319_amoris-laetitia_en.pdf (accessed 8.7.23).

Pope Francis, 2018, *Letter of His Holiness Pope Francis to the People of God*, 20 August, https://www.vatican.va/content/francesco/en/letters/2018/documents/papa-francesco_20180820_lettera-popolo-didio.html (accessed 27.6.23).

Pope John Paul II, 1981, *Familiaris consortio*, section 11, https://www.vatican.va/content/john-paul-ii/en/apost_exhortations/documents/hf_jp-ii_exh_19811122_familiaris-consortio.html (accessed 27.6.23).

Pope John Paul II, 1994, *Ordinatio sacerdotalis* ('On Reserving Priestly Ordination to Men Alone'), http://www.vatican.va/content/john-paul-ii/en/apost_letters/1994/documents/hf_jp-ii_apl_19940522_ordinatio-sacerdotalis.html (accessed 27.6.23).

Pope Paul VI, 1965, *Dogmatic Constitution on Divine Revelation: Dei Verbum*, 18 November, https://www.vatican.va/archive/hist_councils/ii_vatican_council/documents/vat-ii_const_19651118_dei-verbum_en.html (accessed 27.6.23).

Pope Paul VI, 1967, *Sacerdotalis Caelibatus*, 24 June, https://www.vatican.va/content/paul-vi/en/encyclicals/documents/hf_p-vi_enc_24061967_sacerdotalis.html (accessed 27.6.23).

Pope Paul VI, 1968, *Humanae Vitae*, https://www.vatican.va/content/paul-vi/en/encyclicals/documents/hf_p-vi_enc_25071968_humanae-vitae.html (accessed 27.6.23).

Pope Pius XI, 1930, *Casti connubii (Chaste Marriage)*, para. 56, http://www.vatican.va/content/pius-xi/en/encyclicals/documents/hf_p-xi_enc_19301231_casti-connubii.html (accessed 27.6.23).

Power, Kim, 1995, *Veiled Desire: Augustine's Writing on Women*, London: Darton, Longman & Todd.

Protoevangelium of James, https://www.newadvent.org/fathers/0847.htm (accessed 27.6.23).

Provan, Charles D., 1989, *The Bible and Birth Control*, Monongahela, PA: Zimmer Printing.

Puff, Helmut, 2013, 'Same-sex Possibilities', in Judith M. Bennett and Ruth Karras (eds), *The Oxford Handbook of Women and Gender in Medieval Europe*, Oxford: Oxford University Press, pp. 379–92.

Quick, Laura, 2021, 'Bitenosh's Orgasm, Galen's Two Seeds and Conception Theory in the Hebrew Bible', *Dead Sea Discoveries* 28.1, pp. 38–63.

Rainbow Catholics, https://rainbowcatholics.org/ (accessed 27.6.23).

Rambo, Shelley, 2020, 'Foreword', in Karen O'Donnell and Katie Cross (eds), *Feminist Trauma Theologies: Body, Scripture and Church in Critical Perspective*, London: SCM Press, 2020.

Ranke-Heinemann, Uta, 1990, *Eunuchs for the Kingdom of Heaven: The Catholic Church and Sexuality*, New York: Penguin.

Ratzinger, Joseph Cardinal, 1986, 'Letter to the Bishops of the Catholic Church on the Pastoral Care of Homosexual Persons', https://www.vatican.va/roman_curia/congregations/cfaith/documents/rc_con_cfaith_doc_19861001_homosexual-persons_en.html (accessed 27.6.23).

RCT Abuse Law Team, 2017, https://rctlaw.com.au/legal-blog/2017/child-abuse-in-catholic-church-here-are-the-statistics (accessed 27.10.22).

Reaves, Jayme R., David Tombs and Rocío Figueroa (eds), 2021, *When Did We See You Naked? Jesus as a Victim of Sexual Abuse*, London: SCM Press.

Reddie, Anthony G., 2009, *Is God Colour-Blind? Insights from Black Theology for Christian Ministry*, London: SPCK.

Roberts, Alexander, James Donaldson and A. Cleveland Coxe (eds), 1885, *Tertullian, On Monogamy, Ante-Nicene Fathers*, Vol. 4, trans. S. Thelwall, Buffalo, NY: Christian Literature Publishing Co.

Robinson, John A. T., 1973, *The Human Face of God*, London: SCM Press.

Robinson-Brown, Jarel, 2021, *Black, Gay, British, Christian, Queer: The Church and the Famine of Grace*, London: SCM Press.

Rollo, David, 2022, *Medieval Writings on Sex between Men: Peter Damian's* The Book of Gomorrah *and Alain de Lille's* The Plaint of Nature, Leiden: Brill.

Ruether, Rosemary Radford, 1998, *Women and Redemption: A Theological History*, London: SCM Press.

Ruttenberg, Danya , 2012, 'Jewish Sexual Ethics', in Elliot N. Dorff and Jonathan K. Crane (eds), *The Oxford Handbook of Jewish Ethics and Morality*, Oxford: Oxford University Press, pp. 383–96.

Said, Edward W., 1979, *Orientalism*, New York: Knopf Doubleday.

Salzman, Todd A. and Michael G. Lawler, *The Sexual Person: Toward a Renewed Catholic Anthropology*, Washington, DC: Georgetown University Press.

Sanchez, Melissa E., 2019, *Queer Faith: Reading Promiscuity and Race in the Secular Love Tradition*, New York: New York University Press.

Scheck, Thomas P., 1985, *St. Jerome: Commentary on Matthew*, The Fathers of the Church, Vol. 117, Book 2, Washington, DC: Catholic University of America Press.

Schüssler Fiorenza, Elisabeth, 1985, *Bread Not Stones: The Challenge of Feminist Biblical Interpretation*, Boston, MA: Beacon Press.

Shaw, Teresa M., 1998, 'Askesis and the Appearance of Holiness', *Journal of Early Christian Studies* 6.3, pp. 485–99.

Shaw, Teresa, 1998, *The Burden of the Flesh: Fasting and Sexuality in Early Christianity*, Minneapolis, MN: Augsburg: Fortress Publishers.

Shaw, Teresa M., 2000, 'Sex and Sexual Renunciation', in Philip Esler (ed.), *The Early Christian World, Volume I–II*, London: Routledge, pp. 401–21.

Sheehan, E., 1981, 'Victorian Clitoridectomy: Isaac Baker Brown and his Harmless Operative Procedure', *Medical Anthropology Newsletter* 4, August, pp. 9–15.

Shiloh Project, 2023, https://www.shilohproject.blog/about/ (accessed 27.6.23).

Sinkewicz, Robert E., 2011, *Evagrius of Pontus: The Greek Ascetic Corpus*, Oxford: Oxford University Press.

Slater, Jack and Susannah Cornwall, 2022, 'Queer Theology', *St Andrews Encyclopaedia of Theology*, https://www.saet.ac.uk/Christianity/QueerTheology (accessed 27.6.23).

Sommar, Mary E., 2020, *The Slaves of the Churches: A History*, New York: Oxford University Press.

Southern, Robert, 1970, *Western Society and the Church in the Middle Ages*, Harmondsworth: Penguin.

Spivak, Gayatri, 1987, 'Can the Subaltern Speak?' in Cary Nelson and Lawrence Grossberg (eds), *Marxism and the Interpretation of Culture*, Urbana, IL: University of Illinois Press, pp. 282–3.

Starr, Rachel, 2018, *Reimagining Theologies of Marriage in Contexts of Domestic Violence*, Abingdon: Routledge.

Starr, Rachel, 2023, 'Marriage and *LLF*', *Modern Believing* 64.1, pp. 17–25.

Stavrakopoulou, Francesca, 2021, *God: An Anatomy*, London: Picador.

Stewart, Charles, 2002, 'Erotic Dreams and Nightmares from Antiquity to the Present', *Journal of the Royal Anthropological Institute* 8.2, pp. 279–309.

Stiebert, Johanna, 2018, 'Brother, Sister, Rape: The Hebrew Bible and Popular Culture', in Caroline Blyth, Emily Colgan and Katie Edwards (eds), *Rape Culture, Gender Violence, and Religion: Biblical Perspectives*, Cham, Switzerland: Palgrave Macmillan, pp. 31–50.

Stiebert, Johanna, 2019, 'Divinely Sanctioned Violence Against Women: Biblical Marriage and the Example of the *Sotah* of Numbers 5', *The Bible and Critical Theory* 15.2, pp. 83–108, p. 88.

Stiebert, Johanna, 2023, 'Abusive Theology and *LLF*', *Modern Believing* 64.1, pp. 8–16.

Stokes, Laura, 2013, 'Toward the Witch Craze', in Judith Bennett and Ruth Karras (eds), *The Oxford Handbook of Women and Gender in Medieval Europe*, Oxford: Oxford University Press, pp. 577–89.

Storkey, Elaine, 2015, *Scars Across Humanity: Understanding and Overcoming Violence Against Women*, London: SPCK.

Stuart, E. and Adrian Thatcher, 1997, *People of Passion: What the Churches Teach about Sex*, London: Mowbray.

Summers, Steve, 2015, 'Friends and Friendship', in Adrian Thatcher (ed.), *The Oxford Handbook of Theology, Sexuality, and Gender*, Oxford: Oxford University Press, pp. 688–704.

Swancutt, Diana, 2003, '"The Disease of Effemination": The Charge of Effeminacy and the Verdict of God (Romans 1:18–26)', in Stephen D. Moore and Janice Capel Anderson (eds), *New Testament Masculinities*, Atlanta, GA: Society of Biblical Literature, pp. 193–234.

Swancutt, Diana, 2006, 'Sexing the Pauline Body of Christ: Scriptural Sex in the Context of the American Christian Culture War', in Virginia Burrus and Catherine Keller (eds), *Towards a Theology of Eros: Transfiguring Passion at the Limits of Discipline*, New York: Fordham University Press, pp. 65–98.

Sweeney, Marvin A., 2008, *Reading the Hebrew Bible after the Shoah: Engaging Holocaust Theology*, Minneapolis, MN: Fortress Press.

Taylor, Charles, 2007, *A Secular Age*, Cambridge, MA: Harvard University Press.

Teller Report, 2021, *Report of the Sauvé Commission: The Church of France, Between Shame and Astonishment*, 5 October, https://www.tellerreport.com/news/2021-10-05-report-of-the-sauv%C3%A9-commission--the-church-of-france--between-shame-and-astonishment.B1_xWrc4t.html (accessed 27.6.23).

Tertullian, 1885, *On the Veiling of Virgins*, in Alexander Roberts, James Donaldson, and A. Cleveland Coxe (eds), trans. S. Thelwall, *Ante-Nicene Fathers, Vol. 4*, Buffalo, NY: Christian Literature Publishing Co., https://www.newadvent.org/fathers/0403.htm (accessed 27.6.23).

Tertullian, n.d., *Five Books Against Marcion*, http://gnosis.org/library/ter_marc1.htm (accessed 27.6.23).

Tertullian, n.d., *Treatise on the Soul*, https://www.newadvent.org/fathers/0310.htm (accessed 27.6.23).

Tertullian, n.d., *On the Apparel of Women (de cultu feminarum)*, in *The Early Church Fathers and Other Works*, https://www.ewtn.com/catholicism/library/on-the-apparel-of-women-on-the-dress-of-women-de-cultu-feminarum-11398 (accessed 27.6.23).

Thatcher, Adrian, 1993, *Liberating Sex: A Christian Sexual Theology*, London, SPCK.

Thatcher, Adrian, 1999, *Marriage after Modernity: Christian Marriage in Postmodern Times*, Sheffield: Sheffield Academic Press/New York: New York University Press.

Thatcher, Adrian, 2000, 'A Strange Convergence? Popes and Feminists on Contraception', in Lisa Isherwood (ed.), *The Good News of the Body: Sexual Theology and Feminism*. Sheffield: Sheffield Academic Press, pp. 136–48.

Thatcher, Adrian, 2008, *The Savage Text: The Use and Abuse of the Bible*, Chichester: Wiley-Blackwell.

Thatcher, Adrian, 2011, *God, Sex, and Gender: An Introduction*, Chichester: Wiley-Blackwell.

Thatcher, Adrian, 2012, *Making Sense of Sex*, London: SPCK.

Thatcher, Adrian, 2016, *Redeeming Gender*, Oxford: Oxford University Press.

Thatcher, Adrian, 2020, *Gender and Christian Ethics*, Cambridge: Cambridge University Press.

Thatcher, Adrian, 2021, 'The Harm Principle and Christian Belief', *Journal for Interdisciplinary Biblical Studies* 2.1, Spring, pp. 5–24.

Thiessen, Matthew, 2018, 'The Legislation of Leviticus 12 in Light of Ancient Embryology', *Vetus Testamentum* 68.2, pp. 297–319.

Tollerton, David, 2021, 'The Religious Challenges of Linking Holocaust Memory with Colonial Violence', in Sara E. Brown and Stephen D. Smith (eds), *The Routledge Handbook of Religion, Mass Atrocity, and Genocide*, Abingdon: Routledge, pp. 87–95.

Tombs, David, 2022, *The Crucifixion of Jesus: Torture, Sexual Abuse, and the Scandal of the Cross*, London: Routledge.

Udis-Kessler, A., 2000, 'The Holy Leper and the Bisexual Christian', in D. R. Kolodny (ed.), *Blessed Bi Spirit: Bisexual People of Faith*, New York: Continuum Press, pp. 11–16.

UNAIDS, n.d., 'Global HIV and AIDS Statistics – Fact Sheet', https://www.unaids.org/en/resources/fact-sheet (accessed 27.6.23).

United States Conference of Catholic Bishops, n.d., 'Unitive and Procreative Nature of Intercourse', https://www.usccb.org/issues-and-action/marriage-and-family/natural-family-planning/catholic-teaching/upload/Unitive-and-Proc-Nature-of-Interc.pdf (accessed 27.6.23).

Vasey, Michael, 1995, *Strangers and Friends: A New Exploration of Homosexuality and the Bible*, London: Hodder & Stoughton.

ViaMedia.News, n.d., https://viamedia.news/ (accessed 27.6.23).

Wahlquist, Calla, 2020, 'The sole function of the clitoris is female orgasm. Is that why it's ignored by medical science?', *The Guardian*, 31 October, https://www.theguardian.com/lifeandstyle/2020/nov/01/the-sole-function-of-the-clitoris-is-female-orgasm-is-that-why-its-ignored-by-medical-science (accessed 27.6.23).

WATCH (Women and the Church), 2020, 'Male Headship Churches' Transparency about their PCCs' Resolutions on Women's Ministry', March, https://womenandthechurch.org/features/transparency-statistics-march-2020/ (accessed 27.6.23).

Weber, Saskia and Nicolas Glimois, 2022, 'Children of Shame', YouTube, https://www.youtube.com/watch?v=7RJK8eR9IzM (accessed 27.6.23).

Webster, Danny, 2021, 'The Challenges Around Conversion Therapy', *Evangelical Alliance*, 16 March, https://www.eauk.org/news-and-views/the-challenges-around-conversion-therapy (accessed 27.6.23).

Wei, Simon Lienyueh, 2012, 'The Absence of Sin in Sexual Dreams in the Writings of Augustine and Cassian', *Vigiliae Christianae* 66.4, pp. 362–78.

Wiesner, Merry, 1990, 'Luther and Women: The Death of Two Marys', in Ann Loades (ed.), *Feminist Theology: A Reader*, London: SPCK, pp. 123–37.

Wiesner-Hanks, Merry E., 2000, *Christianity and Sexuality in the Early Modern World: Regulating Desire, Reforming Practice*, New York: Routledge.

Wijngaards Institute for Catholic Research (The Wijngaards Report), 2018, *Christian Objections to Same Sex Relationships: An Academic Assessment*, https://www.wijngaardsinstitute.com/research-report-christian-objections-same-sex-unions/ (accessed 27.6.23).

Wilkerson, Isabel, 2020, *Caste: The Lies that Divide Us*, London: Allen Lane.

Williams, Frank (ed. and trans.), 2013, *The Panarion of Epiphanius of Salamis Books II and III. De Fide*, Leiden: Brill.

Williams, Rowan, 2002, 'The Body's Grace', in Eugene F. Rogers, Jr. (ed.), *Theology and Sexuality: Classic and Contemporary Readings*, Oxford: Blackwell, pp. 309–21.

Wilson, Anna, 2003, 'Sexing the Hyena: Intraspecies Readings of the Female Phallus', *Signs* 28.3, pp. 755–90.

Wonderley, Anthony, 2017, *Oneida Utopia: A Community Searching for Human Happiness and Prosperity*, Ithaca, NY: Cornell University Press.

Wood, Simon, 1954, *Christ the Educator*, Fathers of the Church Series, Washington, DC: Catholic University of America Press, pp. 159–89.

Woolley, Jasmine, 2016, 'The Social Construct of Gender', in Christina Beardsley and Michelle O'Brien (eds), *This is My Body: Hearing the Theology of Transgender Christians*, London: Darton, Longman & Todd, pp. 45–56.

World Health Organization, 2018, 'United Nations Agencies call for Ban on Virginity Testing', https://www.who.int/news/item/17-10-2018-united-nations-agencies-call-for-ban-on-virginity-testing#:~:text=WHO%20recommends%20that%20this%20test%20should%20not%20be%20performed%20under%20any%20circumstances.&text=There%20is%20an%20urgent%20need,need%20to%20eliminate%20its%20use (accessed 27.6.23).

Young, M., 2000, *King James VI and I and the History of Homosexuality*, London: Palgrave Macmillan.

Young, Serinity, 2018, *Women Who Fly: Goddesses, Witches, Mystics, and Other Airborne Females*, New York: Oxford University Press.

Zion, William Basil, 1992, *Eros and Transformation: Sexuality and Marriage; An Eastern Orthodox Perspective*, Lanham, MD: University Press of America.

Index of Bible References

Hebrew Bible

New Testament

Index of Names and Subjects